Great Battles of the
Early Roman Empire

By the same author

Great Battles of the Early Roman Empire

Simon Elliott

Pen & Sword
MILITARY

First published in Great Britain in 2023 by
Pen & Sword Military
An imprint of Pen & Sword Books Limited
Yorkshire – Philadelphia

ISBN 978 1 39906 983 0

Typeset by Mac Style
Printed in the UK by CPI Group (UK) Ltd, Croydon, CR0 4YY.

Pen & Sword Books Limited incorporates the imprints of After
the Battle, Atlas, Archaeology, Aviation, Discovery, Family History,
Fiction, History, Maritime, Military, Military Classics, Politics,
Select, Transport, True Crime, Air World, Frontline Publishing, Leo
Cooper, Remember When, Seaforth Publishing, The Praetorian Press,
Wharncliffe Local History, Wharncliffe Transport, Wharncliffe True
Crime and White Owl.

For a complete list of Pen & Sword titles please contact

PEN & SWORD BOOKS LIMITED
47 Church Street, Barnsley, South Yorkshire, S70 2AS, England
E-mail: enquiries@pen-and-sword.co.uk
Website: www.pen-and-sword.co.uk
or
PEN AND SWORD BOOKS
1950 Lawrence Rd, Havertown, PA 19083, USA
E-mail: uspen-and-sword@casematepublishers.com
Website: www.penandswordbooks.com

Contents

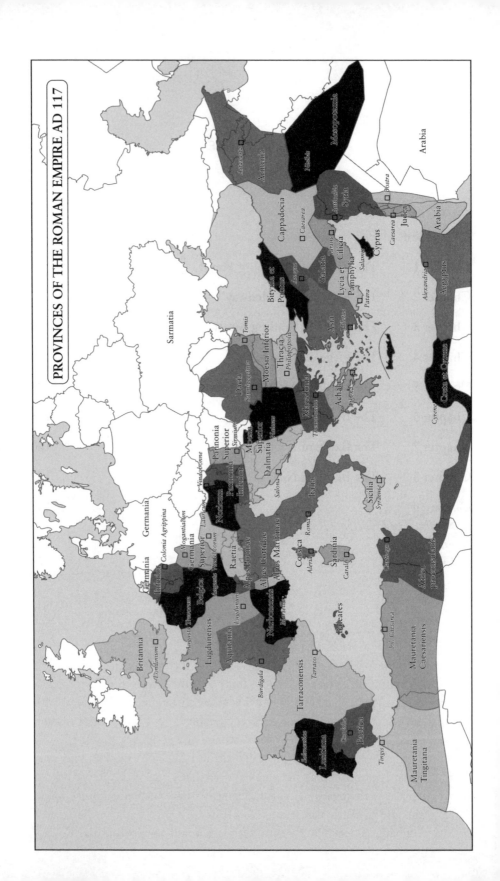

PROVINCES OF THE ROMAN EMPIRE AD 117

Introduction

The Roman Empire was always at war. Across its vast territory, even in times of relative peace, conflict could always be found. This was an empire defined by martial prowess, one where the entire Roman economy was bent towards supporting its enormous military establishment. Yet few books have been written in the modern era specifically addressing the key battles in the early imperial period, when the Roman Empire was at the height of its power. I address that here.

I have chosen my eight encounters very carefully, aiming to provide a balance between those well-known and others less so. In particular, I have taken into account the importance given to each by the Romans themselves, as well as by us today. Specifically, the battles covered in this book are the AD 9 Varian Disaster in the Teutoburg Forest, Plautius' AD 43 victory over the Britons in the Battle of the Medway, Paulinus' tactical masterstroke defeating Boudicca when saving the province of Britannia in the AD 60/61 at the Battle of Watling Street, the brutal siege of Masada in AD 73 which ended the First 'Great' Jewish Revolt, Agricola's victory in the far north of Britain at Mons Graupius in AD 83, the shattering Marcomanni victory over the Romans at *Carnuntum* in AD 170 which allowed the first 'barbarian' invasion of Italy itself for centuries, Septimius Severus' victory over the usurper Clodius Albinus to secure his throne in AD 197, and finally the Battle of Nisibis in AD 217 when the Romans and Parthians last fought each other. Each chapter is broken down into three key components, these the strategic build-up to the battle, the key engagement itself, and the aftermath and legacy. This approach avoids each battle being viewed in isolation, providing the full context to enable a wider understanding. My conclusion then examines the common threads evident in all of the engagements considered, with the book completed with an Appendix detailing the Roman military establishment of the early Roman Empire to assist the reader with less knowledge of the subject matter.

Some battles here have long proved controversial. For example, it is only through recently published archaeological data that a reasonable narrative can be set in place with regard to Varus' defeat in the Teutoburg Forest, while locating the site of Agricola's victory at Mons Graupius remains the subject of heated debate, as does whether it took place at all. Meanwhile, the Roman defeat on the Danube at *Carnuntum* in AD 170 has never been tackled at length given the lack of data until now. I have personally gathered much of this over the last decade researching the Marcomannic Wars. Where controversies exist, I have addressed them directly in the relevant chapter, and when new data has been used, I set this out in full. It goes without saying that all of the analysis and interpretation you read here are my own, and as usual I am more than happy for others to disagree. The more debate my writing prompts, the better.

The battles detailed here are deliberately set out in chronological order, helping build a timeline of the early Roman Empire through to the third century AD. This approach has proved most insightful given it quickly became evident when I was writing the book that each Roman commander was clearly aware of the success or otherwise of their forebears, often learning from clever stratagems or mistakes. In particular, all were mindful of Varus' woeful performance in AD 9 and its terrible consequences, which still resonate in popular culture today.

Next, some housekeeping notes. First, Roman fortifications play a key role in this book. In that regard I have used the size-based hierarchy currently utilized by those studying the Roman military as a means of describing their size. Specifically, these are:

- Fortress, a permanent base for one or more legions, some 20ha or more in size.
- Vexillation fortress, a large fort of between 8 and 12ha holding a mixed force of legionary cohorts and auxiliaries.
- Fort, a garrison outpost occupied by an auxiliary unit or units, usually 1 to 6ha in size.
- Fortlet, a small garrison outpost large enough to hold only part of an auxiliary unit.

Additionally, marching camps are also important when detailing the Roman military. These were temporary fortifications built by every Roman force at the end of every day's march in enemy territory. They effectively replicated the permanent fortifications detailed above in their layout, size on size, but were temporary. Key features included surrounding ditches, and an internal bank with a palisade.

Next, the various time periods discussed in this book fit broadly into phases. These are the Roman Republic, and the Principate (when the battles discussed took place) and Dominate phases of the Roman Empire. The first began in 509 BC with the overthrow of the last Etrusco-Roman king Tarquin the Proud. It ended, and the Principate Empire began, following the Senate's acclamation of Augustus as the first emperor in 27 BC. The name is derived from the term *princeps* (chief or master), referencing the emperor as the leading citizen of the empire. This phase lasted until AD 284 with the accession of Diocletian. Faced with dragging the empire out of the disastrous 'Crisis of the 3rd Century', he instituted a series of structural changes that changed the very nature of the Roman world. This featured a new, far more overtly imperial system of government that set the emperor up as something more akin to an eastern potentate. The name of this last phase of empire, the Dominate, is based on the word *dominus*, referencing lord or master.

Next, an understanding of the social structure of the Roman world is useful given it played a key role in the command structure of the Roman military. At the top were three levels of aristocracy, the most senior the Senatorial class. Its members were said to be endowed with wealth, high birth and 'moral excellence'. There were around 600 Senators in the mid-second century AD. Those of this class were patricians, a social as well as political rank; all those below, including other aristocrats, were plebeians. Next was the equestrian class, the old 'knights' of the Republic, having slightly less wealth but usually with a reputable lineage. They numbered some 30,000 across the empire in the mid-second century AD. Finally there was the curial class, with the bar set slightly lower again. These were usually merchants and mid-level landowners, making up a large percentage of the town councillors in the Principate Empire. Below this were freemen who were free in the sense that they had never been slaves. Freemen included the majority of smaller-scale merchants, artisans and professionals in Roman society. All of the above classes were also full *cives Romani*, citizens of the Roman Empire, if they came from Italy. They enjoyed the widest range of protections and privileges as defined by the Roman state, and could travel the breadth of the empire pursuing their professional ambitions. Roman women had a limited type of citizenship and were not allowed to vote or stand for public or civil office. Freemen born outside of Italy in the imperial provinces were called *peregrini* (meaning in Latin 'one from abroad') until Caracalla's AD 212 *constitutio Antoniniana*, an edict that made all freemen of the empire into citizens. In the first and second centuries AD *peregrini* made up the vast majority of the empire's inhabitants.

Further down the social ladder were freedmen, former slaves who had been manumitted by their masters. Once free these former slaves often remained with the wider family of their *pater familias* (head of family) former owner, frequently taking that person's name in some way. Providing the correct process of manumission was followed, freedmen could become citizens/*peregrini*, though with fewer civic rights than a freeman including not being able to stand for the vast number of public offices. Their children were freemen. Many freedmen became highly successful, and since they were not allowed to stand for public office found other ways to celebrate their lives. A common choice was the creation of monumentalized funerary memorials. Meanwhile, at the bottom of society were slaves.

Moving on, I frequently reference the provincial structure of the Principate Empire in this work. Understanding this is therefore important. The word province provides interesting insight into the Roman attitude to its empire, the Latin *provincia* meaning land 'for conquering' (Matyszak, 2009, 60). There were actually two kinds of province in this period. These were Senatorial provinces left to the Senate to administer, these dating back to the Republic whose governors were officially called *proconsuls* and remained in post for a year, and imperial provinces retained under the supervision of the emperor which post-dated the Republic. The emperor personally chose the governors for the latter, they often being styled *legati Augusti pro praetor* to mark them out officially as deputies of the emperor. Given their early origins, Senatorial provinces tended to be those deep within the empire where less trouble was expected. At the beginning of the first century AD these were:

- Baetica (in southern Spain).
- Narbonensis (in southern France).
- Corsica et Sardinia.
- Africa Proconsularis (in North Africa).
- Cyrenaica et Creta (in eastern Libya and Crete).
- Epirus (in modern Albania and Greece).
- Macedonia.
- Achaia (in Greece's Peloponnese).
- Asia (in western Anatolia).
- Bithynia et Pontus (on Turkey's Black Sea coast).

In this work I specifically use *proconsul* to refer to the governor of these Senatorial provinces, and governor to refer to this position in an imperial province.

Next, a note on nomenclature. In the book the words German and Goth are frequently used, confusingly perhaps given that the Goths themselves were of German descent. Both words are problematic given they infer a tribal identity that in reality did not exist. While each grouping may have often shared the same blood and cultural practices, the tribes within more often fought themselves than the Romans, and indeed later in the empire provided many of the troops and military leaders in the Dominate Roman army. Even the term tribe itself is problematic given many were confederations of various regional groupings. While acknowledging these issues, I retain the use of the words here for ease of reference, especially given they were terms well understood by the Romans.

More broadly, regarding the use of classical and modern names, I have attempted to ensure the research here is as accessible as possible to the reader. For example, I have used the modern name where a place is mentioned, referencing its Roman name at that first point of use. When an ancient place is referenced with no modern successor, it has been italicized to illustrate this. Meanwhile, where a classical name for a position or role is well understood, I use that, for example *legate* (a Roman general). Further, when emperors are detailed in the main narrative I have listed the dates of their reigns at the point where they are first mentioned.

Finally, a number of terms are frequently used in this book which the reader will benefit from understanding at an early stage. Therefore, I detail them here:

- *Battlespace.* The wider region of conflict in which a given battle took place.
- *Guerilla Warfare.* Irregular warfare fought by asymmetrically inferior combatants using unconventional tactics (see below).
- *Legionaries and Auxiliaries.* For the majority of the Roman Republic, and the Principate phase of empire, the premier Roman warrior was the legionary, a heavily armed and armoured infantryman who most often formed the main line of battle. From the time of Augustus, supporting troops were then organized into formal units known as auxiliaries, often lesser in quality to the legionaries but still a match for most opponents the Romans faced. Auxiliaries provided both foot troops and most of the cavalry in Principate Roman armies (see Appendix for full detail).
- *Symmetric and Asymmetric Warfare.* In the first instance, war between fairly evenly matched belligerents. In the second, conflict where one is so dominant that the other is forced to use unconventional strategies and tactics, for example guerilla warfare. By way of example, in the Roman world their many conflicts with the Sassanid Persians can be described as symmetrical given both sides were so evenly matched, while their campaigns against the natives in the far north of Britain often forced the latter to respond asymmetrically.
- *Romanisation.* From the onset of the Roman occupation of a new province many economic and social changes unfolded. Romanisation is a term often used to describe this process. The word has proved controversial academically given it is often associated with modern concepts of imperialism. However, if taken at face value, it is a useful term given the broad appreciation it gives showing how conquered territory became 'Roman', and so I use it here.

Lastly, I would like to thank those who have helped make this book possible. Firstly, as always, Professor Andrew Lambert of the War Studies Department at KCL, Dr Andrew Gardner at UCL's Institute of Archaeology and Dr Steve Willis at the University of Kent (where I am an Honorary Research Fellow). All continue to encourage my research on the Roman military. Also Professor Sir Barry Cunliffe of the School of Archaeology at Oxford University, and Professor Martin Millett at the Faculty of Classics, Cambridge University. Next, my patient proofreader and amazing wife Sara. As with all my literary work, all have contributed greatly and freely, enabling me to complete this work on Great Battles of Early Imperial Rome. Finally I would like to thank my family, especially my tolerant wife Sara once again and children Alex (also a student of military history) and Lizzie.

Thank you all.

Dr Simon Elliott
August 2023

Chapter 1

The Battle of Teutoburg Forest

Augustus Loses His Legions, AD 9

Augustus was Rome's first emperor, and arguably the greatest. Yet it was under his rule that the early empire suffered its most shocking defeat when a rash campaign through the dense forests of *Germania* (as the Romans knew the arboreal vastness north and east of the river Rhine) cost him three entire legions, and even more of his recently formed auxiliary foot units and cavalry.

The doomed Roman campaign was led by Publius Quinctilius Varus, newly-appointed by Augustus to 'Romanise' newly-conquered territory there. The subsequent Varian Disaster, called the *Clades Variana* by the Romans, had such a psychological impact in the imperial capital that plans to expand the empire's frontiers in the northwest were shelved for generations, if not permanently.

Context is important here to understand why the Romans failed so spectacularly in the Teutoburg Forest, and where so many of their elite soldiers endured a miserable end. After years of civil war savagery, Augustus' initial aim as the new *princeps* had been to provide stability across the now-vast territories incorporated into the Roman world. However, even though the new *pax romana* promised a newfound peace within the embryonic empire's borders, Augustus' foreign policy remained expansionist. This was a classically Augustan smoke-and-mirrors strategy, designed to deflect popular attention away from domestic issues where he was terrified civil war could ignite at any time. Instead, he shrewdly directed the public's gaze towards what seemed a never-ending process of Romanisation as the empire grew.

As a priority, Augustus initially completed the pacification of northern Spain, bringing the Cantabrian Wars there to an end by 19 BC. His legions and auxiliaries then campaigned in North Africa to consolidate his newly-named province of Africa Proconsularis. Next, he targeted the Danube where he established a new imperial frontier, bringing huge tracts of new territory under imperial control. However, his most high profile campaign was the attempt to expand Rome's northern footprint beyond Caesar's Rhine frontier. Augustus had alighted on the idea of occupying the lands between the Rhine and Elbe as the first century BC came to an end after abandoning three high

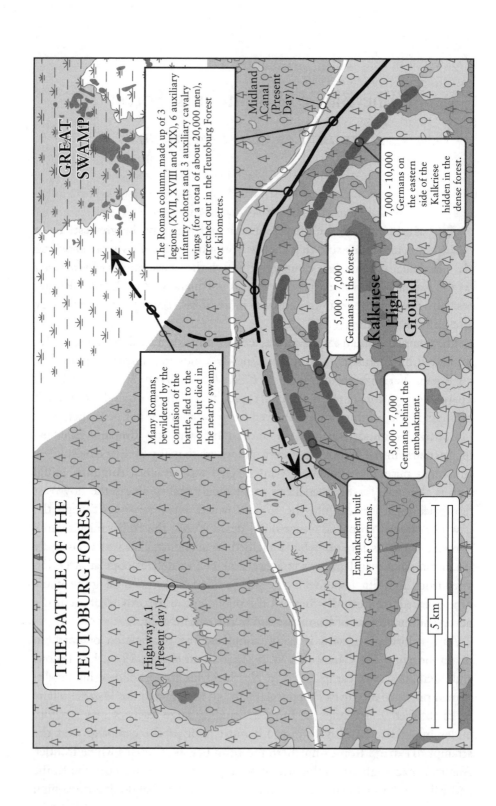

THE BATTLE OF THE
TEUTOBURG FOREST

GREAT SWAMP

The Roman column, made up of 3 legions (XVII, XVIII and XIX), 6 auxiliary infantry cohorts and 3 auxiliary cavalry wings (for a total of about 20,000 men), stretched out in the Teutoburg Forest for kilometres.

Midland Canal (Present Day)

7,000 - 10,000 Germans on the eastern side of the Kallriese hidden in the dense forest.

5,000 - 7,000 Germans in the forest.

Kallriese High Ground

Many Romans, bewildered by the confusion of the battle, fled to the north, but died in the nearby swamp.

5,000 - 7,000 Germans behind the embankment.

Embankment built by the Germans.

Highway A1 (Present day)

5 km

profile incursions to Britain in 34 BC while still Octavian, and then in 27 BC and 25 BC when emperor (Elliott, 2021b, 68).

Augustus' initial aim in *Germania* was to create a buffer zone to prevent the increasingly frequent raids by predating German tribes across the Rhine. This proved highly successful, with new territory soon coming under full imperial control. The emperor now saw the opportunity to go further than his initial plan, looking to create a new province that he would call *Germania* beyond the Rhine. The man he chose to consolidate his gains there as a first step was Varus, the experienced administrator (if not warrior) who was soon busy establishing *Romanitas* in the region. However, at exactly the wrong moment Augustus' attention was diverted away. This was towards Illyricum in the western Balkans, where in AD 6 a huge rebellion broke out in territory only recently incorporated into the empire. This completely undermined Augustus' northern ambitions given the region linked the Rhine with the Danube (Cornell and Matthews, 1982, 60). Augustus now intervened in Illyricum in person, leaving Varus to his own devices. So began a series of missteps that were to lead to disaster.

Strategic Build-Up to the Battle

Here I first discuss the early German armies fought by the Romans at the time of the Teutoburg Forest campaign. I then consider the initial early imperial Roman campaigns in *Germania*, including those of Drusus and Tiberius, setting the scene for Varus' doomed AD 9 expedition.

Early German Armies

The Germanic peoples of continental northern Europe were a major opponent of the later Roman Republic, and then empire throughout the entirety of its existence. After their initial encounters, the Romans early on identified them as a distinct ethnic group when compared to the Gauls to their south.

The Germans originated in the westward Indo-European migrations from the Pontic-Eurasian steppe, and by 3,300 BC had split off from the main migratory group, heading northwest to the southern coastline of the Baltic Sea. The Germanic confederations and tribes known to the Romans originated in these southern Scandinavian homelands, and later in the far north of Germany where they later settled. Writing at the end of the early first century AD, Strabo provides contemporary insight into how the Romans viewed the Germans, saying (7.1.3):

Now the parts beyond the Rhenus (Rhine), immediately after the country of the Gauls, slope towards the east and are occupied by the Germans, who, though they vary slightly from the Celtic stock in that they are wilder, taller, and have yellower hair, are in all other respects similar, for in build, habits, and modes of life they are such as I have said the Gauls are. And I also think that it was for this reason that the Romans assigned to them the name Germani, as though they wished to indicate thereby that they were 'genuine' Gauls, for in the language of the Romans Germani means genuine.

The last point above, referencing the Germans as 'genuine' Gauls, is most likely a literary device by Strabo reflecting what he believed was their superior martial prowess following the conquest of Gaul by Caesar in the 50s BC, and the comparative ease with which the Gallic provinces were later incorporated into the Empire.

The later Republican Romans described four broad Germanic groupings, the first being the Ingaevones. These comprised the Cimbri, Teutones and Chauci tribes. These were based in the Jutland Peninsula, Frisia and northern Saxony. Another early Germanic grouping were the Irimones, these situated further to the east between the Oder and Elbe rivers. A third grouping was called the Istvaeones, later located on the Rhine and around the Weser, which included the Sicambri, Batavi and Frisii tribes. The final group were called the Herminones, comprising the Suebi (from whom the Marcomanni descended, as well as the Quadi, Semnones and Lombards), Chatti and Hermunduri tribes, these later dominating the Elbe region. All four of these early terms for the large confederations gradually fell out of use as individual tribes within them came to be known to the Romans.

Soon the German tribes began a new wave of migrations south from their original southern Scandinavian and north German homelands, carving out new territories between the Rhine and the Pripet Marshes in modern Belarus. There they slowly consolidated until they eventually coalesced into even larger confederations. It was these that caused so much trouble to the later Roman Empire, particularly after the Hunnic expansions westward from the Central Asian steppe drove them increasingly against the Roman limes along the Rhine and Danube. By then six major confederations had emerged, these being the western Visigoths, eastern Ostrogoths, Vandals, Burgundians, Langobards and Franks, all later playing a key role in the fall of the Roman Empire in the west.

Back to the time of Augustus, the early German armies which fought the Romans, for example in the Teutoburg campaign, were very similar to their Gallic counterparts though lacked chariots. The cavalry in these armies fought in much the same way as the Gauls, though the horses tended to be smaller. However, a particular innovation of early German armies was the deployment of light troops among the ranks of their own cavalry. Armed with javelins and shields, these swarmed around the flanks of opposing troops, hamstringing their mounts if they were cavalry.

Early German infantry formations often fought in a wedge formation rather than a standard shield wall. Most warriors wore little armour, though often carried a shield, usually square in design. Their principal weapons were javelins which they carried in quantity, aiming to shower an opposing formation with volleys prior to contact. A common type was called the *framea*, which featured a narrow blade and long socket. Some German tribes also deployed troops armed with long thrusting spears in their front ranks, for example Arminius' Cherusci and the Batavians. The main side arm was the long dagger, for example the Saxon *seax*, though a few warriors also carried a sword if they could afford it.

German troops of all periods were known for their blood-chilling war-cry called the *barritus*. This started in a low voice and rose to a high-pitched chilling scream immediately prior to a charge. It proved so effective it was later copied by the Romans themselves.

The Romans in Germania

The first series of Roman campaigns against the Germans were highly successful, with Augustus initially appointing members of his wider imperial family to positions of command. For example, the best-known early campaigns were those of his stepson Nero Claudius Drusus. He arrived in the region in 15 BC when appointed *legatus Augusti pro praetor* in charge of Augustus' newly-created Gallic provinces. Soon his stepfather was encouraging him to look north to *Germania* beyond the Rhine where the emperor was eying fresh conquest. Drusus' planning was meticulous. First, in 14 BC he built fifty vexillation forts along the Rhine frontier to support the huge force of seven legions he now gathered for his planned invasion. Then, after a series of armed reconnaissance expeditions in 13 BC to determine the key points of access into the thickly forested German interior, he launched his first campaign in 12 BC. This proved a great success, he leading his legionary spearheads deep into German territory, using waterways wherever possible. Where these weren't available he relied on the engineering excellence of his legionaries to build new roadways to ensure continuing logistics support for his troops.

Drusus' first campaign was very effective and set the bar high for subsequent Roman incursions north of the Rhine. In the first instance he subjugated the Sicambri immediately north of the Rhine frontier, before building a new fleet which later became the *Classis Germanica* Augustan regional fleet on the Rhine (Elliott, 2016, 45). This he led on a naval expedition through the Rhine Delta, pacifying the Batavi there, before reaching the North Sea. Having secured his lines of supply through building more forts, including the legionary fortress at Nijmegen (later, Roman *Noviomagus*), he then set off along the North Sea coast, taking two battle-hardened legions with him. These were *legio* I *Germanica* and *legio* V *Alaudae*, both veterans of the northern frontier, with the latter founded by Gaius Julius Caesar to help conquer Gaul and the former long based there (Pollard and Berry, 2012, 61). In particular, the hard fighting I *Germanica* had a point to prove, having earlier lost its Augusta *cognomen* for disobeying orders given by the emperor's general and close confidant Marcus Agrippa (Cassius Dio, *Roman History*, 54.11). Drusus drove his legions and fleet with great vigour and soon the Frisii were subjugated, followed by the fierce Chauci at the mouth of the River Weser.

Here he stopped, built even more forts and then overwintered. Next, at the beginning of the 11 BC campaigning season, he launched his legionary spearheads up the Weser valley, quickly defeating the Usipetes and Marsi tribes there and conquering the entire Upper Weser region. Drusus paused again to overwinter, before launching a new lightning campaign in 10 BC against the Chatti, briefly returning to the Rhine frontier to defeat a rebellion amongst the Sicambri. Then, in his final campaign in 9 BC, having been newly-elected *consul*, he defeated the Mattiaci, Marcomanni and Cherusci, finally arriving on the western bank of the Elbe. Here the latter sued for peace, a fateful event given their leader Sigimer (also known as Segimerus) agreed to send his sons Arminius and Flavus to Rome as tribute. It was there the former, soon to become Rome's nemesis in the Teutoburg Forest, received a Roman civil and military education, and where he became a Roman citizen with the rank of equestrian. This allowed him to lead an auxiliary unit in combat (Hornblower and Spawforth, 1996, 173).

However, sadly for Drusus, when at the height of his martial success he fell from his horse while returning from the Elbe and died within a month. Always popular with his legionaries, they erected a monument today called the Dursusstein in his honour at the legionary fortress of Mainz (Roman *Mogontiacum*), while the Senate granted him the cognomen *Germanicus* in honour of his victories.

Drusus was succeeded in command of the Roman forces on the Rhine frontier by his younger brother Tiberius, who had arrived there at the behest of Augustus just before his brother passed away. Tiberius proved a highly effective if less glamorous commander there, with Holland saying (2015, 120):

'...it was the accomplishments of Drusus that glittered the more brightly, but those of Tiberius were the harder won.'

Tiberius was tasked with consolidating the vast tracts of territory conquered by Drusus. It quickly became apparent his main problem would be the Marcomanni, a huge tribe that was part of the Suebi confederation Caesar had repeatedly fought when conquering Gaul. Led by their leader Maroboduus, a recent returnee from Rome where he'd also been held as tribute by Augustus, they rebelled as soon as imperial attention was directed away. Tiberius, determined to deal with them once and for all, adopted a complex plan involving a pincer movement. Here, his *legate* Gaius Sentius Saturninus would fix the Marcomanni in place using a large force deploying east from Mainz, while he would personally lead a legionary spearhead comprising four legions and auxiliaries west from the Danube legionary fortress of Carnuntum in Pannonia. This proved a great success, with Tiberius soon carving his way through the lands of the Quadi before entering Marcomanni territory where he adopted a scorched-earth policy, completely destroying the local economy and forcing any German survivors to flee. The campaign was a huge success, though Tiberius failed to pacify the wider region given he had to return to the Rhine frontier where trouble had broken out with the Sicambri again. These were once more subjugated, after which the victorious Tiberius was recalled to Rome in early 5 BC where he was granted the title *tribunicia potestas* (making him the senior magistrate in Rome after the two *consuls*). Augustus then posted his imperial trouble-shooter to the eastern frontier with orders to take over command of the legions there facing the Parthians.

His replacement on the Rhine was another member of the imperial family, Lucius Domitius Ahenobarbus who was married to Augustus' niece Antonia the Elder, and who had earlier been *consul* in 16 BC (Goldsworthy, 2014, 391). Though described by Suetonius as '...arrogant, cruel, notorious and extravagant...' (*The Twelve Caesars, Nero*, 4), he proved a highly effective leader, with his legionary spearheads hacking new roadways through the forested German interior and soon crossing the Elbe for the first time where he set up an altar to Augustus at the end of the campaigning season in 5 BC. Having penetrated further north than any previous Roman expedition, Lucius then turned back, on the way building a sophisticated walkway tens of kilometres long called the *pontes longi* that joined the Ems with the Rhine frontier.

Augustus now addressed the administration of his Rhine frontier, with a view to the future creation of his new province of *Germania* to the north. As a first step he reformed the provincial structure of Gallia Belgica, his northernmost Gallic province. Here he stripped away the territory immediately south of the Rhine to create two new provinces, *Germania* Inferior and Superior. His plan was to use these as the springboard to finally secure the Germanic interior to the north, and then begin the process of establishing Roman administration and stone-built settlement there. At some point, when critical mass had been reached and security fully established, he then planned to announce *Germania* a full Roman province and appoint a governor and procurator there.

However, even in the regions in the far north wholly pacified by the Romans, internecine conflict between the various German tribes continued, with some more agreeable to the process of 'Romanisation' than others. For example, the Cherusci chieftain Sigimer was declared a coward by the leaders of his tribal neighbours for treating with Rome, this being symptomatic of a deteriorating political situation. Eventually, the anti-Roman faction among the German tribes gained ascendancy and Augustus was forced to act. He turned once more to Tiberius, bringing him back from the east and tasking him with bringing the troublesome Germans to heel again.

In AD 4 Tiberius was ready for action and advanced north of the Rhine yet again, into territory that should already have been under full Roman control but clearly wasn't.

With a huge army, again using river systems and newly-built roads, he soon subjugated the Cananefates tribe, then the rebelling Chatti, and finally the Bructeri in Lower Saxony. He then advanced across the Weser where he handed over command of the key river crossings there to Saturninus who had once more been deployed to the region. The *legate* then performed heroically holding off repeated German attacks trying to force the Romans back over the Weser. This allowed Tiberius to go back on the offensive, this time east of the Rhine. First he appointed Marcus Aemilius Lepidus his deputy, and then together they led a huge army of thirteen legions and auxiliaries against Maroboduus and the Marcomanni who were again causing trouble. This force may have comprised up to 100,000 men, with Maroboduus quickly surrendering when faced with such overwhelming odds.

Once more Augustus thought Germany pacified, with Saturninus awarded the honours of *ornamenta triumphalia* on his return to Rome for his heroics on the Weser. This allowed him to receive the privileges and wear the dress normally granted a *triumphator*, though by this time Augustus had restricted the honour of a full triumph to family members only. The emperor now planned an aggressive process of 'Romanisation' in *Germania* to prevent rebellion breaking out again. Perhaps here he was badly guided by his *Consilium Principis*, the main imperial advisory council he had created. They were clearly unaware that military matters were far from resolved in *Germania*.

The man Augustus chose for the job was Varus, husband of his great-niece Claudia Pulchra. His exact title here is unclear, some arguing he was appointed the *legatus augusti pro praetor* governor of what would become *Germania*, though that may have been premature even for the ever-optimistic Augustus. Most likely, at this initial stage, he was simply appointed commander of the military forces along the Rhine frontier, with the specific 'Romanisation' task in mind. This is important, given his role wasn't one of conquest as with his predecessors, but to establish the structures needed to bring the new province into being.

Varus' skill set reflected this, and on paper the strict, old-school patrician was a shrewd choice. Earlier, he'd been *proconsul* in the plumb posting of Africa Proconsularis, a position guaranteed to make him very rich, where he'd moved to establish the administrative structure of Augustus' new North African province. Later he'd served as a *legate* in Syria, helping put down a revolt in Judaea to the south after the death of King Herod. However, Goldsworthy says that in this operation, and indeed in any of his other earlier military appointments, there is no evidence he actually led troops in battle (2014, 447). Now in his fifties, he was an experienced governor, successful diplomat and reliable bureaucrat. But not soldier. The picture painted by the contemporary Roman historian, soldier and Senator Marcus Velleius Paterculus is one of blandness. He says Varus was (*Roman History*, 2.117):

A man of gentle character and quiet habits, rather inert in both mind and body, more familiar with leisurely life in the camp than with service on campaign.

Posted to the Rhine, Augustus' go-to administrator was now ready to impose order in the far north. Or so he thought. Initially Varus' posting went well, a thriving cross-border trade developing which saw the German tribes supplying wood, cattle, food, iron and slaves in exchange for Roman currency and luxury goods. As time went on, even more tribes pledged their allegiance to Rome, with large numbers of German warriors joining the ranks of the Roman auxilia. Varus was helped here by the overwhelming force he had inherited, with thirteen legions remaining in theatre. However, as detailed earlier, in AD 6 imperial attention suddenly turned to Illyricum where a huge insurrection had broken out. This was a direct threat to the structure of Augustus' growing empire, demanding an immediate response to deal with the situation. The big loser here was Varus, for two reasons. First, he immediately lost eight of his legions which quickly redeployed to the Balkans, leaving him with just five. Three were forward deployed to the Rhine, with two held back as a theatre reserve. The three on the frontier were *legio* XVII, *legio* XVIII and *legio* XIX, these variously given the cognomens *Gallica* and *Germanica* at one time or another. All were originally Caesarian foundings disbanded after the dictator's death and then refounded by Octavian to fight in the final round of Republican civil wars (Pollard and Berry, 2015, 55). Second, he was overlooked to take command of the new military operation in Illyricum. Augustus knew Varus was an administrator and not a soldier, better suited to his task on the Rhine, with Goldsworthy adding this showed Augustus believed him '… capable rather than gifted…' (2014, 447).

Soon Varus was setting up new administrative structures in the fully pacified regions of *Germania*. This included the introduction of Roman law, and the imposition of new taxes. However, the latter infuriated the native Germans who were unused to Roman ways, and soon even the tribal leaders who'd signed peace treaties with Rome began to push back. Unwisely, Varus ignored this and accelerated his programme of Romanisation. This proved even more unpopular, with some chiefs now cannily making up fictitious lawsuits against each other to occupy Varus and his administrators while ignoring his tax collectors. Here the Romans were clearly lured into a false sense of security, with the German leaders heaping praise on him every time he settled one of their 'disputes'. However, in reality they were playing for time, gathering resources for a new rebellion against Roman rule. And here they had a deadly surprise ready, one of staggering magnitude. This was Sigimer's son Arminius. Already an experienced Roman military leader having led auxiliary units in battle, the now apparently 'Romanised' tribune had recently joined the staff of Varus on the Rhine frontier. This set the scene for one of the greatest betrayals in military history.

The Key Engagement

Here I first consider the key role Arminius played in sending Varus and his troops to their doom, then address some key questions raised when studying the Teutoburg Forest battle, before finally detailing the engagement itself.

The Treachery of Arminius

Soon Varus realised the German tribal leaders were stalling his planned Romanisation of *Germania*. Therefore, in early AD 9 he introduced martial law to deal with any Germans who refused to accept Roman law or pay their new taxes. He had a reputation as a harsh disciplinarian, and before long summary executions were taking place, families were being enslaved for sale in Trier (Roman *Augusta Treverorum*) and Mainz, and German property was being seized or destroyed. Unsurprisingly, what had begun as German obstinacy now turned much darker, with relations totally breaking down with the Romans. It is now the primary sources say Arminius began his betrayal of Varus, though historiography is an issue given we have no detail of his specific motivation. It is worth remembering he'd spent most of his adult life among the Romans, and as far as they were concerned was fully Romanised. Goldsworthy suggests he was driven by '…anger at his own and other tribes' loss of independence…' (2014, 449), though I would go further. This was a dramatic, life-altering decision for one so used to the luxuries of 'civilised' living. Perhaps some extreme slight occurred against Arminius' close family, as later happened with Boudicca in Britain (see Chapter 3 for detail). Sadly, the likelihood is we will never know exactly what happened, but we can be sure of one thing: the result was a terrible disaster for Augustus and the Romans.

In the first instance, Arminius began to secretly forge an anti-Roman alliance among the most fractious German tribes, including his native Cherusci, the Chatti, Marsi and Bructeri. Warming to his task while still serving on Varus' command team, he then looked to bring the Romans to battle on his own terms. That meant an ambush. Here, he proved a skilful diplomat as well as warrior. At the beginning of August, he convinced some of the leading tribal groupings to stage a minor rebellion, on a scale just large enough to oblige Varus to respond in force given the Roman leader knew he would lose face if it wasn't quickly stamped out. Varus received news of the revolt while travelling from the Weser to his winter headquarters at Mainz and quickly set about planning a short campaign. The last thing he wanted was a delay to his plans for Romanising *Germania*, with Augustus expecting his new province to come into being shortly.

We now have the curious tale of Varus being warned of Arminius' treachery. Tacitus says that another Cheruscan nobleman called Segestes, leader of the tribe's pro-Roman faction, told Varus the night before the Roman forces departed that they were being led into a trap. Segestes then went further, suggesting Varus apprehend Arminius along with some other Germanic leaders he identified as the perpetrators of the insurrection (*The Annals*, 9.16). Tacitus adds that Segestes was Arminius' father-in-law, the latter having married the former's daughter Thusnelda against her father's wishes. For some reason, perhaps because of the bad blood between Arminius and Segestes, Varus ignored the warning. This is the more surprising given the Germans had form here, with the Marcomanni chief Maroboduus having earlier turned on the Romans as soon as he'd returned from Rome. Nevertheless, Varus left Arminius to his own devices. The German quickly left the Roman camp under the pretext of drumming up native support in advance of the Romans launching their campaign. Sadly for Varus though, once Arminius was free from prying eyes he quickly took command of those Cherusci warriors loyal to him, and shortly afterwards the whole German army.

The Big Questions

Having dismissed Segestes warning, the unwary Varus was ready and set off. It was now the beginning of September, late in the campaigning season, and he expected a short campaign with little opposition once his troops confronted the German rebels. His army comprised the three legions deployed on the Rhine frontier, *legio* XVII, *legio* XVIII and *legio* XIX, together with six *cohorts* of auxiliary foot troops and three *alae* of auxiliary cavalry. Given an early imperial legion numbered (at full strength) 5,500 men, an auxiliary foot *cohort* was either 480 troops in a *quingenary* unit or 800 in a *milliary unit*, and an auxiliary cavalry *ala* 512 in a *quingenary* unit or 768 in a *milliary* unit, this gave Varus a total force of between 20,916 and 30,900 men. Either way this was a sizeable army, the latter the same scale as that used by Agricola in his AD 83 Mons Graupius campaign in modern Scotland (see Chapter 5). Though nowhere near the size of the vast armies earlier commanded so successfully by Drusus, Tiberius, Lucius and Saturninus, Varus still believed it easily up to the task at hand given he chose not to call up his two theatre reserve legions. These were the highly experienced *legio* I *Germanica* and *legio* V *Alaudae*, both based at Trier under the command of his own nephew Lucius Asprenas (Pollard and Berry, 2012, 57).

As Varus' campaign got underway, commentators ancient and modern now reference three issues that significantly undermined his chances of success. These were the apparent inexperience of the three legions with him, the fact he allegedly chose not to deploy his army in the standard Roman formation when marching through dangerous enemy territory, and finally the bad weather that he encountered. I consider each here.

First, some key modern sources reference the lack of combat experience of Varus' three legions, especially in the theatre they were now operating in. Given Paterculus specifically says his force was '...an army unexcelled in bravery, the first of Roman armies in discipline, in energy, and in experience in the field...' (*Roman History*, 2.119), something is clearly amiss here. Taking each legion in turn, sadly we lack any real detail regarding *legio* XVII, so have no way of knowing if it was experienced or not. However, both of the other legions were definitely veterans in theatre, with Pollard and Berry highlighting that *legio* XVIII took part in the German campaigns of both Drusus and Tiberius (2012, 55). Meanwhile, *legio* XIX had long campaigned on both the Danube and Rhine frontiers. For example, an inscription on an iron catapult bolt places it helping conquer Raetia in 15 BC, while another inscription later locates it based at the legionary fortress of Dangstetten on the upper Rhine north of modern Basel at the end of the first century BC. These legions were therefore clearly not novice formations unused to combat on the northern frontier. Meanwhile, though no mention is made of the specific auxiliary mounted and foot units used in Varus' campaign, they were also most likely veterans who had served under Drusus and Tiberius. On this basis, I think we can discount the suggestion that the Romans engaged in Teutoburg Forest were inexperienced, this backed up by the fact Varus didn't call upon his two theatre reserve legions.

Next, did Varus ignore standard Roman military procedure when marching through hostile territory, which prioritised logistics as well as safety? In the first instance, a strong logistics chain underpinned any Roman military activity, with the use of maritime routes preferred given much larger quantities of supplies could be carried on water than on land. This played a key role in determining Varus' route when chasing down what he thought a minor German rebellion, and here he did follow standard practice.

Meanwhile, in normal circumstances Varus' army would have deployed on the march in a tight formation for protection, no matter what the size. Where possible, one flank would be protected by a waterway on which the *libernae* war galleys, *myoparo* cutters and *scapha* skiffs of the Rhine fleet would be deployed. By way of analogy, Tacitus later describes Drusus' son Germanicus Julius Caesar doing just this when leading his campaigns of retribution against the Germans in AD 14 (*The Annals*, 1.60, see below). At the same time, outriders from *ala* of auxiliary cavalry would range far and wide to protect any open flanks on the landward side, and to provide a scouting function. Meanwhile, the main marching column would feature any land-based supply train (including the light and medium legionary artillery) at the centre, then the legions either side, and finally the auxiliary foot on the column flanks, front and rear (Elliott, 2018, 151). Finally, at the end of every day's march in enemy territory the whole force, again no matter the size, would build and then spend the night in well-protected marching camps.

Did Varus follow this practice? Well, based on some key primary source references, the answer is ostensibly no. For example, Cassius Dio says (*Roman History*, 56.19): '...he did not keep his legions together, as was proper in a hostile country, but distributed many of the soldiers to local communities...'

The latter seems a reference to the Roman commander being fooled about the peaceful intentions of some of the tribes whose territory he passed through. However, I find it hard to believe given the reason Varus was deploying in such force north of the Rhine was to put down a rebellion, at least as he perceived things. Further, Roman military strategists had long argued against any move that strayed away from mainstream military practice. For example, the leading first century AD governor and military leader Frontinus later wrote in his *Strategemata* that following training, orders and procedure provided the flexibility to deal with any situation the legionaries and auxilia found themselves in, even guerrilla warfare in the most hostile territory (1.6.3). As Goldsworthy, in his detailed analysis of the Roman army on campaign, says (2003, 168):

> ...the Romans were always able to adapt to any local situation. The sophisticated structure, training and well organized supply system gave them advantages in all levels of warfare.

Further, Varus was not commanding in isolation. Whether officially the *legatus augusti pro praetor* at this point or not, Augustus had clearly appointed him to be the governor of *Germania* once the new province had been established. This meant he would have a full *officium consularis* command team with him, including the three *legatus legionis* commanders of his legions, at least five younger Senatorial-level military *tribunes*, the commanders of each of his auxiliary units, and any additional equestrian-rank officers seconded to him for the campaign. Further, his staff was bolstered with any *beneficiarii consularis* legionary and auxiliary officers and experts seconded from the ranks to join his command team. Finally, the commanders of any of his *speculatores* or *exploratores* intelligence gathering and scouting units would have reported directly to him.

Overall, this meant he led a highly experienced military organization, even if he himself was less experienced in the field. I therefore think suggesting Varus ignored standard military practice at the outset of the campaign is a contemporary Roman trope, designed to ensure he alone was held responsible for the disaster to come, and to deliberately diminish the success of the Germans. In reality, while Varus had his route dictated by the use of rivers to help his logistics supply and was unable in places to effectively use his cavalry at distance due to the densely-wooded terrain, his command team would have certainly ensured correct procedures were followed. This was especially the case given these same campaigning procedures were used to such great effect earlier by Drusus, Tiberius, Lucius and Saturninus. Many of Varus' officers served in these campaigns. Why would they change a successful pattern of behaviour? Based on this level of detail, I therefore believe that Varus' formation only began to lose coherence after the initial point of contact when the German trap was finally sprung, as I detail below.

Finally, with regard to the weather, Cassius Dio says a violent storm beset the Romans while on their march through enemy territory, with heavy rain making the line of march treacherous and slippery, and with strong winds breaking off the tops of trees which slowed Varus' advance (*Roman History*, 56.20). This is very believable, for two reasons. First, as detailed, Varus set out late in the campaign season. This was perhaps part of Arminius' plan, he knowing the weather in the region at this time of year would be problematic for the Romans. Second, Roman historians usually recorded weather events accurately when they impacted a key campaign or battle. For example, both Cassius Dio (76.13) and Herodian (3.14) reference the terrible weather later endured by the army of Septimius Severus when he led his two ultimately failed attempts to conquer the far north of Britain in AD 209 and AD 210. Therefore, I do believe contemporary reports that the weather was against Varus as he entered *Germania*.

The Trap is Sprung

At first, and despite the weather, Varus' huge force made good progress. Given the size of his army, any German tribes they came across quickly submitted. Soon his vast column, which Goldsworthy suggests may have stretched 16km long (2014, 451), was snaking well to the northeast of modern Osnabrück in Lower Saxony, heading for what Varus thought was the epicentre of the rebellion. No doubt continually fed false information by the Cherusci scouts supplied by Arminius, Varus led his men deeper and deeper into the German forested interior. However, as the end of September approached and the decisive meeting engagement he'd been expecting failed to materialise, Varus came to the conclusion his mission was accomplished. Keen to continue establishing his new province, he ordered the Roman column to slowly turn around and head back to the Rhine. However, Arminius was watching. The rebel leader had been busy planning his assault, and now Varus' guard was down he determined the time right to spring his trap.

Before I set out my own view on how the battle unfolded from this point, I now consider three key issues to set the scene and provide context. First, the nature of the engagement, second its exact location, and third the size of the German army involved.

In terms of the type of encounter, each primary source differs with regard to the finer detail. This is not surprising given all had different motivations in how they depicted Varus' shocking defeat. Further, some are broadly contemporary, while others were written long after the event. I begin with the earliest, the account of Paterculus who knew both Varus and Arminius. He describes a classic large-scale ambush in the field, saying (*Roman History*, 2.119):

Varus was surrounded and attacked, with no opportunity as he had wished to give the soldiers a chance of either fighting or of extricating themselves, except against heavy odds. Hemmed in by forests and marshes and ambuscades, his army was exterminated almost to a man by the very enemy who it had earlier always slaughtered like cattle, and whose life or death had depended solely upon the wrath or the pity of the Romans.

Next, writing in the early second century AD, Tacitus is briefer given his focus on the later punitive campaigns of Tiberius and Germanicus. He says only that (*Annals*, I.55): '…Varus succumbed to his fate and the sword of Arminius rather than listen to the warnings of his father-in-law Segestes to have him arrested.'

Meanwhile, the contemporary North African-born poet, orator and historian Julius Florus says Varus was actually engaged in diplomacy with the German confederations and tribes when attacked, possibly while still in camp. Specifically, he says (*Epitome of Roman History*, 30.1):

At a moment when, such was his confidence, he was actually summoning the German leaders to appear before his tribunal, they rose and attacked him from all sides with his camp seized and three legions overwhelmed.

Also writing at this time, Suetonius covers the Varian Disaster in his chapters on Augustus and Tiberius. In the first instance, he says (*The Twelve Caesars*, Augustus, 23):

Augustus suffered two severe and ignominious defeats, those of Lollius and Varus. Of these the former was more humiliating than serious, but the latter was almost fatal, since three legions were cut to pieces with their general, his lieutenants, and all the auxiliaries. When the news of this came, he ordered that watch be kept by night throughout the city, to prevent an outbreak of violence and protest, and prolonged the terms of the governors of the provinces, that the allies might be held to their allegiance by experienced men with whom they were acquainted. He also vowed great games to Jupiter Optimus Maximus, hoping the condition of the commonwealth would improve, a thing which had last been done in the Cimbrian War.

The reference to the Cimbrian War in the late second century BC is particularly relevant given this also proved disastrous for the Roman military, with huge numbers of legionaries lost fighting Germans then invading southern Gaul.

This led to the *terror cimbricus* in Rome itself, where the population feared a repeat of the Gallic sack of Rome in 390 BC was on the way. In the event, it took the seven times *consul* Gaius Marius to take matters in hand, completely reforming the Roman military system before finally defeating the Germans. For Suetonius to use such an analogy here shows how severe Varus' defeat really was.

Meanwhile, in his chapter on Tiberius, Suetonius adds that defeat of the Illyrian revolt at around the same time as the Varian Disaster proved timely given it stopped a likely alliance between the victorious Germans on the Rhine and the various German tribes on the Danube frontier (*The Twelve Caesars, Tiberius,* 17).

Finally, when writing in the early third century AD, Cassius Dio presents the Roman defeat as a classic large scale trap in the field, saying that while the Romans were returning to the Rhine frontier and were struggling with the weather conditions, Arminius struck. He says (*Roman History*, 56.20):

> The barbarians suddenly surrounded the Romans on all sides at once, coming through the densest thickets, as they were acquainted with the paths. At first they hurled their volleys from a distance; then, as no one defended himself and many were wounded, they approached closer to them.

The key point to note in all of these narratives is the broad agreement that Varus was ambushed by Arminius on a large scale, and as we will see, more than once.

Next, regarding the location of the main engagement, until recently this was very difficult to determine given we have so little historical detail about the battle. Early theories emerged in the late fifteenth century AD with the rediscovery of key classical texts including new chapters of Tacitus' *Germania* and *The Annals*. In particular, the latter records a region called the *saltus Teutoburgiensis*. This was the first mention of the Teutoburg Forest, which Tacitus said was a huge wooded region in *Germania*. Early antiquarians quickly identified this as the land between the upper reaches of the Ems and Lippe rivers. However, by the early nineteenth century AD academic opinion had changed, with the vast forest now located along a huge wooded ridge called the Osning Forest near Bielefeld in North Rhine-Westphalia. Soon, this had been officially renamed the Teutoburg Forest, a name it retains to this day.

With the location of the forest, academic attention then turned to where within it the actual main Varian Disaster engagement took place. By the mid-1960s four broad theories were in circulation. These were that it occurred in the Weser Hills, in the eastern half of the Teutoburg Forest near the Weser itself, in the southern Teutoburg Forest near Beckum in the northern part of North Rhine-Westphalia, and finally southeast of the Westphalian lowlands.

However, by the late twentieth century AD archaeology began to play a key role in finally locating the specific Teutoburg Forest battle site. Here, finds of Augustan coins and lead Roman slingshots at Kalkriese Hill between the villages of Venne and Engter near Osnabrück led to an intensive investigation there. Soon large quantities of early first century AD Roman and German battlefield debris were found, these numbering over 6,000 artifacts to date. Most recently, an almost complete set of early *lorica segmentata* banded-iron armour was excavated there. This was the thorax protection of choice for the early Principate legionary, a recent addition to their panoply at the time of the battle, with the set found weighing an impressive 8kg when originally complete.

Subsequent archaeological research after the initial finds at Kalkriese Hill has revealed the battlefield archaeology in the region is actually spread along a 24km long, 1.6km wide corridor running south from the deepest Roman penetration back towards Kalkriese Hill, this Varus' most likely route back to the Rhine frontier as we will see. Further, likely German field defences have also been discovered at Kalkriese Hill which fit the hypothesis I set out below. The whole region is also beset with deep ravines and rough terrain, a key aspect of contemporary descriptions of the battle. Together, all of this historical, archaeological, analogous and anecdotal evidence has led to Kalkriese Hill becoming the most popular location for the main Teutoburg Forest engagement. Indeed, it is here the Kalkriese Hill Archaeological Museum and Park is now located, with its fine collection of archaeological artefacts, recreations and displays commemorating the battle.

In terms of the German force engaged in the battle, Pollard and Berry say Arminius' army initially comprised a large gathering of nobles and warriors from his own Cherusci, and also from the Bructeri and Marsi (2012, 56). Contingents from other German tribes later joined after his initial ambush, when its success attracted other Germans after fame and loot, as I detail below. His force may also have featured deserting Germanic recruits from Roman auxiliary units in the region, as later occurred en masse during the Batavian Revolt in AD 69/70. Such troops would have been better equipped than most Germans fighting in their native manner. Regarding numbers for Arminius' force, this is difficult to determine. Initially, his army may have only been 15,000 strong, far smaller than Varus' huge army. This was later bolstered by other Germans joining once victory seemed certain.

Having set the scene for the battle and provided key context, I now detail my own narrative of events in the Teutoburg Forest based on a personal interpretation of the available data. Broadly, I believe it comprised three phases over two days and one night. First, Arminius' initial ambush deep in the forested interior. Second, Varus' night-time attempt to extricate his army. Third, Arminius' final ambush at Kalkriese Hill, which I determine was the main encounter.

Back to the chronological narrative, Arminius planned his initial challenge to the Romans in full knowledge of how they would enter his planned battlespace, and how they would react once engaged. He'd already observed Varus turning his huge column back towards the Rhine frontier, and carefully chose a location for his initial ambush that would funnel the panicking Romans into a pre-planned killing zone. He now deployed his Cherusci, Bructeri and Marsi warriors in ambuscade positions, and waited for the Romans to march past. As the head of the lengthy Roman column almost cleared his warriors late in the morning, he struck at the front and sides en masse, the Germans launching themselves on the unsuspecting Romans from deep within the forest with savage ferocity. This initial ambush shocked Varus and his troops, with many panicking in the bad weather and difficult terrain. Soon the Roman column had been disarticulated into large but isolated units along their line of march. In some places where the Germans managed to achieve local numerical superiority they overwhelmed the Romans and their camp followers, with the first of many massacres taking place. In other areas large groups of Romans maintained coherence, standing their ground and fighting off the German onrush. However, Varus then made a crucial error by ordering the main baggage train to be burnt. Though intended to lighten his men's load, allowing them to march more quickly out of the danger zone, the move actually caused morale to plummet given it signalled the true jeopardy they were in.

Varus now ordered his surviving units to break out into open country. Assuming my interpretation of the battle space is correct, with the line of march heading back to Kalkriese Hill, this was towards the Wiehen Hills near modern Ostercappeln. As the day went on, his Romans were harried all the way by parties of Germans darting out of the murky undergrowth to pick off weaker units. Soon, as late afternoon approached, Roman casualties began to mount again. Goldsworthy says that by this point only an exceptional commander would have been able to extricate the Romans from their desperate predicament (2014, 452). Varus was certainly not that.

Meanwhile, Arminius now knew total victory was within his grasp and as word spread of his amazing success other warriors from neighbouring tribes now began to join him. Cassius Dio adds detail here, saying that by this point (Roman History, 16.21):

...the German forces had greatly increased, as many of those who had at
first wavered joined them, largely in the hope of plunder, and thus they
could more easily encircle and strike down the Romans, whose ranks
were now thinned, many having perished in the earlier fighting.

Still, many Romans survived the day, in places in sufficient numbers to
maintain their increasingly isolated formations and begin the process of
building marching camps. However, before they could complete the task,
Varus ordered a drastic change of strategy. With no idea how many Germans
were surrounding him as night fell, he convinced himself a desperate march in
the darkness was their only hope of reaching safety. The canny Arminius had
anticipated this and knew exactly where the Romans would travel, this along
a wide sandy expanse of open terrain that led directly to the foot of Kalkriese
Hill. There the Germans prepared their final, huge ambush.

As the Romans approached in the dark, their way lit by damp torches, the
route began to narrow. Finally, they were funnelled onto a 100m wide sand bar,
with dense woodland and swamps closing in on either side. Given the weight
of numbers to their rear, those at the front had no choice but to continue. As
they did, they were increasingly attacked from all sides, with small groups
of legionaries, auxilia and camp followers dragged screaming into the pitch-
black night. Florus graphically describes their fate, saying (*Epitome of Roman
History*, 30.37):

> The Germans put out the eyes of some men and cut off the hands of
> others. They cut off the tongue of one man and sewed up his mouth, and
> one of the barbarians, holding the tongue in his hands, exclaimed 'That
> stopped your hissing, you viper.'

Finally, as a rainy dawn broke on the second day, the head of the Roman
column came to a shuddering halt when, out of the gloom, it reached a freshly
built series of German fortifications on Kalkriese Hill. These comprised deep
trenches behind which sat palisaded earthen walls swarming with German
warriors. As terror and confusion rippled down the Roman line of march,
Arminius now launched his final mass ambush. Those Romans to the rear
were soon overpowered, but those near the front made a final desperate
attempt to storm the German defences. The frenzy here is still evident in
today's landscape, with the still visible German defences scattered with a huge
amount of Roman battlefield archaeology. Given much of this has been found
on the far side of the earthen walls, many Romans managed to fight their
way over in their desperation, only to be slaughtered on the far side. Animal

remains have also been found, including a mule skeleton with a broken neck where it had fallen down the far side, and another with the remains of grass stuffed into its bell to muffle the sound during the earlier night march. As Varus had already ordered the baggage train to be destroyed earlier in the engagement, these may have been carrying Roman wounded.

Sadly for Varus, despite the heroism of these surviving troops, the Roman attempt to force their way through Arminius' barrier failed. At that point command and control finally broke down in the Roman ranks. Varus' second in command, the *legate* Numonius Vala, fled with the remaining auxiliary cavalry, but was soon hunted down by Germans and killed (Paterculus, *Roman History*, 2.119). Two other senior officers also soon fell, the *prefect* Eggius dying while leading a last stand with his bodyguard, while another called Ceionius took his own life after being captured. Cassius Dio describes a brutal endgame, with any surviving Romans butchered or taking their own lives. The last surviving members of Varus' command team chose the last option, including their commander, with Dio saying (*Roman History*, 16.21):

> Varus, therefore, and all the more prominent officers, fearing that they should either be captured alive or be killed by their bitterest foes (for they had already been wounded), made bold to do a thing that was terrible yet unavoidable: they took their own lives.

The battle was over. Varus was dead, his army entirely destroyed. Roman losses numbered in the tens of thousands, including all of the legionaries and most of the auxiliaries. Tacitus says that any captive Roman officers were gruesomely sacrificed as part of the German tribal ceremonies celebrating the victory, graphically adding some were cooked in pots, their bleached bones then used in religious rituals (*The Annals*, 1.61). Meanwhile, any other Roman captives who survived German brutality were quickly enslaved, disappearing into the German interior never to be seen again.

Crucially for morale back in Rome, Varus' army also lost hundreds of battle standards. These included the *Aquila* eagle standards of the three legions, which only left the chapel of the standards in a legionary fortress when the entire legion was marching to battle. The loss of one was viewed as shameful. The loss of three was beyond the understanding of many Romans, with Augustus decreeing their numbers – XVII, XVIII and XIX – suffer *damnatio memoriae* and be officially struck from the Senatorial record.

In Rome the blame game began straight away, with Varus in the frame immediately. This wasn't undeserved, he arrogantly ignoring Segestes' earlier warning of Arminius' treachery and then leading his army on a doomed march into a heart of darkness he clearly did not understand. Augustus undoubtedly blamed him, with Suetonius graphically describing the emperor's response which, based on this narrative, caused a psychotic episode (*The Twelve Caesars*, *Augustus*, 23):

> Augustus was so greatly affected that for several months in succession he cut neither his beard nor his hair, and sometimes he would dash his head against a door, crying: 'Quintilius Varus, give me back my legions!' And he observed the day of the disaster each year as one of sorrow and mourning.

Varus certainly paid a terrible price for his catastrophic failure, even post-mortem. Paterculus morbidly describes the fate of his remains, discovered by the Germans after his suicide (*Roman History*, 2.119):

> The body of Varus, partially burned, was mangled by the enemy in their barbarity; his head was cut off and taken to Maroboduus [king of the Marcomanni] and was sent by him to Augustus; but in spite of the disaster it was honoured by burial in the tomb of his family.

Arminius clearly hoped the arrival of Varus' severed head would encourage the Marcomanni into joining their assault on the Roman frontier. However, the shrewd Maroboduus knew the Romans would never let such a defeat stand.

Based on the contemporary written record, this was Arminius' only misstep. The focus on the failures and shortcomings of Varus in modern commentary (and on Augustus' decision to appoint him in the first place) often masks how skilful a campaign Arminius fought. Teutoburg Forest was as much a German victory as a Roman defeat, and in its aftermath Arminius joined the pantheon of literary foes the Romans thought worthy enemies. Tacitus for example calls him '…beyond doubt the liberator of Germany…' (*The Annals*, 2.88). However, now the initiative switched to Rome. Retribution was on the way.

Aftermath and Legacy

In the immediate aftermath of his mighty victory Arminius targeted the remaining imperial outposts in *Germania*, keen to sweep any remaining Roman presence back over the Rhine. However, his force was now much diminished. Most of the warriors engaged in the various stages of the Teutoburg Forest battle with Varus left for home as soon as the engagement had finished, taking any captured Roman loot with them. Given the battle took place late in the campaigning season, many had delayed harvests to gather. This left Arminius with a cadre of his best Cherusci warriors, together with a few others from other tribes still in search of plunder.

Unsurprisingly, word of the massacred legions quickly reached imperial territory. The Roman military establishment now swung into gear in a way that put Varus' inadequacies to shame. In the first instance, the two theatre reserve legions in Trier were swiftly deployed to the Rhine under Varus' nephew Asprenas. They then held the frontier to prevent any German incursions into Gaul until an emergency relief force under Tiberius arrived from the imperial centre. This numbered over 20,000 men and included *legio* II *Augusta*, *legio* XX *Valeria Victrix* and *legio* XIII *Gemina*, all veterans of conflict along the northern frontier.

Here, Asprenas was helped by some heroic resistance in the forts north of the frontier as Arminius strove to squeeze any Roman presence out of *Germania*, for example that at Haltern am See (Roman *Aliso*). Here, the auxiliary garrison under the *prefect* Lucius Caedicius held out until early November, before breaking through the German siege lines to reach the Rhine and safety.

With their northern frontier secure again, the Romans now planned a series of massive campaigns of retribution. The first was launched in AD 10 by Tiberius himself, and here Suetonius details how the Romans had learned from the Varian Disaster. He says (*The Twelve Caesars, Tiberius*, 18):

When Tiberius came to Germany, realising that the disaster to Varus was due to that general's rashness and lack of care, he took no step without the approval of a special advisory council he set up; while he had always before been a man of independent judgment and self-reliance, then contrary to his habit he consulted with many advisers about the conduct of the campaign. He also observed more scrupulous care than usual. When on the point of crossing the Rhine, he reduced all the baggage to a prescribed limit, and would not start without standing on the bank and inspecting the loads of the wagons, to make sure that nothing was taken except what was allowed or necessary. Once on the other side, he adopted the following manner of life: he took his meals sitting on the bare turf, often passed the night without a tent, and gave all his orders for the following day, as well as notice of any sudden emergency, in writing; adding the injunction that if anyone was in doubt about any matter, he was to consult him personally at any hour whatsoever, even of the night.

Clearly, the meticulous Tiberius was leaving no stone unturned in ensuring the success of his mission, knowing another disaster in *Germania* would put the very existence of Augustus' new empire in doubt.

However, it fell to another Julio-Claudian family member to mount the main post-Varian Roman incursions into *Germania*. These were under the command of Tiberius' nephew Germanicus, already a veteran campaigning in the theatre. The first was launched across the Rhine in AD 14, just after Augustus' death and after the accession of Tiberius. It comprised a huge force of up to 70,000 men, with Germanicus initially targeting the Marsi in a surprise thrust that caught the Germans by surprise, leading to a massacre in their tribal centre. Here, he recovered one of the lost *aquila* eagle standards from the Varian Disaster. This prompted the neighbouring Bructeri, Tubanti and Usipeti to intervene. They attempted to ambush Germanicus' huge column as it strove to reopen the old Roman trunk roads through the German forests, but the Romans had learned from Varus' mistakes and quickly deployed to defeat the Germans with huge loss of life. Germanicus then consolidated his gains, rebuilding the long-abandoned Roman forts in the region.

Germanicus' next campaign in AD 15 replicated that of his father, first marching through Bructeri territory where he recovered a second *aquila* lost in AD 9, that of *legio* XIX, before reaching the North Sea coast where he deployed his fleet to support his legionary spearheads. To ensure the Marsi didn't regroup he ordered his *legates* to fully occupy their territory. When the survivors of the previous campaign objected, another massacre of the Germans took place. Germanicus himself then led a campaign against the fierce Chatti, though any German resistance here quickly faded when faced with such huge numbers of imperial troops. The Romans then destroyed the Chatti tribal centre, where Germanicus also captured Arminius' wife Thusnelda.

By late summer Germanicus had reached the site of the Varian Disaster. Around Kalkriese Hill his troops found enormous mounds of bleached bones piled in the dense woodland, with severed Roman skulls nailed to trees. Here, Tacitus describes the Roman leader's shocked reaction (*The Annals*, 1.61):

> Germanicus, upon seeing the remains, was seized with anger and an eager longing to pay the last honor to those soldiers and their general, while the whole army present was moved to compassion by the thought of their kinsfolk and friends, and, indeed, of the calamities of wars and the lot of mankind. Having sent on Caecina in advance to reconnoitre the obscure forest-passes, and to raise bridges and causeways over watery swamps and treacherous plains, Germanicus then visited the mournful scenes, with their horrible sights and associations.

However, Arminius now heard that his Roman foes had returned to the site of his greatest victory. Leading a force of his native Cherusci he quickly attacked, catching Germanicus' auxiliary cavalry scouts in an ambush where he inflicted minor casualties. Again the Romans were ready, with Germanicus ordering his legionaries to swiftly engage the Germans. Soon the mounted troops were relieved. A sporadic two-day battle ensued for control of the Roman roads through the forest in the region, with neither side victorious. As the campaigning season came to an end, Germanicus then returned to the Rhine frontier where he prepared for the following year's campaign. Meanwhile, over the winter, Arminius was distracted when challenged by his old opponent Segestes for control of the Cherusci. A short civil war occurred, ending inconclusively in early AD 16 (Hornblower and Spawforth, 1996, 173).

By this time many German tribes had made their peace with the Romans, and soon German warriors were gathering to fight as allies with Germanicus in his AD 16 campaign. This featured a deep penetration into *Germania* where he forced a crossing of the Weser near Minden. Once across the river, Germanicus then succeeded where Varus had failed, forcing Arminius to engage in a set piece battle. Contemporary historians called the location Idistaviso, though the site has never been satisfactorily identified. Most argue it was east of the Weser between Minden and Hamlin. Today the engagement is therefore either called the Battle of Idistaviso or the Battle of the Weser River.

Here, Germanicus' legions and German allies inflicted huge casualties on Arminius' army, while sustaining only minor losses themselves. Arminius then fled eastwards with his survivors deeper into the forests of *Germania*, but Germanicus pursued, building new roads and clearing woodland to ensure there was no prospect of a desperate German ambush. He then forced Arminius into a final battle at another open-field site, this called the Angrivarian Wall by our primary sources, and thought to be near Hanover. Here the Germans again suffered huge losses, with Arminius now fleeing even further east beyond the Elbe.

Free of Arminius, Germanicus still had time at the end of his AD 16 campaigning season to continue his offensive, targeting the only German tribe still holding out against him. This was the Chatti. Here, he ordered the *legate* Gaius Silius to lead a mixed force comprising 3,000 auxiliary cavalry and 30,000 legionaries, auxiliary foot and German allies to invade their territory. There they carried out a scorched-earth policy, laying waste to anything of value they came across, including any crops in the field. The surviving Chatti then endured a terrible famine through the following winter.

Meanwhile, as the campaigning season came to a close, Germanicus invaded Marsi territory for a third time, even though those left alive after his earlier predations had signed a peace treaty. Here he was clearly reacting to intelligence that yet another revolt was in the offing and deployed an army even larger than that of Silius. Soon the lands of the Marsi were devastated once more, with the Romans killing any Germans they could get their hands on. Any survivors fled east to join Arminius (Tacitus, *The Annals*, 2.25). Germanicus' objectives for the year finally achieved, he ordered his army back to the Rhine frontier, though when his fleet was transferring troops down the North Sea coast back to the Rhine Delta some ships were damaged in a storm.

Though Germanicus was planning a new campaign across the Rhine for AD 17, Tiberius judged Roman honour restored and the German threat to Gaul ended, at least in the short term. He therefore ordered a halt and recalled Germanicus to Rome where he was awarded a triumph. He then sent his nephew to the eastern frontier with orders to reorder the various provinces and client states there, though sadly Germanicus then died in mysterious circumstances near Antioch in October AD 19 (Hornblower and Spawforth, 1996, 783). Arminius himself was then killed two years later by opponents from his own Cherusci tribe, allegedly after Tiberius refused an offer from a Chatti nobleman to poison the German hero (Tacitus, *The Annals*, 2.27).

Meanwhile, the final act of the Varian Disaster was played out two decades later when, in AD 41, the third lost legionary standard was recovered from the Chauci by the *legate* Publius Gabinius in the reign of Claudius, Germanicus' brother (Cassius Dio, *Roman History*, 60.8).

What was the true legacy of the Varian Disaster? In short, it stopped Roman plans to expand the Gallic frontier into northern and eastern Germany dead in the water. Before that, Augustus assumed it was only a matter of time before a new province he would call *Germania* was established between the Rhine and Elbe. This would then give him access to the rich resources of southern Scandinavia and the continental Baltic coast. However, afterwards he knew the price he would have to pay to establish *Romanitas* so far north and east would be too high, with successive emperors understanding this too.

Meanwhile, Arminius' success in holding back those who strove to conquer Germany at the beginning of the first millennium AD was resurrected in the later nineteenth and early twentieth centuries AD by German nationalists in the aftermath of the unification of the country in 1871. Today, a huge statue of him commemorates his victory over Varus, this being situated southwest of Detmold in North Rhine-Westphalia, a reminder to any would-be conqueror that even the Romans didn't win every time.

Chapter 2

The Battle of the Medway

Plautius Invades Britain, AD 43

The Claudian invasion of Britain in AD 43 was one of the highest-risk military operations ever carried out by Rome, in either Republic or empire. Large-scale amphibious assaults are always problematic given the variables involved, including weather, tides and defensive response. However, here the 40,000 men led by Claudius' leading general Aulus Plautius were also crossing *Oceanus*, the terrifying (as the Romans believed) waters of the English Channel and North Sea. Further, their target was a land about which the Romans knew comparatively little, even after Gaius Julius Caesar's two incursions there in 55 BC and 54 BC. The fact the emperor's legionaries and auxiliaries succeeded was testament to a military establishment operating at its highest tempo, with the subsequent creation of the new province of Britannia a high point of the Julio-Claudian dynasty. The campaign's decisive action was the Battle of the Medway, which I detail in full here, including brand-new data published for the first time.

Strategic Build-Up to the Battle

To set the scene for the battle, here I first consider the military capabilities of the native Britons Plautius faced in AD 43, then Rome's initial encounters with Britain prior to the Claudian invasion, and finally the build-up to the campaign itself.

The Britons

At the time of the Claudian invasion Britain featured a dense network of tribes often at war with each other. Starting in modern Kent and heading roughly clockwise, these included the Cantiaci, the Trinovantes to their north in eastern Essex, the Catuvellauni in western Essex through to Oxfordshire, the Atrebates in the Thames Valley, and the Regni and Belgae on the south coast. In the south west, one then had the Durotriges and Dumnonii, with the Dobunni and Cornovii to their north reaching into the Welsh Marches. Into Wales proper were the Silures, Demetae, Ordovices and Deceangli ranging

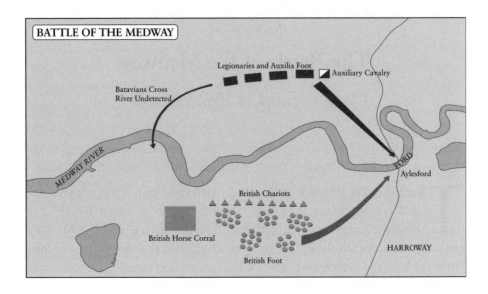

south to north, with the Brigantes in the north of modern England, the Carvetii in the north west, the Parisi north of the Humber, Coritani south of the Humber and finally the Iceni in modern north Norfolk (note I consider the tribes in the far north of Britain in the context of Agricola's AD 83 Mons Graupius campaign in Chapter 5).

In terms of army size, given few native British troops were professional warriors, various sized gatherings are reported in contemporary history. For example when Cassivellaunus fought Caesar in 54 BC he fielded 4,000 chariots at one stage, having sent the rest of his force home. However, as he was the leader of all resistance to Caesar in the south east of Britain, it has been estimated he could have led up to 80,000 men in total. Larger and smaller native British armies are discussed in this and later chapters.

The elite troops in native British armies were the chariot-riding nobility. They were most popular among the tribes in the south east and east of the main island of Britain, but were used throughout the British Isles given the status they bestowed on the chariot rider. Native British chariots featured two ponies harnessed with a yoke and breast straps to a draft pole, a wooden fighting platform with plank or wicker sides, and two wheels on a centrally-mounted axle. They featured two crewmembers, these being an unarmed driver and the noble. The latter carried a Gallic-style shield that was either oval, oval with the upper and lower ends removed or round with a central boss. All were of plank construction. The noble also wore various kinds of iron or bronze Gallic helmet and a chainmail hauberk. He was armed with javelins and the long iron Gallic slashing sword. Contemporary historians describe these native chariots in action, reporting how manoeuverable they were and stating that the Britons deliberately rode them across the front of an enemy battle line which they showered with javelins and insults. The noble then often jumped down to fight on foot, leading his own war band.

Meanwhile, British cavalry acted in a supporting role to the chariots, skirmishing with javelins, attacking flanks and pursuing routers. When used in conjunction with the chariots they proved a particular nuisance for Caesar in his two incursions to Britain, and later against Plautius in AD 43.

By far the biggest component of native British armies were their line of battle spearmen. Mostly farmers called up in a mass levy when needed, they were armed in a similar manner to the Gallic foot troops faced by Caesar in his Gallic conquests. The main defensive equipment was the Gallic shield, or a simpler wicker and hide design. Few wore helmets and fewer any form of armour. The main weapon was a light spear or javelin, with some troops also armed with the long Gallic slashing sword or a dagger. In Britain these warriors formed a spear wall if required, usually in a strong defensive position as with those opposing Plautius in the Battle of the Medway detailed here. However, the preferred tactic was the use of natural terrain to ambush their opponents, often as part of a guerilla campaign.

In Britain the favoured missile weapon used by skirmishers was the sling, particularly in the south west. The Durotriges and Dumnonii tribes who fought Vespasian there in the later AD 40s are a good example of this. Javelin-armed skirmishers are also reported, though no bowmen.

Rome and Britain

The British Isles are the most northwesterly archipelago of the European landmass. Prior to their first contact with the world of Rome the indigenous peoples there had a rich cultural history dating back almost 10,000 years to a time when reoccupation began after the end of the last Ice Age. Throughout this lengthy period they maintained strong links with their continental neighbours, sharing each societal and technological development. This reached its height with the La Tène culture that dominated much of Britain at the time of Rome's first serious engagement here, this in the form of the Julius Caesar's two incursions in 55 BC and 54 BC.

Immediately prior to Caesar's Gallic campaigns, Britain's strong links with its continental neighbours were manifest in many ways. For example key tribes here shared their names with counterparts on the continent, including the Belgae on the south coast, Atrebates in the Thames Valley and Parisi above the Humber. The export of goods from Britain to the continent was also well-known to contemporary audiences, for example iron as detailed by the Greek geographer Strabo (*The Geography*, IV.5) and Caesar himself (*The Conquest of Gaul*, V.135). This connectivity was then brutally dislocated by Caesar's conquest of Gaul. From that time Britain became a place of refuge for those on the continent fleeing Caesar's sanguineous campaigns there which Plutarch (*Life of Caesar*, 15.5) later calculated cost the lives of one million Gauls and the enslavement of another million.

It is in the context of Caesar's Gallic conquests that he mounted his two British incursions. As I have recently argued, here he had no intention to overwinter on either occasion, with both campaigns in effect large-scale armed reconnaissance (2021, 63). His first attempt in 55 BC was one of his worst military operations, showing an uncharacteristic lack of planning, particularly in intelligence gathering. The failure of his allied cavalry to arrive then hobbled his two legions on the east Kent coast, they being unable to scout ahead effectively or protect their line of march. After bad weather intervened, Caesar soon returned to Gaul. His next campaign in Britain in 54 BC was on a much larger scale, with five legions involved, and despite bad weather again hampering him, here he was able to force a peace deal on Roman terms with the leader of native British resistance, Cassivellaunus (likely the tribal leader of the Catuvellauni). Here, the latter agreed to supply hostages from his family and nobility who were sent to Rome, and also pay a huge annual tribute.

Caesar's assassination in 44 BC initiated the final vicious round of late Republican Roman civil wars. In these circumstances Britain was, for a time, forgotten as a potential candidate territory for the next phase of Roman territorial expansion. However, trade did continue through Roman mercantile activity, with Strabo indicating just how profitable this was (*Geography*, 5.8): 'At the moment more revenue is gained from customs duties than tribute could bring in, if you deduct the cost of the forces that would be needed to garrison the country and collect the tribute.'

Interestingly, it is not clear from this statement whether the tribute promised to Caesar by Cassivellaunus and other leaders in Britain was still being paid at the time Strabo was writing in the 20s BC. However, even if not, it seems Britain was for a time still seen as a source of steady revenue for the Republic.

However, foreign adventure was soon back on the agenda. Octavian was by now the last man standing at the close of the Republican civil wars, and from that time onwards the Romans increasingly cast their eyes avariciously towards the archipelago less than a day's sailing from Gaul. Three serious phases of planned invasion of Britain followed. The first involved a number of initiatives by Octavian, or Augustus as he came to be known after his acclamation as emperor by the Senate in 27 BC. The next involved the unlikely-sounding Caligula, while the last was the successful AD 43 invasion of Claudius.

Augustus' interest in Britain actually began before he became emperor, and even before his climactic victory at the naval Battle of Actium in 30 BC against Mark Antony and Cleopatra VII Philopator. We know this through Dio who says that in 34 BC he planned an expedition to Britain, but called it off because of a revolt in Dalmatia, the newly-conquered territories to the north and east of Caesar's old province of Illyricum (*Roman History*, 49.38). He next planned to invade Britain in 27 BC, with the political classes in Rome clearly wanting another successful foreign adventure and grand triumph after he had been declared emperor. For example, the late first century BC Latin poet Albius Tibullus wrote in anticipation ahead of this planned departure (III, 7,147f): 'Where ocean embraces the world with its waters, no kingdom will meet you with hostile intent, only the Briton remains, still undefeated by Rome's might.'

However, once more the new conquest was not to be, with Dio saying (53.22):

He set out to make his expedition to Britain, but on coming to the provinces of Gaul lingered there. For the Britons seemed likely to make terms with him, and the affairs of the Gauls were…unsettled.

Southern (2013, 48) makes the case that the context for this second planned invasion was the cessation of tribute payment to the Romans at some stage by the British. She argues that the tribal elites there would have been far more comfortable dealing with a specific individual, this initially in the form of Caesar himself, than with the comparatively amorphous Roman state. Under this hypothesis, the tribute would have been paid as normal until his murder in 44 BC, and then may have gradually fallen off. Indeed, this may also have been the reason Augustus had planned to launch his earlier 34 BC expedition to Britain.

Even if the threat of his second invasion was enough to have the tribute from Britain resume, this clearly wasn't for long because in 25 BC Augustus planned a third incursion to Britain, with Dio saying that in that year (53.25): 'Augustus was planning an expedition into Britain, since the people there would not come to terms, but he was detained by the revolt of the Salassi and by the hostility of the Cantabri and Astures.'

Here Augustus, already in Gaul with his legions preparing to invade Britain, suddenly found himself fighting on two unexpected fronts. The Salassi were a particularly troublesome Gallic or Celticized Ligurian tribe whose lands were located on the Italian side of the Little St Bernard Pass and the Great St Bernard Pass over the Pennine Alps. Only recently conquered by Rome, they now rose in revolt, though were quickly defeated and then disappear from history. Meanwhile, in Spain Augustus' armies were in the midst of his

Cantabrian Wars, the lengthy campaign from 29 BC to 19 BC where he aimed to conquer the far north of the Iberian Peninsula. There, the Cantabri and Astures now went on the offensive, forcing Augustus to redeploy some his legions south from Gaul to bolster the Roman forces already engaged in Spain.

The timing of the Spanish belligerence here is interesting. The lands of the Cantabri and Astures were the only free regions left in the Iberian Peninsula. The peoples there had long engaged in a once expansive long-range maritime trade with Britain (Cunliffe, 2008, 231). In that context, it is not unreasonable to suggest that the Britons still in contact with Spain encouraged their trading partners to turn Augustus' attention away from Britain. This was clearly successful, with Augustus having to maintain a significant military presence in Spain for another six years. Ultimately he would have to commit eight legions before he was finally victorious, and even afterwards the Romans always maintained a legion at modern León (the Roman legionary fortress of *Castra Legionis*) to maintain order there.

Augustus had two final opportunities to engage directly with Britain. He recorded these himself in his *Res Gestae Divi Augusti* (The Deeds of the Divine Augustus) list of his own accomplishments. This was written down at some stage before his death in AD 14, and then left in his will with instructions for the Senate to set up inscriptions of it across the Empire to celebrate his life. Many copies were made, some of which survive today. The most complete was found in the ruins of a temple to Augustus in Ankara (Roman *Ankrya*, capital of the province of Galatia).

In his *Res Gestae* Augustus details two British kings who came to visit him, either separately or together, to ask for help fighting off their aggressive neighbours. One is named only in part as 'Tin...' on the various surviving sections of the inscription, with the remaining letters missing. This man was initially identified as Tincommius, a son or descendant of the Atrebatian king Commius. However, more recently coins minted in the name of a king called Tincomarus have been found in Atrebatian territory in Hampshire, and it is now thought the latter was most likely the individual named. The two may actually reference the same person. Meanwhile, the other king is named in full as Dubnovellaunus of the Trinovantes (Southern, 2013, 50). The fact that the chiefs were from the Atrebates and Trinovantes tribes seems to point the finger of aggression squarely at the Catuvellauni, with whom they were neighbours to the south and east respectively. By now the latter's territories extended from the Thames Valley to western Essex, and then north as far as Northamptonshire. They were increasingly dominating political and military activity in the south east of Britain, and we are fortunate to have direct evidence of this. Once again this is in the form of minted coins, this time in the name of a king of the Catuvellauni called Tasciovanus, who by 15 BC had succeeded Caesar's protagonist Cassivellaunus. Some of Tasciovanus' coinage has stamps indicating they were minted in Camulodunon (modern Colchester), the usual capital of the Trinovantes. This indicates that by this time the Catuvellauni had conquered much of the territory of the Trinovantes, including their principal settlement. Indeed, later when Aulus Plautius led the Claudian invasion of Britain, this huge *oppida* had become the actual capital of the Catuvellauni's expanded territory. In a further link to the AD 43 campaign, Tasciovanus was the predecessor of the well-known Catuvellauni king Cunobelinus whose later death set in train the events that led to the successful Claudian invasion of Britain (see below).

Returning to Augustus, sadly the *Res Gestae* doesn't provide a date for the visit, or visits, of the two kings he details. It could be that they were associated with Augustus' three known planned campaigns in Britain, detailed above. However, we have no specific evidence to tie either king to these. If they weren't involved with those, then their visits occurred at some stage between 25 BC and AD 7, by which time the *Res Gestae* is thought to have been completed.

We therefore have at least three, and possibly five, occasions when the great Augustus could have campaigned in Britain. The fact he didn't might seem odd given his earlier impeccable campaigning credentials, indicating he was perhaps fighting shy of such an epic undertaking, especially given Caesar's earlier failures to overwinter there. However, the one thing Augustus was above all else by this stage in his career was pragmatic. In that regard, Goldsworthy (2014, 3) notes that although he was at times a gambler, by and large this was a far more common trait earlier when fighting in the last round of Republican civil wars. Later in his career, with regard to Britain, he would certainly have been aware what a mighty undertaking invading there was. I therefore think he simply judged that when each opportunity presented itself, it was ultimately not worth the effort, especially given the known distractions detailed at the time of the three detailed opportunities.

Augustus' failure to conquer Britain certainly played on the wider Roman psyche, with each false start viewed negatively at the time. Even the late first century BC poet Horace, usually a supporter of and apologist for Augustus, reflected that when saying (*Odes*, III.5): '…Augustus will be deemed a God on Earth when the Britons and the deadly Parthians (also targets for early Imperial Roman expansion) have been added to our Empire.'

This poetic quote is noteworthy for two reasons, both relating to the setting of a very high bar for Augustus to achieve deification. The first is the most obvious. Though Horace fought with the *liberators* on the losing side at the Battle of Philippi in 42 BC against Mark Antony and Octavian, he is usually accused of being a propagandist for the Augustan imperial project. Some argue this was through the influence of the poet's patron Gaius Cilnius Maecenas, friend and a chief adviser to Octavian (and later Augustus), which makes it even stranger that Horace should draw attention here to previous failures. The second is the reference to the Arsacid Parthian Empire alongside the Britons. The former, until the arrival of their Sassanid Persian successors, were Rome's principal threat in the east. They were the nearest thing the Roman Republic, and later Principate Empire, faced to a symmetrical threat. For the Britons to be analogously set on this level was high praise indeed, though of the wrong kind given their ultimate fate.

Despite his many successes, Augustus was never to set foot in Britain. In the latter part of his reign, with his attention drawn elsewhere, he instead relied on foreign policy and economic engagement to steadily draw Britain towards the world of Rome. As Moorhead and Stuttard detail (2012, 38): 'There are more ways to conquer than simply through war. Already the south of Britain was being sucked into the economic sphere of Rome. Roman luxury goods, silver, bronze and glass, began to increasingly find their way into the hands of powerful Britons.' His successor Tiberius (AD 14 to AD 37) also showed no interest in the costly prospect of further military adventure in Britain. This was instead left to that most unlikely of candidates, his own successor Caligula (AD 37 to AD 41).

By AD 40 the new emperor was desperate for a successful military adventure to bring him the fame and adulation he openly craved. Actually called Gaius Julius Caesar Germanicus, he'd grown up on campaign with his father Germanicus on the Rhine frontier. While there, he'd worn a child's legionary uniform specially made for him, including diminutive *caligae* marching boots, hence his nickname Caligula. Having been made emperor by the Praetorian Guard prefect Naevius Sutorius Macro after Tiberius' death, he now found himself completely unable to live up to the high martial standards set by his Julio-Claudian forebears. Caligula's first foreign policy venture had shocked Rome, in the context of his annexation of the Roman client state of Mauretania in AD 40. This was because, as a precursor, he'd invited its last king Ptolemy to Rome for discussions. Caligula then promptly had him assassinated, for reasons unknown, before snatching his kingdom.

To remedy his growing ills at home Caligula now decided the solution to his problems lay along the Rhine frontier, with Suetonius explaining (*The Twelve Caesars, Gaius,* 43):

Gaius had only a single taste of warfare, and even that was unpremeditated. At Mevania (a Roman town in Umbria, now modern Bevagna)…someone reminded him that he needed Batavian recruits for his bodyguard (these his preferred close protection): which suggested the idea of a German expedition. He wasted no time in summoning regular legions and auxiliaries from all directions, levied troops everywhere with the utmost strictness, and collected military supplies of all kinds on an unprecedented scale. Then he marched off so rapidly and hurriedly that the guard cohorts could not keep up with him except by breaking tradition: they had to tie their standards on pack mules.

However, once in theatre in northern Gaul Caligula was at a loss what to do next with his huge force. His face was saved when a young British noble arrived at his headquarters, accompanied by a few followers. This was Adminius, son of the now ageing Cunobelinus, king of the Catuvellauni. He'd been banished by his father for some unspecified crime, though it's not clear if the young man sought Caligula's backing to become his father's heir, or had simply arrived to ask for sanctuary. The emperor immediately seized on his good fortune, declaring in an extravagant dispatch to the Senate in Rome that the whole of Britain had submitted to him, adding he planned to invade to claim this new fantastical prize for Rome. He then promptly marched his entire force to the northwestern coast of Gaul, where he set in train plans for a new campaign of conquest across the English Channel. However, as with Augustus, it was once more not to be. Moorhead and Stuttard take up the story (2012, 41):

Plans were made, ships built, supplies sourced and requisitioned, weapons stockpiled, soldiers drilled, all was in place. And then disaster struck. The legionaries gathered on the sea front refused to obey their orders. They would not embark. Not even the threats by the murderous Gaius would induce them to cross the ocean for the nightmare land of Britannia.

Caligula was furious, though impotent given the entire army was set against the invasion. In a rather ill-thought out attempt to cover up his failure, or perhaps as a punishment for the soldiers, Suetonius says he then ordered his legionaries and auxiliaries to gather sea shells in their helmets and tunic laps from the nearby beaches (*The Twelve Caesars, Gaius*, 46). He called this strange harvest the plunder of the ocean and sent it to the Senate as tribute. As a final act he then built the famous Roman *pharos* lighthouse at Boulogne-Sur-Mer (Roman *Gesoriacum*), where extensive harbour works and wharfing had earlier been constructed as part of his abortive invasion. Perhaps realizing he might now be in danger, far from Rome and surrounded by a disgruntled and perhaps humiliated army, he then paid each legionary and auxiliary four gold pieces and then headed quickly back to Rome with his guard. Once there he took his cue from his far more illustrious forebear and namesake Julius Caesar, proclaiming his failed expedition a great success. Celebrations followed, culminating with the Senate awarding him an *ovation* on his birthday on the 31 August. This was a specific form of triumph granted when an opponent was not actually at war with Rome, was considered basely inferior, or where foreign policy success had come without the need to resort to conflict. It seems here the increasingly deluded Caligula really did think gathering pebbles on the Gallic beaches of the English Channel equated to conquering Britain. However, the Roman nobility and people would have none of this nonsense, and only four months later he was assassinated by the acting Praetorian Prefect Cassius Chaerea and another guard officer called Gaius Sabinus.

Enter Claudius

It was left to Caligula's successor, the ill-favoured Claudius, to finally invade Britain and create the new province of Britannia. He came to the throne in the most unlikely of circumstances. Having fled the killing spree carried out in the imperial palace by Caligula's faithful Batavian guard after their master's murder, Claudius hid behind a curtain. There he was later found by Praetorian guardsmen searching for the Germans. They pondered what to do with Claudius, eventually deciding to take him to their *Castra Praetoria* camp. There, to his astonishment, the senior officers decided to proclaim him emperor. They expected him to be their puppet, but he was to prove them dramatically wrong.

Contemporary sources paint a very unflattering picture of Claudius, younger brother of Germanicus who was Caligula's father. For example Suetonius says (*The Twelve Caesars, Claudius*, 3): 'Claudius' mother, Antonia, often called him "a monster: a man whom nature had not finished but had merely begun"; and, if she ever accused anyone of stupidity, would exclaim: "He is a bigger fool even than my son Claudius."'

Modern sources are equally unflattering, with for example Moorhead and Studdart (2012, 42) calling him notoriously absent-minded, short-sighted, limping and drooling, while Kean and Frey (46, 2005) highlight that throughout his education he remained under the same kind of guardianship as would an aristocratic Roman daughter.

However, there was more to Claudius than meets the eye. Southern (2013, 56) suggests that, barred from most aspects of political life except token public appointments, he became a scholarly recluse. This certainly set him in good stead when he did become emperor as, defying all expectations, his was one of the more successful imperial terms of office. In particular, Roman provincial territory grew exponentially in his reign. First defeating a rebellion in the new province of Mauretania, he then invaded Britain in AD 43 as detailed below, where he created perhaps the most unlikely of provinces, before later annexing as new provinces Judea in AD 44, Thrace in AD 46 and northern Palestine in AD 49. The latter was particularly important given it created the Roman province of Syria that was to be the bulwark against the Parthians and later Sassanid Persians in the east. He also continued his academic activities, and by the time he died in AD 54 had written twenty-eight history books, his own autobiography and a treatise on Latin.

At the beginning of his reign, Claudius knew he needed more than the crushing of the Mauritanian revolt to prove himself a worthy emperor to the political classes and people of Rome. Nevertheless, alighting on Britain as his first target for imperial expansion at first seems incredible given the scale of the jeopardy involved. However, two key factors need to be considered here which show it not to be such a strange choice after all. These were the fact that the means were already available to him, and that he was serendipitously presented with a timely motive.

In the first instance, as we have seen above, Caligula had already built a fleet of vessels to carry his army across the English Channel in AD 40. These were still available three years later, and were to provide the core of the fleet of 900 vessels used by Claudius for his AD 43 invasion (Elliott, 2016, 64, these ships later becoming the *Classis Britannica* regional fleet). Further, Caligula had also built the new harbour works detailed above, and had also stocked row-upon-row of warehouses with the provisions needed to support his abortive invasion.

With these preparations for an invasion of Britain already in place, Claudius was able to act swiftly when the opportunity arose to intervene there. The trigger was provided by the death in late AD 40 of Cunobelinus. He was succeeded as king of the Catuvellauni by his two sons Caratacus and Togodumnus. These quickly launched a campaign against their Atrebates neighbours in the Thames Valley, who by this time had strong links with Rome. The Catuvellauni were evidently successful as Verica, the elderly king of the Atrebates, fled to Rome where he sought the support of Claudius. However, instead of consolidating their success, Caratacus and Togodumnus now overplayed their hand by demanding the extradition of Verica. When this was rebuffed by Claudius, the two British leaders vowed vengeance and soon disturbances broke out in Britain against the Roman merchants already embedded there (Suetonius, *The Twelve Caesars*, 17.1).

It was against this backdrop that Claudius was presented with the opportunity to make his name within the Julio-Claudian dynasty. Suetonius provides detail here, saying (*The Twelve Caesars, Claudius*, 17.1): '…he decided

Britain was the country where a real triumph could most readily be earned.' Claudius now had the means thanks to Caligula, and motive thanks to the naïve belligerence of Caratacus and Togodumnus. The scene was now set for one of the greatest amphibious operations of the pre-modern world.

Having committed to the invasion, Claudius set off from the port of Rome at Ostia and was soon in northwestern Gaul. There he set up his headquarters in Boulogne-Sur-Mer (Suetonius, *The Twelve Caesars*, 17.1). Soon he was gathering his army of conquest there, shrewdly appointing the Pannonian governor Aulus Plautius as its commander. Plautius was not only a long-term friend and ally of the Julio-Claudian dynasty, but was also one of the most experienced military leaders in the empire. He in turn appointed the future emperor Vespasian as his leading legionary *legate*. The invasion force numbered 40,000 men, comprising four legions and 20,000 auxiliaries. The former comprised *legio* II *Augusta*, *legio* XIV *Gemina* and *legio* XX *Valeria Victrix*, who travelled from their bases on the Rhine frontier, and Plautius' own *legio* IX *Hispana* which travelled with him from Pannonia. Meanwhile, the auxiliaries provided more foot troops and all of the cavalry, the latter vital to military success as Caesar had found in 55 BC when forced to fight in Britain without them. Claudius also ordered 3,000 tonnes of grain to be loaded onto the larger merchant vessels, guaranteeing food for the invasion force for at least three months after its arrival. This was not a reconnaissance in force as with Caesar, but a full campaign of conquest.

Claudius now readied his fleet for the invasion. The vessels built by Caligula, and the additional ones he'd constructed to boost their number to 900, were built in two different ship-construction traditions. Those designed to provide the escort for the fleet, and then provide fire support for the land forces once they were ashore, were normal Roman war galleys built to a standard Mediterranean design. By this time the most common was the *liburnian* bireme galley, this having taken over from the larger *quinquereme* as the dominant type after the conclusion of the late Republican civil wars. These were lighter and more manoeuverable than earlier types, and much more suited for use in littoral and riparian operations along coastlines and down river systems. Meanwhile, most of the transport vessels employed by Claudius were built in a completely different way. This was in the Romano-Celtic shipbuilding tradition, as used by Julius Caesar in his second incursion to Britain in 54 BC. These featured lower freeboards to enable easier disembarkation, banks of oars, large sails, and wider beams to carry bulkier loads and help ride out the rough seas in northern waters. With the local maritime Gallic tribes such as the Veneti, Morini and Menapii long incorporated into the Empire, both Caligula and later Claudius were able to make much use of their noted shipbuilding skills.

Claudius was therefore able to utilize a substantial, high-quality fleet. To man them he also called on the services of his best sailors and marines, those of the *Classis Misinensis* on the Tyrrhenian coast of Italy, many of whom were now seconded to north western Gaul.

The Key Engagement

Here I detail the AD 43 Roman invasion of Britain under Plautius as Claudius looked on from Boulogne-Sur-Mer. I then move on to the early phase of the campaign as the Roman legionary spearheads cut through to central Kent through the lands of the Cantiaci. There, along the line of the River Medway, the main encounter then occurred. This was one of the most significant battles in British history given that, if the Romans had lost the hard-fought two-day encounter, the narrative of British history may have been considerably different. To that end, I go into great detail about each phase of this key engagement, where Plautius had to use all of his extensive experience as a field commander to overcome a highly motivated and well-positioned enemy.

Aulus Plautius Invades

Late in the summer all was ready and Claudius ordered the invasion to begin, gambling his reputation and future on the successful conquest of fearsome Britain. However, as with Caligula, all almost came to naught before a single ship had sailed. Once again the legionaries and auxiliaries, weary of crossing terrifying *Oceanus*, refused to board the invasion vessels. The day was saved by the most unlikely of imperial champions, Claudius' own freedman Tiberius Claudius Narcissus. This former imperial slave was actually a member of the emperor's *Consilium Principis* main advisory council, and so one of the most powerful men in the Empire. He now stepped forward to address the massed troops, scolding them for their cowardice and disloyalty to the emperor. He then boarded the nearest vessel himself. Shouting '*Io Saturnalia*', referencing the Roman end of year role-reversing winter festival, the chastened soldiery quickly followed, and the invasion proceeded. Plautius positioned himself in the lead ship, with Claudius remaining in Boulogne-Sur-Mer for the time being.

Once persuaded to board the invasion fleet the huge force set sail in three divisions to avoid any congestion when they landed, though Dio (*Roman History*, 60.19) says the weather conditions soon turned against them '...until a light from the east streaked westwards, in the direction they were sailing.' This good omen marked a change in meteorological fortunes and soon the fleet was underway again, arriving in Britain uneventfully and unopposed in late summer. In this regard the later departure of the fleet actually helped the Roman amphibious operation. When the British leaders in the southeast had earlier learned that Claudius' was massing an army of invasion in northwestern Gaul, they had gathered a large force along the east coast of Britain to oppose any attempted Roman landing. However, by the time Plautius arrived this had been dispersed to begin gathering their harvests, the Britons assuming that once more the Romans had changed their minds.

Controversy has long surrounded the exact point where Plautius' force disembarked. Manley (2002, 131) and others have argued in favour of potential landing sites near Chichester and elsewhere. However, given its proximity to the continent, and Roman knowledge of the region gained during Caesar's previous two incursions, I firmly believe the landing site was on the east Kent coast. Others, for example Grainge (2005, 117) in his detailed assessment of the Roman invasions of Britain, agree. If this is accepted, then where were the exact landing beaches for this huge invasion? One candidate would be the beaches between Sandwich and Walmer as used by Caesar in 55 BC and 54 BC, though given the huge size of the AD 43 fleet (even accepting it arrived in three waves) a much larger area would have been needed. In that regard, it seems likely that the shelter of the then navigable Wantsum Channel to the north of Sandwich, together with the safe harbourage of Pegwell Bay with its broad expanses of beach, would also have been used. As Moody (2008, 141) says:

> Given the size of the operation, it is unlikely that a single location can be identified for the Roman landings. More probably, the ships landed where they could, in the network of harbours, beaches and trading ports on the east and western sides of the Wantsum and (the) troops secured themselves, by units, over a wide area.

Wherever the specific landing places were in eastern Kent for this invasion, the locale for the event was later commemorated by the building in the reign of Domitian of a grand monumental arch at Richborough (Roman *Rutupiae*, the arch fully detailed in Chapter 5) which stood from the later first century AD through to the late third century AD, latterly being used as a signal station (Strong, 1968, 72).

Once the majority of his forces and provisions were ashore, and with no enemy to engage as yet, Plautius built an extensive ditch-and-bank fortification to protect his principal beachhead. This has been identified at Richborough, with a section of the vast ditch still visible within the walls of the later Saxon Shore fort. Over 640m of these defences have been excavated, with the overall site likely to have been playing card in shape, as with a standard

Roman marching camp though far larger than normal. Calculations based on its known dimensions suggest a size of up to 57ha, and from this location it would have sealed off the neck of the then promontory on which the later arch and fort were built. The sophistication of the fortification is indicated by the presence of a gate tower on the western side.

Plautius now began his breakout campaign. In terms of the route taken in modern Kent, Bishop (2014, 2) convincingly argues that rather than build new bespoke roads at this early stage of the initial conquest campaign, the Romans would instead have made use of the extensive network of Late Iron Age (LIA) trackways in the region. I believe the route Plautius would have taken is along the Pilgrim's Way, the well-known prehistoric ridgeway running for much of its length in Kent along the south side of the North Downs. Given the south-facing slopes here, this ensured Plautius' force was exposed to the maximum amount of sunlit daylight as the legionary spearheads snaked their way along the route. This helped them stay on the march for longer each day given this was late in the campaigning season.

As Plautius advanced through northern Kent, he finally tracked down his elusive foe. Once again, as with Caesar, the Catuvellauni were the catalyst for regional native resistance, gathering allies from far and wide across Britain. However, in short order the Romans defeated both Caratacus and Togodumnus separately in two small engagements, after which the Dobunni (a tribe based in the Welsh Marches who'd supplied troops to support the British leaders) became the first of the British kingdoms to sue for peace.

The Battle of the Medway

Consolidating for a short period after his victories, Plautius then continued westwards, arriving at a major river defended on the far bank by an arrayed British army. Our main source is Cassius Dio (*Roman History*, 60.20), his narrative considered in detail later. Here Plautius fought his definitive engagement of the AD 43 campaign. This is usually identified as the River Medway given it is the principal waterway bisecting central Kent, hence the name Battle of the Medway, and I agree.

Accepting this argument, Plautius quickly reached Bluebell Hill overlooking the Medway Gap where the River Medway cuts through the North Downs. There, instead of continuing along the route of the Pilgrim's Way as it turned north before crossing the winding river at Cuxton, he instead headed directly westwards, aiming to cross at one of the then well-known fording points on the Medway. Here, there is now some real debate over the actual site of the fords he targeted, this being very important given his choice led directly to the battle taking place there.

The most widely accepted theory is that Plautius aimed for the twin fords at modern Snodland and Aylesford downriver of Maidstone. The former marked the tidal reach of the Medway at the time (Kaye, 2015, 232). Indeed, at Snodland local historians have installed two small monuments on the eastern bank of the river opposite the local church to mark the site. However, I have questioned this location in the past given it features a steep approach down Bluebell Hill, and is then beset with extensive marshland either side of the river. This would not only impede a Roman advance to the fords, but also a British defence on the far side, especially given their extensive use of chariots. From a Roman perspective, having filmed television documentaries wearing Roman *lorica segmentata* banded-iron armour, imperial Gallic helmet and carrying a full-size *scutum* shield, and having also filmed a separate documentary on that very river bank, I can definitively say I would certainly not choose to fight there in the full panoply of a Principate Roman legionary.

However, most recently two potential new Roman marching camp sites have been located at West Farleigh and Mereworth, both upriver of Maidstone. The first is 200m west of the village green, classically playing-card shaped with visible entrances and exactly the right size to house a full legion. In terms of archaeological evidence, a Roman lead slingshot and lead ingot have been found nearby along with Roman ceramic building material (CBM). It also sits within a dense landscape of later Roman industrial and settlement activity.

Meanwhile, the second site is 300m south of St Lawrence's Church in Mereworth, again classically playing-card shaped, and sits on high ground adjacent to Mereworth Castle. In particular, the ditch and bank at its northwest corner and along its western side are very evident in the landscape. Here, the most recent archaeological finds have included whetstone sword-sharpeners, Roman CBM and Roman pottery. At both sites intensive research is now underway to find datable evidence to comprehensively confirm their candidacy as Plautian marching camps, and to also find additional Roman marching camps between the two.

If they do prove to date to the AD 43 campaign, this would then see Plautius' forced crossing of the Medway moved upriver from Snodland/Aylesford to a broad front west of Maidstone along the river at East Farleigh, Barming and Teston, where the Medway has historically been fordable and where modern bridges are located today. Here, the river valley is shallow with gentle slopes leading down to the Medway from the high ground above where the West Farleigh marching camp site is located, with no marshland to impede a gentle approach to the fords along the river. This would be a far more agreeable battlespace for Plautius to operate in. Further, the gently sloping valley would also provide an ideal platform for Plautius' legionary artillery to support his forced river crossing. The legions provided all of the battlefield and siege artillery component of Roman armies when on campaign. This included light *scorpiones* dart-throwers and larger *ballistae*, the latter firing large bolts and shaped stones. When at full strength, each cohort in a legion fielded one of the latter and each century one of the former. This gave an impressive total of 10 *ballistae* and 59 *scorpiones* per legion. Given Plautius fielded four legions in this campaign, that gave him an impressive amount of serious battlefield firepower to utilize, in addition to his auxiliary archers who would also have been able to make good use of the sloping valley sides.

If this location is where Plautius fought his way over the Medway, then the role of the second marching camp site at Mereworth is also explained. This sits on high ground above the Greensand Way, the key prehistoric trackway linking the east Kent coast with Haslemere in southwestern Surrey. From there it provided access to the Solent, the south coast, and the south west of Britain. Controlling it in western Kent at Mereworth would thus have allowed the Romans to seal off the Medway Valley battlespace where Plautius was operating, preventing any native British reinforcements from confederations and tribes on the south coast, in the southwest and in the west from arriving along this vector.

In terms of how Plautius might have arrived here upriver of the tidal reach on the Medway, under this hypothesis he made use of local guides with detailed knowledge of the region who guided him to the easiest crossing points on the river, avoiding the steep approach and marshes around Snodland and Aylesford. Given the distance between Bluebell Hill and the East Farleigh/Barming/Teston fords is only 4km as one tracks the Maidstone bend of the Medway, this would merely add a few hours of travelling time when compared to the Snodland/Aylesford site.

At the time of writing there is no definitive archaeological evidence to support either candidate site as the location of Dio's famous river-crossing battle. However, accepting as I do the engagement was on the Medway, and noting it could have been at either location, we can now consider the battle itself. I begin with Dio's key commentary, which given its importance I record in full (*Roman History*, 60.20):

Plautius advanced farther and came to a river. The barbarians thought that the Romans would not be able to cross it without a bridge and consequently bivouacked in rather careless fashion on the opposite bank; but he sent across a detachment of Germans, who were accustomed to swim easily in full armour across the most turbulent streams. These fell unexpectedly upon the enemy, but instead of shooting at any of the men they confined themselves to wounding the horses that drew their chariots; and in the confusion that followed not even the enemy's mounted warriors could save themselves. Plautius thereupon sent across Flavius Vespasian also and his brother Sabinus, who was acting as his lieutenant. So they, too, got across the river in some way and killed many of the foe, taking them by surprise.

The survivors, however, did not take to flight, but on the next day joined issue with them again. The struggle was indecisive until Gnaeus Hosidius Geta, after narrowly missing being captured, finally managed to defeat the barbarians so soundly that he received the ornamenta triumphalia, though he had not been *consul*.

There is much to unpack in this short description. In the first instance, this was clearly a far closer-run battle than Dio would have us believe. It took the Romans two days to force the crossing, even after Plautius' initial stratagem of sending 'Germans' to swim the river. My interpretation here is that he actually sent them to cross the Medway further downstream, aiming to outflank the Britons, perhaps nearer to modern Rochester if the battle site was at Snodland/Aylesford, or immediately downriver of Maidstone if East Farleigh/Barming/Teston. This shows the native forces were better prepared than Dio describes.

The Germans he details here have often been identified as Batavian auxiliaries, given such troops similarly swam across the River Po near Placentia during the civil wars of AD 69 (Southern, 2013, 68). Among the auxilia in Plautius' army these would have been elite warriors, further showing he viewed the Britons on the opposite bank as a serious threat. In terms of such troops swimming in armour, the likelihood is they used inflated pigskins to float across the river, a tactic familiar to the Batavians given their origins in the Rhine Delta (Elliott, 2016, 115).

Whether they were Batavians or not, Plautius' tactic here was clearly to distract the Britons with their surprise attack on the corrals of British horses and ponies. Vespasian and Sabinus then led a legionary assault across the river. However, no matter how much Dio talks this up, it clearly failed given the Britons remained on the battlefield and continued to resist. As evening approached, Plautius now ordered the building of marching camps on the eastern bank of the river (perhaps that at West Farleigh is one of them) to protect his army overnight.

Plautius knew the importance of this battle, given if he lost then the whole invasion might fail. He therefore lost no time in renewing his assault across the fords at first light the following day. However, even then it took an extraordinary act of bravery on the part of the officer Geta to turn the tide in favour of the Romans. We know this because of the *ornamenta triumphalia* awarded him. This was the highest award possible for a military officer, and one that in Republican times would have allowed him a real triumph in Rome. In imperial times it was usually reserved for army commanders, so clearly his actions were dramatic indeed. As Moorhead and Stuttard say (2012, 48): 'That the Roman's eventual victory hung in the balance, turning on the fierce and determined fighting of Geta and his men, suggests a hard-contested bloody struggle.' Finally, the Britons broke and fled northwards· towards another major river barrier, the Thames.

Aftermath and Legacy

Once on the line of the Thames the Britons deployed on the north bank and prepared to fight a second battle defending a major river crossing. Plautius was unrelenting in his pursuit and soon the Roman army was arrayed in force opposite. The location of the ensuing engagement is again a matter of conjecture, with some arguing it was near to modern Westminster (Moorhead and Studdart, 2012, 48). However, in recently published work I have argued in favour of a location further to the east on the line of the medieval Higham-Tilbury ferry. This was the lowest fordable point on the Thames during the Roman period (Elliott, 2016, 116). It also most closely fits Dio's description of it being '…at a point near where the Thames empties into the ocean and at flood-tide forms a lake' (*Roman History*, 60.20).

If this indeed were the location of the Thames-crossing battle, then Plautius would have reached it by marching north down the Medway past modern Cuxton and Strood, then continuing northwards through Higham and Church Street before hitting the line of the Thames. Viewing the Britons opposite, he then decided on another forced crossing. Once more Plautius employed the stratagem of crossing the river to flank the Britons, but this time both upriver and downriver of their deployment. This again featured his auxilia 'swimming' across downriver according to Dio (*Roman History*, 60.20), but he also made use of a bridge upriver. This latter must have been a Roman bridge of boats given it is highly unlikely the Britons had the technological capability to build a substantial bridge capable of carrying such a large body of heavily armed men over a major waterway, even taking into account the numerous islands and marshes in the pre-modern Thames.

A key point to note here is that while Plautius didn't use his fleet in the earlier Medway-crossing battle, he did here on the Thames. In fact it played a key role, helping him force the river with the bridge of boats and also, perhaps, ferrying the auxilia rather than them swimming, as Dio improbably suggests.

The deployed ships, including *libernae* war galleys, *myoparo* cutters and *scapha* skiffs, also participated in the combat itself, using their *ballistae* and other missile weapons to provide covering fire while the legionaries and auxiliaries crossed. This combination, using ground and naval forces fighting together, proved highly effective and later became a key feature of the Claudian campaigns of conquest.

Dio says that, as the Romans forced the river crossing, they '...assailed the barbarians from several sides at once and cut down many of them...' (*Roman History*, 60.20). A likely scenario here would see the Britons engaged on each flank by the troops who had crossed both downriver and upriver of their position, with the fleet enfilading them with missile fire at the same time. Once the Britons were disrupted, a reserve of legionaries and auxilia then used known crossing points to complete the destruction of the native army.

Once more the Britons fled northwards, though Dio (*Roman History*, 60.21) says they used their knowledge of the local marshy terrain to make good their escape, with many of the pursuing Romans getting into difficulty and some being surrounded and killed. However, to all intents and purposes this first phase of the Claudian campaign of conquest in Britain was over, with Togodumnus somehow dead and Caratacus fleeing to the west to find sanctuary with the Silures and Ordovices tribes in Wales.

Having successfully crossed the Thames, and about to enter the home territory of the leaderless Catuvellauni, Plautius now paused to consolidate his position. Here he may have taken into account Caesar's difficulties during his two incursions and took care not to overextend his lines of supply. However, this seems unlikely to me given he had his fleet in attendance, able to support his advance from the line of the Thames Estuary, up the eastern coast, and down the river systems of modern Essex and Suffolk. Dio, in his commentary, gives a very different reason for the pause. He says (*Roman History*, 60.22):

> ...because of the difficulties he had encountered at the Thames, Plautius became afraid, and instead of advancing any farther, proceeded to guard what he had already won, and sent for Claudius. For he had been instructed to do this in case he met with any particularly stubborn resistance, and, in fact, extensive equipment, including elephants, had already been got together for the expedition.

There is an unusual hagiographic quality in this comment by Dio, seeming to indicate that Plautius needed the emperor to help him complete the first season of campaigning in Britain. This presents two problems for the modern historian. First, there is no evidence elsewhere that Plautius had any difficulty in the Thames engagement other than controlling the pursuit of the routed Britons across the marshes. Second, as we will see, there was no other subsequent set-piece engagement in the campaign. To my mind, this is therefore a clear example of well thought out imperial propaganda. Claudius and Plautius had agreed the emperor would travel to Britain in time to take the final submission of their opponents, and this he did.

When Claudius did arrive in Britain from Boulogne-Sur-Mer, the Romans lost no time in driving home their advantage to bring the campaign to a swift conclusion. First, as a propaganda exercise, Dio says Claudius arrived with the elephants he had earlier gathered in Gaul (*Roman History*, 60.22). Given the last time the Romans had used trained war-elephants was a century earlier, it is likely these were beasts from the emperor's personal menagerie, or those destined for use in the arena. Plautius then targeted the now leaderless Catuvellaunian capital Camulodunon in a lightning strike, with any remaining resistance quickly crushed. The Catuvellauni finally defeated, they and ten other British confederations and tribes now voluntarily submitted to Roman rule. It is at this point Tacitus says the province of Britannia was founded, with Plautius becoming its first governor (*The Agricola*, 14.11). The army then acclaimed Claudius as *imperator* several times, allowing him to later hold a triumph in Rome, this number of acclamations an unheard of precedent given only one was usually reserved per individual campaign.

Having achieved his career-defining conquest, Claudius didn't stay in his new province for long. First he gave Plautius instructions to continue campaigning, given only the south east had, to that point, been conquered. Then, after only sixteen days he crossed back to Boulogne-Sur-Mer, before taking an overland route back to Rome given the increasingly difficult sea conditions this late in the year. However, he had no such concern for his son-in-laws Magnus and Silanus who Dio (*Roman History*, 60.21) says he sent back to Rome by the fastest means to carry the news of his great victory to the Senate and people there. The former quickly granted him the title *Britannicus*, confirmed his triumph, and voted that there should be an annual festival to commemorate this most unlikely of conquests given their previous qualms about Claudius. Further, two triumphal arches were erected in his honour which detailed his success in Britain, one in Rome itself and one in Gaul (most likely Boulogne-Sur-Mer given its key role in the campaign). Finally, by the time Claudius himself had arrived back the returning hero, the Senate had also given the title *Britannicus* to his two-year-old son Tiberius Claudius Caesar. Claudius' dramatic gamble had paid off, his name now secure as one of the leading members of Julio-Claudian pantheon. However, the Roman campaigns of conquest in Britain were far from over.

Chapter 3

The Battle of Watling Street

The End of Boudicca, AD 60/61

In Rome the Claudian invasion of AD 43 was considered a great success, with at least part of fearsome Britain tamed and incorporated into the world of Rome as a new province. However, the empire had a voracious appetite for territory it deemed *pretium victoriae* (worth the conquest), and no time was lost in the rapid growth of imperially-controlled land there. The first breakout campaigns saw the legions of Rome expanding out from the initial province in the south east to conquer the south west, Midlands, the north up to The Wash, and the Welsh Marches. Soon Wales itself was invaded. Then, just as the warrior governor Gaius Suetonius Paulinus was on the verge of victory there, he received news of a terrible disaster. Back in the south east, a furious rebellion had broken out. Led by Boudicca, queen of the Iceni tribe in north Norfolk, this had spread like wildfire across much of Roman-occupied Britain. The province was now in danger of falling. Paulinus, cut off from the continent in distant Wales, headed back at speed. Soon he was on Watling Street, the major military trunk road running through central Britain to Kent. This now became the setting for one of the most important battles in British history, and certainly its most sanguineous.

Strategic Build-Up to the Battle

The Boudiccan Revolt was the culmination of nearly twenty years of Roman conquest campaigning in Britain. To understand it, and the resulting Battle of Watling Street, an appreciation is needed of the various phases of Roman occupation as its province here grew. Therefore, first I set out each of these initial campaigns of conquest, ending with the final breaking point as tensions with the native Britons exploded into open rebellion. I then conclude this first section by outlining the initial stages of the Boudiccan Revolt, building to Paulinus' final confrontation with the Iceni queen, the stakes being the future of the very province itself.

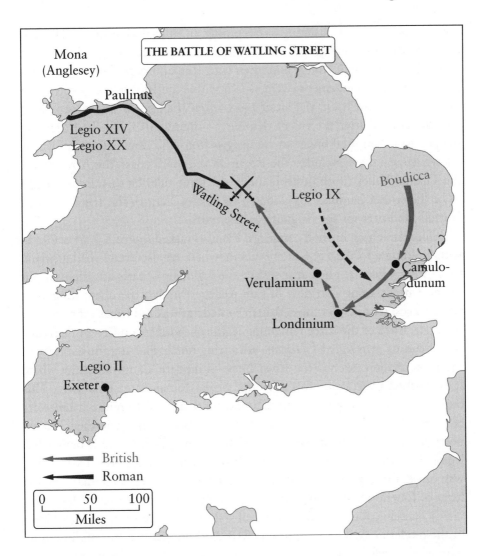

Early Breakout Campaigns

At the point Claudius left his new province it only comprised southeastern Britain. However, the emperor made it clear to Aulus Plautius before his departure that his newly-conquered territory must be expanded swiftly. The new governor responded immediately, guided by the tribal landscape set out before him. Already the territories of the Cantiaci, Catuvellauni and Trinovantes had been assimilated by Rome to establish the core province. Looking further afield, the Romans now followed a familiar pattern of imperial conquest. First, those confederations and tribes politically closest to Rome became client kingdoms. This was a formal process where the king or queen of the nation in question became a *clientes* of the empire, in a procedure called *rex sociusque amicus* (translating as becoming an official king/queen, ally and friend of Rome). Such kingdoms continued to function 'independently', but under the guidance of Rome, and often with Roman troops deployed in their territory. These arrangements were usually with a specific king or queen rather than the kingdom itself, the latter more often than not being incorporated into the empire after the ruler's demise (Southern, 2013, 75). In Britain, at the point of the initial breakout campaigns from Claudius' original province, known *clientes* there included the Regni on the south coast, the Atrebates in the Thames Valley (both possibly under the same ruler by this time, thought to be Tiberius Claudius Cogidubnus, an heir of Verica), the Iceni in north Norfolk, and perhaps the Brigantes in the north.

Before launching his first campaign Plautius tasked *legio* XX *Valeria Victrix* with building a fortress at Camulodunon, where he also established a *colonia* for retiring veterans. Their rear secure, the legionary spearheads then set out in short order, using corridors of safe passage through the client kingdoms where necessary to target those British confederations and tribes yet to submit to Rome. Each of the three remaining legions headed in a different direction, with Plautius' own *legio* IX *Hispana* advancing north. Skirting the territory of the Iceni, it soon reached the River Nene in modern Cambridgeshire where it established a vexillation fort at Longthorpe (Roman name unknown). This built, the legion continued north to found another vexillation fort at Leicester (Roman *Ratae Corieltauvorum*) on the River Soar. Finally, it then headed northeast to the lands of the Coritani above The Wash where it built a full legionary fortress at Lincoln on the River Witham. There the IXth legion was based for a generation, with its legionaries leaving their mark in the form of funerary inscriptions. A fine example is the tombstone of legionary Gaius Saufeius, found at the corner of Salthouse Lane on the High Street in the modern city. The inscription (RIB 255) on his fine 2m-tall limestone monument reads: 'To Gaius Saufeius, son of Gaius, of the Fabian voting-tribe, from Heraclea, soldier of *legio* IX, aged 40, of 22 years' service: he lies here.'

If Saufeius' tombstone is contemporary with the IXth legion's stay in Lincoln then here is a warrior that, given his 22 years' service at death, could easily have taken part in the Claudian invasion itself, and the subsequent breakout campaign.

Meanwhile *legio* XIV *Gemina* headed northwest deep into the Midlands, establishing vexillation forts at Great Chesterford (Roman name unknown), Mancetter (Roman *Manduessedum*) and Alchester (Roman name unknown). Finally, and most famously, *legio* II *Augusta* under the future emperor Vespasian (AD 69 to AD 79) struck out for the still-hostile south west. His route from modern Essex, or perhaps Kent if some of his troops had remained in the lands of the Cantiaci, is unclear. One option would be through the territory of the Atrebates in the Thames Valley. Another would be direct from Kent along the Greensand Way (detailed in Chapter 2), skirting the impenetrable Weald to the south. If the latter were the case, a working hypothesis sees the newly-located marching camp at Mereworth, built to secure the western flank of Plautius' AD 43 Medway Valley battlespace, later becoming a logistics base to support Vespasian's initial advance into Surrey and Hampshire. The fact Roman period CBM has been found there supports this view that it later became a more permanent structure.

Whichever route Vespasian took, once in theatre Suetonius (*The Twelve Caesars, Vespasian*, 4) goes into great detail about the hard-fought campaign, saying that the senior *legate*: '...fought 30 battles, subjugated two warlike tribes (the Durotriges and Dumnonii), captured more than 20 oppida (fortified native urban centres), and took the Isle of Wight.'

On leaving the south east, Vespasian headed directly for the coast where his speedy advance was greatly aided by the use of the British fleet to provide close support in the littoral zone along the seaboard and down the river systems. This included exercising military control there, scouting and raiding ahead of the land forces, carrying out all of the logistical heavy lifting, and building fortified harbours to supply the troops as they advanced (Elliott, 2016, 120). An extreme example of this was the capture of the Isle of Wight early in Vespasian's campaign, as detailed by Dio. Analogously this would have featured an AD 43 Claudian-style invasion in microcosm, with the fleet displaying all of its military roles to facilitate the swift conquest of this significant landmass opposite the vital Solent waterway.

Archaeological data supporting the rapid progress of Vespasian's offensive from that point comes in the form of large-scale Claudian-period storage buildings and Claudian pottery on the site of the later Roman settlement of *Clausentum* (today a suburb of Southampton) at the tip of the Bitterne Peninsula. From here supplies arriving via the regional fleet would have been ideally placed for forward deployment up the River Itchen to the advancing legions and auxilia. Vespasian's ongoing progress can be tracked today by each new coastal base he established during his westward progression. The next step from Bitterne can be found at Wimbourne in Dorset where he built an early vexillation fort with an associated port and storage facility, this time on Poole Harbour. Weymouth Bay would then have been the location of the next fleet base given its proximity to the major military engagement site at Maiden Castle, where Vespasian's legionaries famously stormed the extensive hill fort defended by the Durotriges. Then heading deeper into Dumnonian territory, a key fleet base was established at Topsham, immediately to the south of the later legionary fortress and *civitas capital* of Exeter (Roman *Isca Dumnoniorum*, of which it became the port). After four seasons of intense campaigning, with Vespasian using this combination of land-based shock troops supplied by his new series of fortified harbours, the south west was conquered and incorporated into Britannia.

Plautius returned to Rome in AD 47, accompanied by Vespasian. The Romans could be forgiven for thinking at this point that the conquest of Britain was following the same pattern as Caesar's conquest of Gaul. Soon they expected the whole main island of Britain to be filling the emperor's *fiscus* treasury with taxes as one large province. However, nothing could be further from the truth, with years of campaigning still to come and the conquest of the far north never fully completed.

At the point of Plautius' departure, the territory of the new province had been greatly expanded. Britannia now comprised the region below a line from the River Severn to the River Trent, excepting the territories of the Regni, Atrebates and Iceni client kingdoms. This new stop line is often called the 'Fosse Way Frontier' after the major Roman road that later ran along its length from the legionary fortress at Exeter to that at Lincoln. This routeway almost certainly derived the name by which it was later known from the Latin word *fossa*, meaning ditch. This not only reflects its origins as the late AD 40s stop line of the initial Roman campaigns of conquest in Britain, but also indicates that for at least some of its length the ditched barrier remained visible hundreds of years later. Back to the late AD 40s, along the 'Fosse Way Frontier' a number of vexillation forts were then built, for example at Newton-on-Trent and Great Casterton (Roman names unknown), joining already established bases including Longthope and Leicester. These forts later became logistics bases for the next phase of conquest into the west and north.

By this time manifestations of *Romanitas* had begun to emerge across the conquered territory, with the former native British nobility encouraged to learn formal Latin, wear togas on official business and invest in grand stone-built public building enterprises, conveniently for the Romans, funded with loans from the leading Senatorial families back in Rome. More practically, given the always-urgent need to make a new province pay its own way, Roman patterns of local Government were also imposed. As Oosthuizen (2019, 27) details:

> The [new] administration of Roman Britain was based on a set of nested hierarchies: broadly speaking from vicus, a small local centre [as opposed to the vici civilian settlements associated with Roman forts], to pagus, the locality, to civitates, a region often reproducing a prehistoric territory [as for example with the Cantiacii in modern Kent].

The next governor in Britain was called Publius Ostorius Scapula, arriving just as winter set in in AD 47. His first task was to pacify those areas already conquered by Rome below the 'Fosse Way Frontier', in the first instance disarming any Britons still under arms. This included the client kingdoms there and prompted the first revolt against the new Roman presence in Britain, this among the Iceni in north Norfolk. The rebels there fortified themselves in a promontory with a narrow entrance, sometimes identified as Stonea Camp in the Cambridgeshire Fens, later the site of a Roman agricultural imperial estate (Potter and Jackson, 1982, 118). Ostorius knew there was real danger here as a native victory could begin to unravel the Roman conquests in Britain to date. He advanced swiftly on the rebels and defeated them in short order, only needing his auxiliaries to do so with his cavalry fighting dismounted.

Ostorius now turned his attention to the expansion of imperial territory north and west of the 'Fosse Way Frontier' stop line. First he campaigned against the Deceangli tribe in northwestern Wales, with the Roman fleet deploying to the Dee Estuary to protect his littoral flank and supply his troops along the coast and down the local river systems. To support this extensive campaign the governor built a large 18ha legionary fortress-sized supply base at Rhyn Park in modern Shropshire on the English side of the River Ceiriog. However, his campaigning in Wales was cut short when he was called away to deal with a disturbance among the northern Brigantes.

This large confederation, whose name translated as 'High Ones' or 'Hill Dwellers', had yet to feel the might of Rome. Their territory covered a huge region in the north, including modern Yorkshire excepting the east coast, Lancashire, Cumbria, Northumberland and southwestern Scotland. Their power is evident in the size of the pre-Roman tribal capital located at Stanwick in North Yorkshire, this an enormous *oppida* enclosing almost 300ha surrounded by 9km of ditches and ramparts (Moorhead and Stuttard, 2012, 93). Given the scale of his opponents here Ostorius took no chances, marching north with a large force of legionaries and auxilia, swiftly wiping out any opposition and then putting to death the ringleaders.

Matters in the north resolved, Ostorius then returned to Wales where this time he targeted the Silures and Ordovices tribes in the south and centre who between them were still harbouring the fugitive Caratacus. First Ostorius redeployed *legio* XX *Valeria Victrix* from Colchester to Kingsholm near modern Gloucester where they built a vexillation-size fort. This location became a key site for the various campaigns of conquest in Wales given it was the lowest easily bridgeable point on the River Severn, while also being navigable for the sea-going transport vessels of the fleet. Once the campaign was underway, with the XXth legion driving hard into the territory of the

Silures, the governor then deployed *legio* XIV *Gemina* for her in the eyes of the Welsh Marches. From there they opened a new front against the Ordovices. Progress for both legions and their auxiliaries was slow, but eventually Roman military prowess prevailed with the tribes submitting after Caratacus was defeated when the Romans assaulted the fortified site he was defending deep in Ordovician territory. The rebel leader fled once more, this time leaving behind his wife and daughter to be captured by the Romans. Heading north, in AD 51 he eventually arrived at the court of Cartimandua, now the queen of the Brigantes. Here she was presented with a dilemma. The Roman conquest of Britain was still in its early years, with resistance still evident in many areas, even below the 'Fosse Way Frontier'. To that end, handing him over to the Romans would be an embarrassing loss of face to those Britons still fighting Rome. However, after the failed unrest in Brigantian territory at the beginning of Ostorius' governorship (the event which may have placed her on the throne there) she was clearly aware of the military might of the Empire. In the end she made the pragmatic choice to hand the former leader of the Catuvellauni over to the Romans in chains. Caratacus was later presented to Claudius, with the emperor deciding to spare him. He was allowed to live out the rest of his life in Rome where he made a positive impression on the nobility and people there. Meanwhile, Tacitus (*The Histories*, 3.45) says Cartimandua was rewarded with great wealth for her support for Rome.

Back in Wales, if Ostorius thought the region pacified then he couldn't have been more wrong, for the Silures now rose in revolt. The governor made it known he intended to exterminate the whole confederation as a punishment, this unsurprising given Rome's usual attitude to recalcitrant foes. As Mattingly says (2006, 89):

> A key ingredient in the Roman approach to war was their ruthless attitude, which frequently extended to their use of exemplary force. Rebellious peoples were slaughtered or enslaved without qualms, massive resources being poured into the crushing of even small groups of dissenters

On this occasion this was a mistake, as with nothing to lose the Silures now fought a vicious guerilla campaign (Southern, 2013, 88). On one occasion they inflicted a major defeat on the Romans, ambushing a sizeable force of legionaries when they were building a marching camp. In this engagement Roman losses were heavy, with the *praefectus castrorum* camp prefect, eight centurions and hundreds of soldiers killed. However, the Silures then made a mistake, being drawn into a set piece encounter when, having ambushed a Roman foraging party, Ostorius arrived with a sizeable force of legionaries and wiped out the Britons there. Despite this setback the Silures still refused to submit, knowing the fate that awaited them. The conflict fizzled on unresolved, its ultimate outcome the death of Ostorius in AD 52, worn out by years of campaigning in Wales and the north.

Britannia's next governor was Aulus Didius Gallus who relocated *legio* XX *Valeria Victrix* to a new legionary fortress at Usk (Roman *Burrium*) in southeastern Wales, *legio* XIV *Gemina* to a similar new fortress at Wroxeter (Roman *Viroconium Cornoviorum*) and *legio* II *Augusta* to the existing fortress at Gloucester. Both the new sites were specifically chosen for the access provided to the Bristol Channel by the rivers Usk and Severn respectively, with maritime supply remaining vital to Rome's continued military success in its Welsh campaigning. This observation is reinforced by the next two forts built as the campaign continued, these vexillation-sized structures at Chepstow on the mouth of the River Wye and Cardiff on the River Taff.

The gruelling Welsh campaign continued throughout the AD 50s, with the use of three complete legions showing the intensity of the campaigning there. However, the most noteworthy event in Didius' time as governor in Britain was his intervention in Brigantian territory again. There, in the mid AD 50s, a schism occurred between Cartimandua and her husband Venutius. We have no insight into what caused this, but we do of the outcome, he being banished from the northern kingdom. Soon he was raising a force to invade the queen's territory. This was a serious threat to the Roman client kingdom, with Tacitus (*Annals*, 12.40) calling him the leading British military leader now Caratacus had been captured. Didius realized the queen was under threat and quickly intervened. At first the governor sent *exploratores* scouts and auxiliaries, but soon realized he'd misjudged the seriousness of the threat. He therefore deployed a full legion to the north, either *legio* IX *Hispana* or *legio* XIV *Gemina*, and soon the situation was under control after a series of decisive clashes, with Venutius again banished. The queen later divorced him and married his armour bearer, a man called Vellocatus.

By this time the never-ending conquest campaign in Britain was proving onerous back in Rome, with Suetonius saying that after Claudius died in AD 54 the new emperor Nero (AD 54 to AD 68) for a time considered abandoning the province altogether (*The Twelve Caesars, Nero*, 18). However, he eventually decided his forces would stay and the province continue, though only because he feared the negative publicity if he withdrew.

Didius departed back to Rome in AD 57 and was replaced by Quintus Veranius Nepos, a noted military leader with a hardman reputation. Here, clearly Nero had determined that if Rome was to stay in the main island of Britain then all resistance in Wales must be crushed once and for all. However, the new governor only had time to lead a few skirmishes against the still-resisting Silures before he died in office.

His replacement was one of the truly great British governors, Gaius Suetonius Paulinus, appointed by Nero in AD 58. Another seasoned military leader, he set to work in his new province immediately, picking up where Verianus had left off in Wales. First, to consolidate his position in Silurian territory he built a series of forts to secure the key valleys in the interior which the natives had been using to access the rich farmlands along the coast. Then, in AD 60, he targeted the region he determined to be real centre of resistance to Roman power in Wales. This was Anglesey, deep in the heart of Ordovician territory, the mysterious island that was home to the druids, leaders of Late Iron Age religion in pre-Roman Britain. It was also a place of refuge for the thousands of Britons fleeing the gradual scouring campaigns of the Romans, not only in Wales but elsewhere in the main island of Britain.

As with Vespasian's conquest of the Isle of Wight a decade earlier, here Paulinus staged a Claudian invasion in miniature, with an army of around 20,000 men. This included *legio* XIV *Gemina*, most of *legio* XX *Valeria Victrix* and an equivalent number of auxiliaries. The governor was a meticulous planner and built hundreds of flat-bottomed boats in the estuary of the River Dee to transport his legionaries and auxilia foot troops across the shallow Menai Strait, with the auxiliary cavalry swimming across. However, his amphibious assault was heavily opposed, despite the war galleys from the regional fleet enfilading the landing zone with *ballistae* and other missile weapons. Tacitus here provides a detailed description of the desperate engagement, saying (*Annals*, 14.29):

> On the beach stood the adverse array, a serried mass of arms and men, with women flitting between the ranks. In the style of Furies, in robes of deathly black and with dishevelled hair, they brandished their torches; while a circle of Druids, lifting their hands to heaven and showering imprecations, struck our troops with such an awe at the extraordinary spectacle that, as though their limbs were paralysed, they exposed their bodies to wounds without an attempt at movement. Then, reassured by their general, and inciting each other never to flinch before a band of females and fanatics, they charged behind the standards, cut down all who met them, and enveloped the enemy in his own flames. The next step was to install a garrison among the conquered population, and to demolish the groves consecrated to their savage cults: for they considered it a duty to consult their deities by means of human entrails.

So far so good for the new governor. However, next he faced an existential threat to the survival of the province from a totally unexpected direction. This was the AD 60/61 revolt of Boudicca, queen of the Iceni in north Norfolk.

The Boudiccan Revolt

The blood-soaked rebellion of Boudicca is arguably the most famous event in the story of the Roman occupation of Britain. It almost ended the Roman presence in the islands here and saw the legionaries and auxilia fighting in the most extreme conditions. Defeat would have meant the destruction of four whole legions, on a scale even larger than the loss of Varus' three legions in the Teutoburg Forest in AD 9.

The context behind this dramatic event was the earlier death of the Iceni king Prasutagus, Boudicca's husband. A Roman client king, in his will he left his kingdom to his two daughters and also to Nero. As detailed above, ruling *clientes* of the Romans usually left their kingdom entirely to the Romans after their deaths, and the emperor reacted predictably when he heard news of Prasutagus' unusual arrangement. The dead king's will was ignored and the territory of the Iceni quickly folded into the expanding province of Britannia. It is now that Boudicca enters history, with Dio describing her appearance as very much the warrior queen, saying (*Roman History*, 62.2):

> She was very tall and stern; her look was penetrating; her voice harsh; a mass of auburn hair fell to her hips and around her neck was a heavy golden torc; she wore a patterned cloak with a thick cape over it fastened with a brooch.

Boudicca protested against the treatment of her kingdom. Tacitus says the Roman response was brutal in the extreme (*The Annals*, 14.31). He details Iceni territory was pillaged by centurions, the dead king's household ransacked by slaves, Boudicca lashed and her two daughters raped. It is worth noting here that Dio gives a completely different and far more mundane reason for Boudicca leading her revolt, saying (*Roman History*, 62.2):

> An excuse for the revolt was found in the confiscation of the sums of money that Claudius had given to the foremost Britons; for these sums, as Catus Decanius, the procurator of the island, maintained, were to be paid back. This was one reason for the uprising; another was found in the fact that Seneca (a leading statesman in Rome), in the hope of receiving a good rate of interest, had lent to the islanders 40,000,000 sesterces that

they did not want, and had afterwards called in this loan all at once and had resorted to severe measures in exacting it.

Whatever the cause, the result was incendiary in the extreme. Tacitus has Boudicca addressing her people, setting them on course for savage rebellion, the queen saying (*The Annals*, 14.35):

> It is not as a woman descended from noble ancestry, but as one of the people that I am avenging lost freedom, my scourged body, the outraged chastity of my daughters. This is a woman's resolve; as for men, they may live and be slaves.

Dio also has the queen exhorting the masses to revolt, grasping a spear and then saying (*Roman History*, 62.3):

> Have we not been robbed entirely of most of our possessions, and those the greatest, while for those that remain we pay taxes? Besides pasturing and tilling for them all our other possessions, do we not pay a yearly tribute for our very bodies? How much better it would be to have been sold to masters once and for all than, possessing empty titles of freedom, to have to ransom ourselves every year! How much better to have been slain and to have perished than to go about with a tax on our heads! Yet why do I mention death? For even dying is not free of cost with them; nay, you know what fees we deposit even for our dead. Among the rest of mankind death frees even those who are in slavery to others; only in the case of the Romans do the very dead remain alive for their profit. Why is it that, though none of us has any money (how, indeed, could we, or where would we get it?), we are stripped and despoiled like a murderer's victims? And why should the Romans be expected to display moderation as time goes on, when they have behaved toward us in this fashion at the very outset, when all men show more consideration even for the beasts they have newly captured?

Soon Boudicca's ferocious insurrection had ignited most of the south east above the Thames against the Romans, giving credence to Dio's reasoning behind the revolt, with all of the local aristocracy affected, not just those of the Iceni. Marching south at the head of an army 120,000 strong according to Dio (*Roman History*, 62.2), she first targeted the then provincial capital at Colchester. The nearest Roman legion was *legio* IX *Hispana* in the Midlands, still holding the northeastern line of the 'Fosse Way Frontier'. Its *legate*

Quintus Petillius Cerialis, a future governor in Britain, moved quickly to lead a large force comprising vexillations of legionaries and auxiliaries to intercept Boudicca. This arrived too late to save Colchester, which by that point had already been torched with great loss of life, with a large number burned alive as they sought shelter in the Temple of Claudius there. This had been built to celebrate Plautius' earlier victory, its enormous foundations still visible beneath modern Colchester Castle. Cerialis' force was then decisively defeated by the main British army, the *legate* fleeing for his life alongside his cavalry, leaving his legionaries to their fate. He then remained incongruously holed-in up in a nearby fort until the insurrection had been finally defeated.

In Wales, Paulinus abandoned his campaign in the north as soon as he heard of Boudicca's revolt and immediately headed for Wroxeter in the Welsh Marches. There he picked up the western end of Watling Street, which by that time was almost complete, running through St Albans to London, and then onwards to Richborough on the east Kent coast (today the A5 and A2 broadly track its route). He was accompanied by *legio* XIV *Gemina*, some vexillations from *legio* XX *Valeria Victrix* and a few auxiliary units including two *ala* of cavalry. Reaching High Cross in modern Leicestershire where Watling Street crossed the Fosse Way, Paulinus then sent for the Exeter-based *legio* II *Augusta* to join him. However, the unit's *legate* and second-in-command were away, with its *praefectus castrorum* in charge. Called Poenius Postumus, he ignored the call, bringing shame on the legion. Clearly he thought the province was about to fall and wanted to stay on the River Ex from where he could evacuate his troops if necessary. Meanwhile, some stragglers from *legio* IX *Hispana* also found their way to Paulinus, giving him a total force of around 6,000 legionaries from the three legions, 4,000 foot auxiliaries and around 1,000 mounted auxiliaries.

At this point Tacitus has Paulinus marching in person to London, the recently founded major trading port on the River Thames, from where the provincial procurator Decianus had fled to Gaul as Boudicca and her growing force continued its march south towards the town. It is useful to quote the historian in full at this point given the real sense of jeopardy he presents as the new province fell into chaos (*The Annals*, 14.33):

> Paulinus...with wonderful resolution, marched amidst a hostile population to Londinium, which, though undistinguished by the name of a colony [it was styled by the Romans a *municipium* mercantile town], was much frequented by a number of merchants and trading vessels. Uncertain whether he should choose it as a seat of war, as he looked round on his scanty force of soldiers...he resolved to save the province

at the cost of a single town. Nor did the tears and weeping of the people, as they implored his aid, deter him from giving the signal of departure and receiving into his army all who would go with him. Those who were chained to the spot by the weakness of their sex, or the infirmity of age, or the attractions of the place, were cut off by the enemy.

The key reference here is that which describes the local population as hostile when Paulinus was marching down Watling Street through the Midlands, to my mind confirming the Catuvellauni certainly, and most likely the Trinovantes to their east, had joined the Iceni in the great revolt. In these circumstances Paulinus' force would have been constructing defended marching camps at the end of each day's march as they travelled southeast. It is therefore unlikely that if Paulinus did indeed travel in person to London, he took his whole army. More likely he would have travelled with a bodyguard of auxiliary cavalrymen, or even more likely have sent an advance guard to assess the situation with authority to order an evacuation if needed.

In the event, when Boudicca did arrive in London, any remaining Romans or Romano-British were butchered and the town burned to the ground. Boudicca then targeted the new *municipium* of St Albans (Roman *Verulamium*), razing this also. The primary sources say that 80,000 were killed in the three sacking events by this point, indicating the scale of the insurrection and its rank savagery. However, the stage was now set for Roman retribution, and on a devastating scale.

By this point Boudicca's force had grown to 230,000, though only 120,000 were still likely warriors. This was an enormous force to keep in the field and she knew that a meeting engagement with Paulinus would be needed quickly to keep her army and its swelling number of dependent camp followers together. She also knew that if the governor was defeated, the Romans might abandon the province for good. Boudicca therefore advanced northwest along Watling Street to seek out the Roman army.

The Key Engagement

As Boudicca progressed she received intelligence about the size of Paulinus' force, and given the disparity with her own no doubt felt the outcome of the forthcoming battle was a foregone conclusion. In that she was wrong, as the wily Paulinus was ready for her and chose the place to make his stand very carefully. This was in a bowl-shaped steep defile, with woods on either side and to the rear and an open end facing Watling Street, Boudicca's line of advance. The woods protected his flanks and limited the frontage of the line of battle, negating the British superiority in numbers, playing to the martial superiority of his own legionaries. The exact location of the battle site is unknown, though all of the leading candidates are along the line of Watling Street, hence the engagement often being referred to as The Battle of Watling Street. These sites are at Mancetter, High Cross where Paulinus had awaited the arrival of *legio* II *Augusta* in vain, Church Stowe in Northamptonshire (my own preference) and Markyate in Hertfordshire. All four sites also have a significant water source, essential with so many engaged in the battle.

Paulinus deployed his legionaries and auxilia uphill of the Britons. He divided his foot troops into four main bodies with a centre, left and right flanks, and with a reserve to the rear of the centre. He then positioned an *ala* of auxiliary cavalry on either extreme flank hard against the woods there, where he finally deployed field defences for additional protection. Dio says he then addressed his legionaries and auxilia as the huge British force approached. He has him say (69.2):

> Up, fellow-soldiers! Up, Romans! Show these accursed wretches how far we surpass them even in the midst of evil fortune. It would shameful, indeed, for you to lose ingloriously now what but a short time ago you won by your valour. Many a time, assuredly, have both we ourselves and our fathers, with far fewer numbers than we have at present, conquered far more numerous antagonists. Fear not, then, their numbers or their spirit of rebellion; for their boldness rests on nothing more than headlong rashness unaided by arms or training. Neither fear them because they have burned a couple of cities; Exact from them now, therefore, the proper penalty for these deeds, and let them learn by actual experience the difference between us, whom they have wronged, and themselves.

Boudicca deployed her enormous force opposite, though in much denser formation, with the chariots in front manned by her own elite warriors. So confident were the Britons of victory that the families of the warriors joined the baggage train at the rear of her battle line to watch events unfold. She now exhorted her own army to more slaughter, then opened the battle with a wild uphill charge with both the chariots and foot warriors. The former rode across the front of the Romans, hurling insults and javelins, before turning square on to close for hand-to-hand combat. The foot troops followed close behind. Soon Boudicca had lost control of her army as each noble and warrior strove to get to grips with the Romans.

By way of contrast, the discipline of the legionaries and auxilia now shone through. The battle proper began with the Roman artillery opening fire as soon as the Britons were in range, first the *ballistae* and then the *scorpions*. Given the nearby proximity of the various logistics bases being used by the Romans, it seems likely there were a larger number of artillery pieces available to Paulinus than usual. Further, having chosen his battlefield, it is certain he would also have set range markers down to ensure the accuracy of his artillery bombardment. Then, as the range narrowed, auxiliary archers and slingers also joined the barrage. By this point the Britons, increasingly disordered by the concentrated missile fire, had begun their ascent up the steep hillside towards the main Roman deployment. At that point, en masse the legionaries released their lighter *pila*, 6,000 iron-barbed javelins arcing high in the air in a steep parabola and then dropping on the heads of the Britons, many without helmets. The auxiliary infantry joined in with their own *lancea*. Then, at point-blank range as the flagging Britons reached the Roman lines, the legionaries unleashed their second, heavier *pila*. These flew in a flat arc, hammering into the front ranks of Britons who came to a shuddering halt in a tangle of dead horses, overturned chariots, bodies and wounded.

Paulinus saw the British advance falter and seized his chance to take the initiative. He now ordered the legionaries to move forward in a series of *cuneus* wedge formations, with centurions and standard bearers to the fore. The auxiliaries followed on the flanks. Swords were drawn and shields set hard forward. The wedges then charged downhill into the dense mass of Britons, causing slaughter everywhere and forcing the natives into a huge, desperate crush where the warriors couldn't use their weapons. A massacre now ensued as the Britons broke and tried to run away. However, they were trapped on the field by the surrounding families and baggage train. All were hacked down where they stood, the slaughter desperate.

The result was a mighty victory for Paulinus, with Tacitus saying (*Annals*, 14.35):

> The troops gave no quarter even to the women: the baggage animals themselves had been speared and added to the pile of bodies. The glory won in the course of the day was remarkable, and equal to that of our older victories: for, by some accounts, little less than eighty thousand Britons fell, at a cost of some four hundred Romans killed and a not much greater number of wounded. Boudicca ended her days by poison; while…Postumus, camp-prefect of the second legion, informed of the exploits of the men of the fourteenth and twentieth, and conscious that he had cheated his own corps of a share in the honours and had violated the rules of the service by ignoring the orders of his commander, ran his sword through his body.

Dio's account of Boudicca's fate differs, stating that after the battle (*Roman History*, 62.12):

> ...Boudicca fell sick and died. The Britons mourned her deeply and gave her a costly burial; but, feeling that now at last they were really defeated, the survivors scattered to their homes.

Thus ended Boudicca's revolt in the desperate Battle of Watling Street, with Roman victory overwhelming and total.

Aftermath and Legacy

In the aftermath of Boudicca's defeat, Nero hurriedly sent 2,000 more legionaries to Britain from the German frontier, together with 1,000 auxiliary cavalry and eight units of auxiliary foot. These helped Paulinus to stamp out the last flames of resistance. This was carried out with such vigour in the Iceni homelands of north Norfolk that the region remained for many years under-developed compared to the rest of the province, with some of the urban plots in the later *civitas* capital at Caistor St Edmunds (Roman *Venta Icenorum*) never used.

However, Paulinus didn't receive the plaudits he might have expected. This was because the absent procurator, Decianus hiding in Gaul, was quickly replaced by Nero with a new man named Gaius Julius Alpinus Classicianus. The latter was critical of Paulinus' post-revolt punitive actions against the Britons, fearing it might spark another revolt. He reported this to the emperor who sent his own freedman Polyclitus to conduct an investigation. Though we don't have the full details of its findings, the investigator did report that Paulinus had lost some ships from the regional fleet. This excuse was used to relieve him, he being replaced by the more conciliatory Publius Petronius Turpilianus as governor. However, Paulinus does not seem to have returned to Rome in disgrace as a lead *tessera* found there features both his and Nero's names alongside symbols of victory, and a man with his name was nominated as *consul* for AD 66. Nevertheless, the Romans had been badly rattled by the rebellion, and in my view if Paulinus had lost his battle Britannia would have fallen, with the Romans perhaps unlikely ever to return.

With a degree of calm restored to Britain, rebuilding and repair began, with consolidation once more the order of the day. In the first instance, the provincial capital was moved from the *colonia* at Colchester to the *municipia* of London on the north bank of the Thames. This triggered a rebuilding programme there paid for by the imperial *fiscus* treasury, the first manifestation being the construction of the 1.5ha Neronian fort at modern Plantation Place on Fenchurch Street. This was found during rescue excavations by Museum of London Archaeology (MOLA) in the early 2010s. The fortification was a timber and earthwork structure, similar in design to a standard Roman marching camp though more robust in its construction. It was enclosed by double ditches each 1.9m wide and 3m deep. Hingley (2018, 62) provides more detail, saying:

> Dominating a strategic point of high ground, the fortification was close to the major road junction and the early marketplace above the bridgehead. Its northern ditches cut through the main northwest road of early Roman Londinium and it is unclear why this road was put out of use. This fortified enclosure overlay timber buildings…burned during the Boudiccan uprising, and the rampart itself contained charred timbers and burnt mud bricks that were reused from destroyed buildings.

The fort could accommodate 500 troops and was occupied for around ten years. Within its walls were located a granary, latrine and cookhouse, with the soldiers housed in tents rather than permanent wooden or stone-built structures. Its construction was a statement to any natives in the region that Rome was here to stay, and from that point the rebuilding of Roman London progressed quickly. By the end of the decade a variety of fine buildings had been built on the high ground around Cornhill, including a new *basilica* and *forum* and temples to the imperial cult and the Capitoline Triad of Jupiter, Juno and Minerva. Meanwhile, on the riverfront beneath modern Cannon Street railway station an impressive governor's palace was built.

The governors who followed Paulinus in the AD 60s are often criticized for not living up to his martial prowess. However, as Jones and Mattingly (1990, 71) argue, the likes of Turpilianus and his own successor Marcus Trebellius Maximus were clearly obeying a new set of orders, not to continue the expansion of Roman-controlled territory but to re-garrison the province, and complete the pacification of the natives in the newly-conquered territories north of the 'Fosse Way Frontier'. It is worth reflecting here that the Romans had only been in Britain for a generation following the Claudian invasion, and many areas within the new province were still coming to terms with their new fate. As Mattingly says (2006, 91): 'The activities of the Roman army in the conquest phase will have had a profound impact on the peoples of Britain. Even in a professional army like the Roman one, the collateral damage to civilian communities was undoubtedly high.'

However, this pacification programme was clearly successful, as by the mid-AD 60s Nero was able to pull the veteran *legio* XIV *Gemina* out of the line in Britain for redeployment to Syria for service against the Parthians.

By this time the territory of the new province had greatly expanded beyond the 'Fosse Way Frontier' stop line of the late AD 40s. Below it the various client kingdoms, including the Regni, Atrebates and Iceni had now been subsumed into Roman controlled territory. Above it, to the northeast, the lands of Coritani south of the Humber were also now part of the province, and perhaps even land belonging to the Parisi to their north. The lands of the Dobunni and Cornovii in the Welsh Marches were now also part of the province, providing the springboard for more campaigns in Wales, some more successful than others. Evidence this region became a new frontier zone for the campaigns there is evident with the later construction of two new branches of Watling Street from Wroxeter, one heading south to Caerleon (Roman *Isca Augusta*) and one north to Chester (Roman *Deva Victrix*). Both sites featured new fortifications, their building fully detailed in Chapter 5.

All of the above detail enables us to roughly establish the northern frontier of the province of Britannia as the AD 60s came to an end. This was now on a line from the River Dee on the west coast to the Humber Estuary on the east, excepting the territory of Wales whose total conquest to that point remained elusive. However, as the decade came to an end, Roman priorities switched from consolidation to conquest once more, with the new focus the far north. Soon the legions were again on the march, as detailed later in Chapter 5.

Chapter 4

The Siege of Masada

Brutal End of the First 'Great' Jewish Revolt, AD 73

Countless archaeological sites across the vast geography of the Roman Empire are steeped in brutal history. However, few can match the 434m-high mountaintop Judean fortress of Masada. Originally the location of two palaces built by Herod the Great atop a plateau overlooking the Dead Sea, it was later fortified and became the final centre of resistance against the Romans at the end of the First 'Great' Jewish Revolt in AD 73. Gazing from the top across the arid emptiness of the Judean Desert, eight huge square or rhomboid shapes are immediately apparent surrounding the mesa. These are the marching camps built to house the Roman troops in their final siege here. Seeing them, the futility of facing the might of Rome there is instantly apparent, especially after the legionaries and auxilia began to build an enormous and still visible siege ramp. Day by day this crept higher and closer to the lofty parapets, defying all attempts by the Jewish rebels to hinder its progress. Then, as the Romans deployed a huge battering ram atop the finished ramp, the famous mass suicide of hardened Zealots followed, with the defenders choosing this awful fate rather than face savage brutalization as captives of Rome. Here I detail this most ferocious of encounters as the Romans were challenged by a region-wide rebellion driven by religious fervour on a scale rarely seen in Roman history.

Strategic Build-Up to the Battle

Rome's interaction with the Jewish population in Judaea was complicated to say the least, their relationship set against the collapse of the last Hellenistic successor kingdoms in the Levant and the subsequent rise of Roman and Parthian power there. Here I first consider late Hellenistic and early imperial Roman history in the region through to the outbreak of the First 'Great' Jewish Revolt in AD 66, and then outline the nature of Jewish armies in this period.

Judaea and the Roman World

Judaea was the most troublesome province of the early Roman Empire, and like Britain had a disproportionately large military presence, even after the

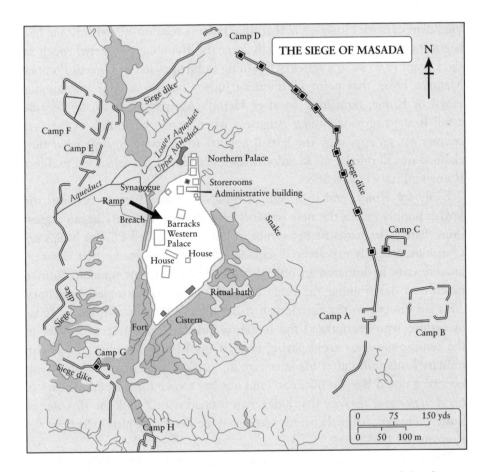

three Jewish Revolts detailed here. It comprised the territory of the former Hasmonean and later Herodian kingdom of Judaea, including Judaea itself, Samaria and Idumaea. The major issue for the Romans here were the native Jewish inhabitants who proved the most recalcitrant adherents to the ways of Rome, even more so than the Britons.

Judaea had originally been under the control of the Hellenistic kingdoms in the eastern Mediterranean, usually the Seleucid Empire or Ptolemaic Egypt dependant on who controlled the Levant at the time. By the second century BC, after six Syrian Wars between 274 BC and 168 BC, the former was dominant, with Judaea fully incorporated into Seleucid territory. Then, as this sprawling empire collapsed, Judaea finally gained its independence after a major Jewish revolt against the Seleucid king Antiochus IV. This was led by the priest Judah Maccabee and lasted from 167 BC to 160 BC. The new Jewish kingdom's ruling dynasty were called the Hasmoneans, with Maccabee's brother Simon Thassi its first king, ruling from 141 BC. The Hasmonean Dynasty lasted 103 years, until Herod the Great overthrew its last ruler Antigonus in 37 BC to found the

Herodian dynasty. However, in that time Judaea's relationship with Rome had begun to change radically, especially after the Republic conquered much of the Levant in 63 BC in a series of lightning campaigns led by Gnaeus Pompey Magnus. From that point Hasmonean Judaea became a semi-autonomous vassal of Rome, remaining so after Herod's usurpation. It finally became a full Roman province under Augustus when, at the beginning of the first century AD, an appeal by the Jewish nobility to intervene against what they claimed was ill rule by the kingdom's last ruler Herod Archelaus led to direct Roman military intervention.

Sadly for Rome, and in a sign of things to come, friction between the Jewish population in the new province and Roman authority began almost immediately. Augustus' first governor in Judaea was called Publius Sulipicius Quirinius, a highly experienced regional administrator. In the first instance, around AD 6, he initiated an official census in Judaea, this standard Roman practice in determining the value of newly-incorporated imperial territory. This led directly to the first Jewish rising against Roman rule, led by Judas of Galilee who encouraged the Jewish population there not to register in the census, and thus avoid paying taxes. Titus Flavius Josephus, the Jewish military leader who after his later capture in the First 'Great' Jewish Revolt became a noted Roman historian (and our key source for the period), says in his *Antiquities of the Jews* that Judas then teamed with Zadok the Pharisee to form a new nationalist theocratic sect called the Zealots to physically fight the Romans (18.1).

Regional tension continued to grow, first through the crucifixion of Jesus of Nazareth which introduced new Jewish Christian sects into the troublesome mix, then with the relocation of the provincial capital away from Jerusalem to Caesarea (Roman *Caesarea Maritima*), a major new port founded by Herod the Great around 10 BC. Then later, Caligula ordered the erection of a statue of himself in the Second Temple in Jerusalem. To that point the Jewish population had largely been left to their own worship. Caligula's ill-considered move now forced them to also pay attention to Roman forms of worship, in this case that of the imperial cult. This was a central feature of the Roman experience, where acknowledging the emperor a God (even if only perfunctorily) was to overtly participate in the full Roman experience. The erection of Caligula's statue in Jewish religion's holiest place thus unsurprisingly provoked outrage, causing what became known as the 'Caligula Crisis', with widespread rioting breaking out across the province.

The imperial centre now began paying close attention to troublesome Judaea, where the population were now overtly pushing back on the two things Rome demanded of its populace, namely payment of taxes and worshipping the imperial cult. However, at first the Romans tried to placate the populace, even after the 'Caligula Crisis'. Here Dougherty provides detail, saying (2008, 194):

> The Romans were keen to diffuse volatile situations there. For example, a Roman soldier who was part of a force assigned to punish local villagers for not helping the authorities deal with brigands, destroyed religious documents uttering blasphemies. The local population were outraged, and the governor agreed with them that the soldier had gone too far in attacking their God. He was publicly beheaded in front of the angry mob, which pacified them for a time.

Other incidents where the Jewish population challenged Roman rule were also allowed to pass while Rome tried hard to set the province on a secure financial footing. However, matters finally came to a head when the procurator of the province, whose job was to ensure it paid its dues into the imperial *fiscus* treasury, was accused of appropriating money from the Second Temple in Jerusalem. This led directly to a full region-wide rebellion breaking out in AD 66, this the First 'Great' Jewish Revolt, of which the siege of Masada was its desperate conclusion.

The Jewish Army

Judaea was a ready supplier of regular troops and mercenaries to later Hellenistic armies, particularly the Seleucid Empire and Ptolemaic Egypt, where they gained a fine reputation fighting as *xystophoroi* lancers, pikemen, *thureophoroi* spearmen and skirmishers. However, the first autonomous Jewish army of the period was the rebel force that fought in the Maccabean Revolt against Antiochus IV. This was triggered by the king intervening in Judaea after Menelaus, his appointed High Priest in Jerusalem, was ousted by a deposed predecessor called Jason. The latter had been emboldened after a false rumour had spread through the region that Antiochus had been killed while fighting against Ptolemaic Egypt.

Second Maccabees, our main source for the period, then has the vengeful Seleucid ruler descending on Judaea '...raging like a wild animal...' to put down what he called a full rebellion. Some 40,000 Jews were then executed, with 40,000 more enslaved (5:11). This episode led to the writing of the *Book of Daniel* where, as the evil 'King in the North', Antiochus set the template for future Jewish and Christian depictions of the devil (The Holy Bible, *Book of Daniel*, 11.21).

However, instead of stamping out opposition to Seleucid rule in Judaea, Antiochus' shocking actions sparked a full seven-year rebellion under Judah

Maccabee and his brothers. They wisely chose not to face the Seleucid army in open battle, but instead formed a guerilla army organised by Jewish veterans who had earlier served in the Seleucid or Ptolemaic armies. Jestice details that they then '...took advantage of the region's broken terrain to fight a war of surprise attack and military ruse' (2008, 17). This proved highly successful, and wise, given the only time the rebels fought Antiochus in set piece battle at Elasa near modern day Ramallah ended in their defeat, with Judah himself killed. Nevertheless the rebellion persisted, and eventually Seleucid forces were driven out of Jerusalem. There, the statues of the deities of the Greek pantheon were then removed from the Second Temple. This was then purified and rededicated, an event still celebrated every year with the Jewish holiday of Hanukkah.

Next, following the establishment of the Hasmonean Dynasty, a formal Jewish army was created. This was based on the later Hellenistic model, featuring *xystophoroi* 'Cavalry of the Army', bow-armed skirmishing cavalry called 'Cavalry of the Phalanx' and *thureophoroi* spearmen called 'Foot of the Phalanx' (Head, 2016, 74). This army proved highly successful, with Jewish troops much sought after by their regional neighbours as allies, including the Parthians and the later Seleucid kings. Indeed, a large Jewish contingent accompanied Antiochus VII Euergetes, the last major Seleucid ruler, on his doomed campaign against the Parthians in 129 BC (Green, 1990, 536). However, this army disappeared with the formal creation of the Roman province of Judaea at the beginning of the first century AD, with many Jewish troops then recruited into various Roman auxiliary mounted and foot units. These provided sterling service across all of the frontiers of the empire.

Over time, as relations with the Romans deteriorated, planning then began to create a new formal Jewish army again. However, this failed when the various Jewish resistance factions argued over the chain of the command, with the Zealots in particular keen to maintain their independence. Thus, when the First 'Great' Jewish Revolt broke out in AD 66, the Jewish rebels lacked military organisation. While Josephus tried to place his troops on some kind of organised footing, most Jewish rebels throughout the conflict were lightly armed guerrillas fighting with javelins, swords, knives (the Romans called the most extreme Zealot warriors *sicarii*, named after their long curved knives) and bows in the same manner as their Maccabean forebears. Some carried a long shield, though very few wore helmets or armour. The only exceptions were warriors later in the revolt who equipped themselves with captured Roman equipment. This even included legionary artillery.

The Key Engagement

Here I first outline the key events of the First 'Great' Jewish Revolt, before detailing the siege of Masada which concluded the region-wide insurrection.

The First 'Great' Jewish Revolt

The revolt broke out in AD 66, the culmination of decades of friction between the Roman authorities and the Jewish population in Judaea. What began as a localised protest in Jerusalem against the Roman procurator quickly spread. Soon Roman citizens in Judaea were being attacked. Nero responded far more aggressively than previously, clearly deciding his earlier policy of placating the local population had failed. He now ordered the Second Temple be fully plundered, and then rounded up and publicly executed 6,000 Jewish rebels. However, far from stamping out the insurrection, this now began a spiral of escalating violence. Soon a full rebellion was underway across the whole province, with its auxiliary garrisons overrun and the Roman officials in Caesarea and Jerusalem fleeing.

Nero now ordered Cestius Gallus, the Roman governor in Syria, to lead a 30,000 strong army based around the veteran *legio* XII *Fulminata* and large numbers of auxiliary units into Judaea to put the rebellion down. As Goldsworthy details, this was a standard Roman response to an insurrection, and exactly the same as Paulinus' earlier response to the Boudiccan Revolt (2000, 144): 'When an uprising did occur, the Roman reaction was always the same. All the troops which could be mustered at short notice were formed into a column and sent immediately to confront the perceived centre of rebellion.'

However, in this case it totally failed, with Gallus' force ambushed and defeated by Jewish rebels at the Battle of Beth Horon. Here 6,000 Roman soldiers were killed and the legion's *aquila* eagle standard lost, an event unheard of in the east since Crassus' disastrous defeat at Carrhae in 53 BC. Worse still, most of the Roman casualties occurred when the army was routed by the ambush, bringing shame on the survivors. Gallus never recovered his reputation and died a broken man in AD 67.

This event shocked the Roman world, with Nero now ordering a huge army to be gathered in Syria featuring four full legions (including *legio* X *Fretensis*, *legio* XV *Apollinaris* and *legio* V *Macedonica*), an equivalent number of auxiliary cavalry and foot, and thousands of regional allied troops. He then appointed the soon to be future emperor Vespasian, veteran of the Claudian conquests of Britain, its commander. In turn Vespasian then appointed his son Titus, also a future emperor, his deputy.

Planning for the campaign was meticulous, and by early summer AD 67 all was ready. Vespasian targeted the Golan Heights in the first instance, the high ground to the east of the Sea of Galilee and key to fertile Upper Galilee, Lower Galilee and the coast. There he besieged the key city of Gamla, originally founded as a Seleucid fort to control the region and later turned into a fortified city under Hasmonean rule. The defenders only numbered 9,000 and were heavily outnumbered by the Romans according to Josephus, who actually participated in the city's defence (*The Jewish War*, 4.10). During the siege, the Romans at first tried to take the city using a siege ramp, but were repulsed. Only on their second attempt did they succeed in breaching the walls in three different locations, which then gave them access to the urban interior. There they engaged the Jewish defenders in brutal hand-to-hand combat up the steep hillsides of the city where, fighting in the cramped streets, the legionaries had to defend themselves from a barrage of rocks and other missiles from the rooftops. Given the number of defenders crowding onto the roofs many collapsed, bringing the supporting walls down too. Not only did this crush the defenders but also many attacking Romans given much of the debris fell into the street. This forced the Romans to retreat, though they re-entered the town a few days later where they eventually destroyed the last remaining redoubts of Jewish resistance.

The siege at Gamla set the template for the remainder of the war, with the Romans steadily grinding away at Jewish resistance through a series of major sieges (Goldsworthy, 2000, 145). However, Vespasian soon had to return to Rome when news of Nero's death reached him in AD 69, and it was Titus who finally besieged Jerusalem in April AD 70 during the Jewish Passover religious holiday. As Dougherty explains, this was a daunting task (2008, 201):

> Jerusalem was built on high ground, with two hills forming natural strong points. The Second Temple itself, surrounded by good strong walls, was a formidable fortress in its own right. Further, the defenders had worked to strengthen the city's defences and were ready to defend it fanatically.

By this time Jerusalem was packed with thousands of rebels who had fled the earlier Roman predations in Galilee and down the coast, with Tacitus saying over 600,000 were within the city (*The Histories*, 5.1). These now deployed to defend the city's three impressive exterior wall circuits. The first two were breached within the first three weeks of the siege. However, a stubborn stand prevented the Romans from breaking through Jerusalem's third and thickest wall, it taking them a further three months to finally force a breach. Soon the Second Temple walls themselves were then breached, resulting in a massacre of its fanatical defenders, with the temple then catching fire and being destroyed, though not before the Romans had systematically looted any remaining treasures there. These later formed the centrepiece of Titus' post-revolt triumph famously recorded on his arch in the *Forum Romanum* in Rome.

Though the fall of Jerusalem broke the back of Jewish resistance, remote pockets of the rebellion remained in the mountainous interior of the province. Vespasian, now emperor, therefore ordered *legio* X *Fretensis* to remain in theatre to carry out a meticulous mopping-up operation. The final centre of resistance proved to be the mountainous stronghold of Masada which the emperor ordered besieged in early AD 73, beginning the epic final confrontation of the First 'Great' Jewish Revolt. Note some argue this event actually occurred in AD 74, but based on the available data I stay with the most commonly referenced date.

The Siege of Masada

Masada is a 434m-high mesa with steep cliffs on all sides, located on the eastern edge of the Judaean Desert 48km south of Jerusalem where it overlooks the Dead Sea. The plateaued top is flat and rhomboid-shaped, with a habitable area 550m by 270m in size. Josephus says the Hasmonean ruler Alexander Jannaeus built a small fortress here at the beginning of the first century BC (*The Jewish War*, 5.13), though to date excavations have failed to find any archaeological evidence of this. Herod the Great then captured the site when seizing power in 37 BC. Over the next six years he built two palaces there, which he later fortified to provide a refuge for his family in case of a revolt. His fortifications included a 4m-high casemate wall around the plateau 1,300m in length, featuring numerous towers. Within the walls he then built storehouses, an armoury, barracks and a large number of cisterns to collect rainwater. Access was provided by three narrow, winding paths that led from the desert floor below to three fortified gateways.

The Romans were keenly aware Masada was the most secure military base in the region and garrisoned it as soon as Judaea became a province at the beginning of the first century AD. However, at the start of the First 'Great' Jewish Revolt a group of *sicarii* Zealots under the rebel leader Eleazar ben Ya'ir used a ruse to seize it, wiping out the Roman garrison (Josephus, *The Jewish War*, 7.274). They then stayed there throughout the revolt, soon falling out with the neighbouring Jewish communities given their extremist views. Their numbers then increased dramatically after the fall of Jerusalem, when Josephus says the population swelled to 960 (*The Jewish War*, 7.402).

With Masada now the last outpost of Jewish resistance, Vespasian knew its capture would bring the revolt to an end. Keen to shine glory on his recently established Flavian Dynasty, he ordered regional governor Sextus Lucilius Bassus to lead *legio* X *Fretensis* and its supporting auxiliaries to the fortress and take it under siege (Titus had returned to Rome to join his father after the fall of Jerusalem). Bassus had just completed the destruction of two of the final rebel strongholds at Herodium and Machaerus and immediately set off for Masada. However, he promptly fell ill on the way and died. His replacement was a highly experienced general, Lucius Flavius Silva, most recently *legate* of *legio* XXI *Rapax* in *Vindonissa*, the Roman legionary fortress near modern Windisch in Switzerland. A Flavian loyalist promoted to his post on the northern *limes* after supporting Vespasian in the AD 69 'Year of the Four Emperors', he'd been deployed to the eastern theatre late in AD 72.

On arrival at Masada Flavius Silva quickly built eight marching camps to house his force. This comprised his legion, mounted and foot auxiliaries, and also thousands of Jewish prisoners of war drafted in to perform manual labour. In total, he fielded around 10,000 fighting men. The number should have been higher, but many units were understrength after years fighting the Jewish rebels.

Flavius Silva's next move was straight from the Roman tactical manuals, the building of a circumvallation wall to isolate the fortress (Josephus, *The Jewish War*, 7.275). Once this was completed he demanded the surrender of the *sicarii* atop the mesa. Unsurprisingly, even though it was clear to the Zealots there was now no possible escape, they refused. This gave the governor two choices. First, he could mount a lengthy siege which, though likely to succeed, could take months given how well stocked Masada was with provisions. In particular, its extensive cistern network collected rain throughout the winter, providing enough water to see the defenders through the dry summer. Second, there was the option of a high-risk assault to capture the near impregnable fortress. Here, Flavius Silva's hand was forced by Vespasian's desire to wrap up military operations in Judaea as quickly as possible. Both emperor and governor knew the longer Masada held out, the more chance its example of standing up to Rome might re-ignite Jewish resistance across the province. Therefore Flavius Silva chose to storm the mesa, using Roman engineering ingenuity to overcome what seemed outwardly impossible.

The engineering specialists in *legio* X *Fretensis*, having already played a key role in the capture of Jerusalem (Dougherty, 2008, 208), were now set to work coming up with a plan to bring the siege to a rapid conclusion. Their solution was radical, the building of the tallest assault ramp ever created by the Romans to that date. Once raised high enough to challenge the 4m Herodian casemate wall directly, a battering ram would then be use to open a breach, allowing the legionaries and auxiliaries to access the mesa top and begin their butchery.

The ramp took three months to complete against the western face of the plateau, and by late Spring AD 73 was ready, with the *sicarii* defenders failing time and again in their desperate attempts to impede its progress. Once complete it stood a mighty 114m high, with its remains still visible today. In the early 1990s Dan Gill of the Geological Survey of Israel used a detailed geological investigation to show how the shrewd Roman legionary engineers made use of a pre-existing natural spur of bedrock to act as the foundation for their ramp (1993, 569). However, often overlooked are the thousands of Jewish captives held in the Roman camps who were used as construction slaves to complete the engineering feat. Thousands perished in the process.

Once the ramp reached the Herodian wall the Romans then deployed a second engineering feat, this an enormous 30m-high wheeled siege tower, featuring a huge battering ram hung through the centre. This was slowly wheeled up the ramp, with Roman artillery fire sweeping the parapets above to prevent any detailed intervention by the *sicarii*. As it neared the top, auxiliary bowmen and slingers in the siege tower then joined in the bombardment, and soon the ram was getting to work. In short order it smashed through the defensive wall, only for the Romans to find the defenders had been equally busy with their own engineering enterprise, the building of a second interior wall comprising heavy timber beams and earth. As the legionaries and auxiliaries entered through the breach in the original wall they now faced this new obstacle, defended by fanatical *sicarii* Zealots ready to martyr themselves.

While Flavius Silva was keen to bring matters to a rapid end, he knew an immediate assault would result in huge numbers of Roman casualties. He therefore ordered his engineers into action again. They quickly set the new fortification alight, leaving the fires to burn for twenty-four hours, after which the Romans prepared to storm the now torched inner defence. However, in that time the *sicarii* took a dramatic decision of their own. Dougherty takes up the story (2008, 215):

> Eleazar ben Ya'ir addressed his followers for the last time. It was obvious that they were doomed. Soon, the fortress would be stormed and everyone in it put to the sword. Alternatively, if they were captured, they would be crucified or otherwise done to death in a gruesome manner to demonstrate the futility of challenging Rome. The Zealots were not prepared to give victory to the Romans in this manner, nor allow such a fate to fall on their wives and children who sheltered within the fortress. There was only one alternative, a suicide pact. Drawing lots, they selected ten of their number to kill all the rest, and one of the ten to kill all of the others. With that done, the last man alive in Masada would slay

himself rather than submit to Rome. They chose this method since their religion frowned upon suicide; this way, only one of the Zealots actually killed himself.

Eleazar ben Ya'ir's last act of defiance was to order the torching of all of the internal structures atop Masada except the storehouses. These were still well stocked, and he wanted the Romans to know they hadn't killed themselves out of hunger. Josephus himself now provides the dramatic detail of what happened next (*The Jewish War*, 7.402):

> The Romans, expecting further combat, armed themselves before dawn and, bridging the approaches from their earthworks (the ramp) with gangways (over the smouldering inner wall) they launched an assault. But they saw not a single enemy and there was a terrible slaughter everywhere, and flames, and silence.

The *sicarii* defenders had carried out their shocking deed, with the Romans looking on stunned. There were no survivors left inside Masada, apart from two women and five children hidden in the cisterns. The siege was over, the Romans victorious, and the First 'Great' Jewish Revolt over.

Aftermath and Legacy

The Romans clearly hoped ending this first region-wide revolt in Judaea would finally bring peace to the province. There they were sadly mistaken, with low-level friction continuing as the norm. For example, instead of being sent back to the eastern *limes* to face the Parthians again, *legio* X *Fretensis* remained in Jerusalem where, based on epigraphy, it spent much of its time on regional policing work. A fine example is provided by the funerary epitaph of one legionary buried around the turn of the first century AD/second century AD. This man was a *beneficiarii* special-duties soldier on the governor's staff who, based on analogy, was a law enforcement specialist. His inscription reads (*CIL* 3, 14155): 'To the spirits of the departed. Lucius Magnius Felix, soldier of *legio* X *Fretensis*, beneficiaries of the governor. He served 19 years, and lived 39 years.'

Animosity between the Roman authorities and the Jewish population continued to build, and eventually rebellion erupted once more. This was in the form of the Second Jewish Revolt, also called the Kitos War.

The Second Jewish Revolt

This brutal conflict broke out in the context of Trajan's invasion of Parthia in AD 114. Here, the ever-restless emperor decided to tackle Rome's 'eastern question' head-on as he sought more martial glory after the enormous success of his two Dacian campaigns. Some have argued that his motivations here were actually economic following his annexation of the key desert trading centre of Petra and creation of the province of Arabia Petraea, after which he built an extensive road network in the east called the *Via Traiana Nova* which stretched from Busra al-Sham (Roman *Bostra*) in Syria to Aqaba (Roman *Aela*) on the Red Sea coast, the later southern terminus of the *Strata Diocletiana*. This meant that the only trading route to import spices and silk from India outside of Roman control was the Parthian port city of Charax Spasinu on the Persian Gulf. Capturing this would give the Roman's a monopoly in this lucrative trade, providing the ambitious (though not notably avaricious) Trajan with a motive for invasion.

As so often when the Romans campaigned in the east, Armenia to the south of the Caucasus Mountains was the first focus of their attention. Trajan had already shown an interest in the region when reports arrived that Sarmatian Alani were arriving on the kingdom's northern borders in large numbers (Kean and Frey, 76, 2005). The Romans feared this would turn into a flood of migrants who would destabilise their eastern provinces, and resolved to use Armenia as a barrier. Trajan began planning the annexation of the kingdom, but the Parthian king Osroes I moved first, placing his nephew Exederes, the son of a favourite brother, on the Armenian throne. Trajan promptly declared war, keen to avoid the humiliation of being outmanoeuvred politically by the Parthians. This gave Osroes pause for thought, he offering to remove Exederes and replace him with another nephew called Parthamasiris. Though Trajan rejected his offer, the Parthian king followed through his suggested plan anyway, hoping it would still placate the Romans. It did not, and it is unclear why he expected Trajan to respond positively to yet another royal Parthian nephew being placed on the Armenian throne. By now all of the Roman plans for a major campaign were in place and Trajan invaded Armenia in late AD 114. He quickly defeated the Armenian forces sent to confront him, together with their Parthian allies, and then killed Parthamasiris before following through on his own plan to annexe Armenia as a Roman province.

Next, in AD 115 Trajan then invaded northern Mesopotamia which he quickly overran, annexing this as another new province which he called Assyria. This secured Trajan's northern flank and rear, allowing him to campaign far down the Tigris and Euphrates valleys. Here he used these vast rivers to transport much of his force, including a large siege train. The latter allowed him to quickly capture and sack the Parthian capital *Ctesiphon*, before next sailing further downriver all the way to the Persian Gulf where he famously bathed in the warm waters there. To mark his success he then founded a third Roman province in the region which he called Mesopotamia, before following in the footsteps of Alexander the Great back to Babylon where he over-wintered. Writing 250 years later, Eutropius (*Historiae Romanae Breviarium*, 8.5) says that he then ordered a fleet to be built in the Red Sea with which he intended to '...lay waste...' to the western coastline of India.

However, this was not to be. As ever with the Romans in the east total victory proved elusive, and later in AD 115 major revolts broke out in the region. This included the Second Jewish Revolt in Judaea which led to the Jewish populations in the province of Aegyptus (especially in Alexandria), the twin Senatorial province of Cyrenaica et Creta to its west, the province of Cyprus, and also the newly-formed Assyrian and Mesopotamian provinces rebelling (Potter, 2009, 206). The latter province was particularly badly hit given the large number of Jewish exiles and refugees living there following the aggressive Roman defeat of the First 'Great' Jewish Revolt. Insurrections also broke out in the latter two new provinces among Parthian remnant populations where some of the wealthy former Hellenistic cities had been used to a large degree of autonomy under the Parthians. As Luttwak explains, simply put Trajan had committed the empire to a degree of geographical control beyond even its means (1976, 111):

> For an empire whose resources of trained manpower had hardly increased since the days of Augustus, the conquests of Trajan were obviously too extensive to be successfully consolidated. Nor did the entrenched cultures of the region offer much scope for long-term Roman policies of cultural-political integration.

Soon Roman military resources were stretched to the limit, with Trajan quickly returning to the eastern Mediterranean coast from Babylon to lead the counter-attack.

The Second Jewish Revolt proved even more sanguineous than the first given its much wider geographic spread. The rebellion was so serious that it threatened to undo Rome's political settlement along the south-eastern shores of the Mediterranean. At first, while Trajan was diverted leading his army back to the coast from Babylon, the rebels were able to massacre many Roman garrisons, officials and citizens across the region. The Romans, used to running their provinces with a light touch, always responded brutally against rebelling populations as earlier detailed, and once in position to strike back

Trajan decided to make a specific example of the Jewish insurrectionists, slaughtering huge numbers of them. This was on such a scale that he was forced to repopulate areas of Judaea now devoid of their original populations, relocating Roman citizens there to avoid good-quality agricultural land falling out of use.

The rebellion was ultimately put down by the Roman general Lusius Quietus whose *nomen*, in corrupted form, later gave the war its contemporary name as the Kitos War. As the conflict came to an end he eventually chased down and killed the Jewish leader Lukuas in Judaea, the *legate* then sentencing to death in absentia Lukuas' two deputies, the brothers Julian and Pappus. These had taken refuge in the Judaean city of Lydda along with a huge number of surviving rebels and refugees. The Romans promptly put this under close siege, eventually capturing it after a vicious assault on a scale similar to that which had earlier captured Masada. Most of the captives were executed including the two brothers, bringing the rebellion to an end in AD 117.

However, conflict in the region was not over. While diverted dealing with the insurrection in Judaea, Trajan's forces had failed to take the key eastern border city of Hatra which had been seized by pro-Parthian rebels. Parthian forces then attacked key Roman positions and garrisons at Seleucia-on-Tigris, Nisibis and Edessa. Trajan eventually subdued the rebels in Assyria and Mesopotamia, then installing a Parthian prince called Parthamaspates as a Roman client ruler in their capital *Ctesiphon*. He then withdrew to Syria where early in AD 117 he became seriously ill and decided to return to Rome. His health gradually declined further as he travelled, with contemporary sources saying that by this time he was suffering from poor circulation, indicating a heart problem. Ultimately he had a stroke that paralysed one side of his body. He finally died on 8 August that year at Gazipasa (Roman *Selinus*) in Cilicia from severe edema. His greatest legacy in the region was the establishment of the short-term provinces of Armenia, Assyria and Mesopotamia.

The Third 'bar Kokhba' Jewish Revolt

Again the Romans could be forgiven for thinking they had established a lasting peace in Judaea given the scale of the slaughter during the second revolt. And once more, they were wrong. Indeed, the Third 'bar Kokhba' Jewish Revolt of AD 132 to AD 136 actually proved the most difficult for the Romans to contain and defeat, even after acknowledging the difficulties they faced in the first two.

This rebellion was named after its leader Simon bar Kokhba, a mysterious figure whose actual family name we may not know given bar Kokhba seems to be an epithet meaning 'son of a star' in Aramaic. This rebellion was more serious than either of its predecessors given that, for the first time, the various Jewish communities in the region closely coordinated their campaigning against the Romans. Led by the charismatic bar Kokhba, who many declared was a heroic messiah who would restore a united kingdom of Israel, the Romans were soon on the back foot in the region again, with many garrisons once more being put to the sword.

In its initial stages the bar Kokhba revolt was surprisingly successful, with one contemporary report saying it resulted in the destruction of an entire Roman legion (this a candidate event for the loss of *legio* IX *Hispana*, Elliott, 2021a, 126). The rebels may also have actually recaptured the city of Jerusalem, and were certainly able to secure much of the province of Judaea under their control given they eventually announced the actual creation of the kingdom of Israel.

However, the Romans soon regrouped. Gathering resources from across the empire, they deployed a massive army featuring six full legions, vexillations from six others, and a large number of mounted and foot auxiliary units to settle matters with the Jewish rebels across the region once and for all. Once in theatre they adopted a scorched-earth strategy that ultimately extirpated most of the rebels, laying waste to much of Judaea. In the final phase of the conflict bar Kokhba fled to his last surviving fortress at *Betar*, near modern-day Battir. The Romans promptly besieged him there, capturing it after a lengthy siege. All inside perished, either in the final assault or in the ensuing massacre of those captured there, excepting one lone rebel who escaped. Among the dead was bar Kokhba himself.

Roman punishment for Judaea and the Jewish rebels was particularly harsh, even by their own extreme standards when stamping out a revolt. Jewish society had already been shattered by seventy years of on-off civil war, with a large proportion of the indigenous population killed, dead through starvation, enslaved or exiled (note the resettlement needed after the Second Jewish Revolt detailed above). Now the emperor Hadrian permanently changed the nature of the province, renaming it Syria Palaestina and turning Jerusalem into a pagan city that he renamed *Aelia Capitolina* after himself. In so doing he set in train a process designed to deliberately erase Jewish history, executing many surviving Jewish religious leaders and scholars, and banning the Torah and the use of the Jewish calendar. Any surviving Jews were banned from living within sight of newly-styled *Aelia Capitolina*, with Eusebius quoting Ariston of Pella in describing the impact of this (*Ecclesiastical History*, 4.6.4):

Thus when the city came to be bereft of the nation of the Jews, and its ancient inhabitants had completely perished, it was colonized by foreigners, and the Roman city which afterwards arose changed its name, and in honour of the reigning emperor Aelius Hadrian was called Aelia.

Given the severe societal dislocation caused by the three failed Jewish Revolts, only small Jewish communities remained in former Judaea, and the demography of the renamed province now shifted in favour of the non-Jewish population. From this point the remaining centres of Jewish cultural and religious life were all to be found outside of the province, particularly in Babylonia still, with other minor communities scattered elsewhere around the Mediterranean. One can therefore say with a degree of confidence that the Roman responses to the three Jewish Revolts, given their scouring nature over seventy years, marked the final classical world dispersal of the Jewish people from their Levantine homelands.

Chapter 5

The Battle of Mons Graupius

Agricola Conquers the Far North, AD *83*

Gnaeus Julius Agricola is the most famous governor of Roman Britain, at least in my opinion, this a bold statement when set against some serious rivals including Aulus Plautius, Gaius Suetonius Paulinus and Quintus Lollius Urbicus. However, Agricola benefits from one of the best public relations campaigns of the classical world given most of what we know of him was written by his son-in-law Tacitus, one of the best Roman historians. He detailed a number of aspects of the history and nature of early occupied Britain in *The Annals* and *The Histories*. However, it is his narrative regarding the campaigns of his father-in-law in *The Agricola* which is most relevant here.

Agricola is the only Roman leader who can claim to have conquered the whole main island of Britain, even if only briefly. He is also the only one to have considered the conquest of modern Ireland. However, his most controversial encounter was the Battle of Mons Graupius, the engagement where Tacitus says he finally defeated the massed tribes in the north of modern Scotland. It is contentious for two main reasons. First, because Tacitus is literally the only source for it, including giving the battle its name, and second because if it did take place we have no idea where the exact site was. Given Tacitus is such a fine classical historian, with a real eye for detail, I choose to accept his narrative that it did occur, hence its inclusion here. I address the debate regarding its actual location in the narrative below.

To provide context for Agricola's later campaigns in modern Scotland, here I first detail the Roman conquest of what is today northern England. Specifically in this chapter, for clarity I refer to the latter region as the north, and the former the far north. Also note that the Britons of the far north at the time of Agricola's campaigns are often called Caledonians. This is confusing given the term is explicitly used for a later confederation there in contemporary literature, as I detail below. Therefore, and again specifically in this chapter, I refer to the natives of the far north encountered by Agricola as Britons.

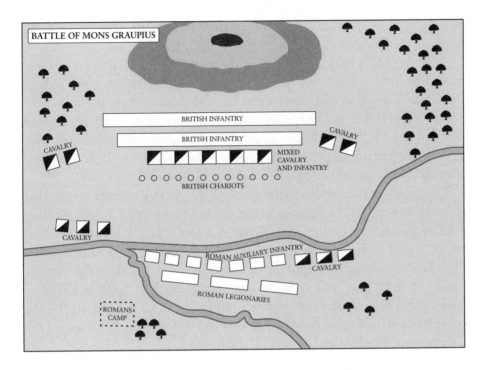

Strategic Build-Up to the Battle

Here I first detail the opponents faced by the Romans in the far north of Britain at the time of Agricola's campaigns there. I then consider the series of military operations that drove the northern frontier of occupied Britain up to the Solway Firth-Tyne line following the post-Boudiccan Revolt consolidation phase that I outlined at the conclusion of Chapter 3. Finally, I set out each of Agricola's campaigns in the far north, leading to the final confrontation with the Britons at the Battle of Mons Graupius.

Armies in the Far North of Britain

The unconquered far north of Britain at the time of Agricola's campaigns featured a quilt of local confederations and tribes just as complex as those encountered in the south by the Romans when establishing their province there. They included the Votadini in the eastern Scottish Borders, the Selgovae in the central Borders, the Novantae in the western Borders, the Dumnonii around the Clyde, and the Epidii in the Mull of Kintyre. Then above the Clyde on the west coast, going south to north, the Creones, the Carnonacae and (at the far north western tip of Scotland) the Caereni. On the east coast in Angus around the River Tay were the Venicones, and above them in Aberdeenshire the Taexali and in Moray the Vacomagi. Broadly, throughout the Grampians, were located the Caledonii, then around the Moray Firth, again going south to north, the Decantae, Lugi, Smertae and finally the Cornacii.

After Agricola's time, by the end of the second century AD many of these tribes had coalesced into two huge confederations, the Maeatae either side of the Clyde-Forth line, and above them the Caledonians. Late in the Roman occupation of Britain the Picts then came to dominate the far north of Scotland down to the Midland Valley. Additionally, the Romans also interacted with the various Scots-Irish peoples of modern Ireland across the Irish Sea, these relevant in the context of Agricola's abortive Irish campaign in AD 81.

The armies of the Britons in the far north fought in a manner very similar to those defeated by the Romans in the south. This included a chariot-riding nobility, skirmishing cavalry on small ponies, a levy of largely unarmoured foot troops armed with short spears and shield, and various types of skirmisher. Here Dio provides great insight through analogy when describing the warriors fought by Septimius Severus in his attempts to emulate Agricola 120 years later. By this time, during the emperor's campaigns in AD 209 and AD 210, the confederations and tribes faced by Agricola had united as the Maeatae and the Caledonians. Specifically, Dio says (77.12.1–4):

> They go into battle in chariots, and have small, swift ponies; there are also foot soldiers, very swift in running and very firm in standing ground. For arms they have a short spear and shield, with bronze apple attached to the end of the spear shaft, so that when the enemy is shaken it may clash and terrify the enemy; and they also have a dagger.

In my own research it has become increasingly apparent that the natives in the far north of Britain proved the most belligerent opponents the Romans fought here, on a scale almost matching the Jewish rebels in Judaea. Indeed, it is no surprise that when Antoninus Pius chose Quintus Lollius Urbicus as his new governor in Britain in the mid-second century AD and tasked him with (briefly as it turned out) driving the northern frontier up to the line of the Antonine Wall, his choice had earlier won the *dona militaria* decoration for playing a key role in brutally defeating the Third 'bar Kokhba' Jewish Revolt. To date, the received wisdom as to why the Romans failed to stay in the lowlands of modern Scotland, despite the two major attempts at full conquest under Agricola and Severus, was economic. However, when travelling through modern Scotland researching Agricola's campaigns, it is clear this region features some of the most fertile land in the north of Britain, for example in Fife. The climate at the time of the Roman occupation was little different to that today, so the experience now would be little different then. Therefore other reasons need to be explored as to why the Romans didn't stay in these fertile northern lands. I firmly believe one is simply the fact that the natives of the far north wanted nothing to do with Rome when not coerced, and were minded to fiercely defend this choice when provoked.

In addition to the animosity of the natives, as one moves above the lowlands even farther north, one can add another reason why the Romans didn't remain there. This is the very inhospitable terrain and climate, as this Mediterranean culture perceived it. For example, when detailing Severus' two campaigns, Dio says the locals lived in '...wild and waterless mountains and desolate and marshy plains...' (*Roman History*, 77.12.1), while for Herodian it was too much water that was the problem. He says '...the land of the Briton's there becomes marshy, being flooded by the continuous ocean tide...' (*History of the Roman Empire*, 3.14.6), adding that because of the mists from the marshes the air in the far north was gloomy. Both sources continue that this combination of ferocious opponent and hostile terrain/climate had a hugely negative impact on the Roman soldiers fighting there. For example, of Severus' AD 209 campaign Dio says that (76.13):

> ...as the emperor advanced through the country in the far north he experienced countless hardships in cutting down the forests, levelling the heights, filling up the swamps, and bridging the rivers; but he fought no battle and beheld no enemy in battle array. The enemy purposely put sheep and cattle in front of the soldiers for them to seize, in order that they might be lured on still further until they were worn out; for in fact the water caused great suffering to the Romans, and when they became scattered, they would be attacked. Then, unable to walk, they would be slain by their own men, in order to avoid capture, so that a full fifty thousand died [clearly a massive exaggeration, but indicative of the difficulties the Romans faced]. But Severus did not desist until he approached the extremity of the island.

The latter comment is clearly a conceit given the archaeological record suggests Severus got no further north than Stonehaven in southern Aberdeenshire, unlike the more ambitious Agricola who, as we will see, got much further north, perhaps as far as the Moray Firth.

Meanwhile, and again very useful by way of analogy, Herodian's account also highlights Severus' difficulty in defeating the Britons given their deep knowledge of the campaigning battlespace above the Scottish lowlands. He says (3.14):

...frequent battles and skirmishes occurred, and in these the Romans were victorious. But it was easy for the Britons to slip away; putting their knowledge of the surrounding area to good use, they disappeared in the woods and marshes. The Romans' unfamiliarity with the terrain prolonged the war.

Finally, Dio also highlights how the Britons above the Scottish lowlands combined the ferocity of those to their south with this deep understanding of their harsh environment, saying (77.12.1–4):

They can endure hunger and cold and any kind of hardship; for they plunge into swamps and exist there for many days with only their heads above water, and in forests they support themselves upon bark and roots, and for all emergencies they prepare a certain kind of food, the eating of a small portion of which, the size of a bean, prevents them from feeling either hunger or thirst.

The hunger-preventing food described here has been identified as the heath pea (*lathyrus linofolius*) by Dr Brian Moffat (2000, 13) of the Soutra Aisle research centre.

Conquest of the North

The post Boudiccan revolt policy of consolidation in Britain continued until the suicide of Nero in AD 68, this leading to the dramatic imperial power struggle in AD 69 called the 'Year of the Four Emperors' (detailed in Chapter 4). Vespasian's ultimate victory ushered in the Flavian Dynasty, providing the impetus for a new series of conquest campaigns in Britain.

As soon as Vespasian became emperor the veteran of the Claudian invasion had to deal with a number of insurrections that broke out across the empire. One involved Britain directly, and one indirectly. The first was a second revolt by the Brigantian queen Cartimandua's former husband Venutius. Taking advantage of the chaos back in Rome, the exile successfully deposed Cartimandua, with her again asking Rome for help (Tacitus, *Histories*, 3.45). By that time Marcus Vettius Bolanus had replaced Trebellius as governor, and the new incumbent headed north immediately. However, he was only able to muster a column of *exploratores* scouts and auxiliaries, with some believing the legions in Britain at the time had become unreliable given the civil war back in Rome. This managed to extract Cartimandua back to safety within the borders of the province to the south. The troops then campaigned further north in Brigantian territory in pursuit of Venutius, with the poet Statius having Bolanus campaigning in the 'Caledonian Plains' (*Silvae*, 53–56). This indicates the governor had penetrated the Scottish Borders, the farthest north the Romans had ventured in force to that date. However, despite this success no meeting engagement took place and, with only his *exploratores* and auxiliaries to hand, Bolanus was eventually forced to withdraw, leaving Venutius in power.

Meanwhile, the insurrection that indirectly involved Britain was the Batavian Revolt in the Rhine Delta led by Gaius Julius Civilis in AD 69, which actually began at the height of the 'Year of the Four Emperors' and concluded after Vespasian had become emperor. Here, the British regional fleet transported *legio* XIV *Gemina* (newly-returned to Britain by Vitellius after it had sided with Otho against him) back to the continent to help put down the uprising. This is an important event in the history of the navy given it is the first time it is actually called the *Classis Britannica* (Tacitus, *Histories*, 4, 79, 3). However, the mention here is ignominious as, having arrived in the Rhineland, the legion's *legate* Fabius Priscus marched his troops inland to attack the neighbouring Tungri and Nervii tribes who were supporting Civilis. In so doing, he left the fleet at anchor and unguarded, excepting its own *milites*, where it became an easy target for the Canninefates, another regional tribe supporting Civilis. Tacitus says that nearly all of the *Classis Britannica*'s vessels were captured or destroyed during a sustained attack on their anchorage (*Histories*, 4, 79, 3). However, Rome being Rome, once Civilis' revolt had been successfully dealt with all the losses were made good, and it continued in service until the mid-third century AD.

Back in Britain, Bolanus never got a second chance of glory in the north. With Vespasian now emperor, he cast around to find a suitable target for early conquest, keen to usher in his new dynasty with a swift victory. He alighted on the Brigantes in the north of Britain. However, rather than give the task to the existing governor he decided to reward a close relative and supporter, and from this point the story of the renewed conquest campaigns in Britain focuses on three great warrior governors, all sent to Britain by the Flavian emperors in search of triumph. The first, Bolanus' replacement, was Quintus Petillius Cerialis (who we first met in Chapter 3 when he ignominiously fled from Boudicca after defeat in his failed attempt to prevent the sack of Colchester). This proved the low point of his career, and by the time of the 'Year of the Four Emperors' he was a leading military commander again, fighting alongside his kinsman Vespasian and playing a key role in the latter's success. His reward was command of the Roman forces that defeated Civilis in the Batavian Revolt, after which he was promoted to the governorship in Britain. He arrived in AD 71, bringing a new legion with him. This was *legio* II *Adiutrix*, an interesting choice given it had been created by Vespasian from the marines of the *Classis*

Ravennate in Ravenna in AD 70 after their support for him in the 'Year of the Four Emperors'. These troops, as with Cerialis, were therefore totally loyal to the Flavians, and their deployment to Britain illustrates the importance the new emperor placed on securing new victories there.

Once in Britain Cerialis headed north immediately to set about Venutius and the Brigantes (Tacitus, *The Agricola*, 17). In the first instance he ordered *legio* IX *Hispana* out from its legionary fortress at Lincoln into Yorkshire where the troops constructed a new fortress at York, deep in Brigantian territory on the River Ouse. He then moved *legio* II *Adiutrix* into the vacated fortress at Lincoln to act as a strategic reserve. Next, Cerialis split the *Classis Britannica* into two divisions, one on the west coast which gathered in the estuary of the River Dee, and another on the east coast off the Humber Estuary. The former was ordered to support a drive north along the west coast by *legio* XX *Valeria Victrix*, whose loyalty the Flavians continued to suspect after the 'Year of the Four Emperors' when it had supported Vespasian's rivals. The emperor had therefore replaced its commander with Agricola, who makes his first appearance in Britain at this time. Meanwhile, the latter was ordered to support a similar drive up the east coast by the units of *legio* IX *Hispana* led by the governor himself, with Cerialis taking command of his old legion once more. Finally, before the campaign began, Cerialis redeployed part of *legio* II *Adiutrix* from Lincoln to the River Dee where a new vexillation-sized fort and naval facility was built at Chester, with the double aim of providing a base for the west-coast division of the *Classis Britannica* and to secure Agricola's left flank against any insurgency in north Wales.

Clear here is the vital importance of the *Classis* to the success of Cerialis' campaign against the Brigantes, for example in controlling the littoral zone to secure the exposed maritime flanks of the legionary spearheads, providing the transport and supply function along the coast and down the river systems to keep the land forces moving, and to scout ahead to provide timely intelligence of any gathering opposition. The parallels of this campaign with that of Vespasian in the south west in the AD 40s are remarkable, not least with the combination of the land forces following routes along the coast supported by a strong naval presence, with again military harbours created along the route as the advance continued. We have strong archaeological data to support this, showing new Roman harbours being built at Wilderspool, Kirkham, Lancaster (later the site of a vexillation fort), Ravenglass and Kirkbride on the west coast (in addition to Chester), and Brough-on-Humber (later Roman *Petuaria*, regional *civitas* capital of the Parisi) and South Shields (Roman *Arbeia*) on the east coast.

Cerialis' campaign followed a familiar pattern, with each legionary spearhead heading inland to subdue the native tribes of the Brigantian confederation on arrival at each estuary and river. Thus, rivers like the Dee, Esk, Ellen and Wampool on the west coast, and the Humber, Tees and Tyne on the east provided highways along which the invading Romans took the fight to the enemy. Soon, Cerialis and his *legate* Agricola began to wrestle regional control from the Brigantes piece by piece. The progression of this campaign is well evidenced by the multitude of vexillation forts built as the operation unfolded, with the end never in doubt given the scale of Roman commitment. The final British stand was at the Brigantian capital Stanwick, with the Romans totally victorious and Venutius killed. Our primary sources are silent at this point regarding Cartimandua so it is unclear whether she regained her crown or not, but we do know that by the time Cerialis returned to Rome in AD 74 the whole of the north of England (and potentially the southern Scottish Borders) was occupied by Rome, with the province extending its frontier further north than ever before.

The next soldier governor was Frontinus, another Flavian favourite who'd fought for Vespasian in the 'Year of Four Emperors'. Famed in his lifetime as a military man of letters, he'd earlier composed a book on strategy called *Strategems*, this being heavily used as source material for the later and more famous *Tactics* by Aelian. Frontinus arrived in Britain with the north for now pacified, and so turned his attention back to the unfinished business in Wales. There, despite the campaigns of Ostorius, Didius, Verianus and Paulinus, the native tribes were still proving troublesome, especially the Silures in the southeast. Deploying *legio* II *Augusta* from Gloucester where it had been based since the mid AD 60s, Frontinus mounted a lightning campaign using the River Severn and Bristol Channel to protect his left flank, where once again the regional fleet played a major role in the now very familiar roles of littoral control, transport and scouting. Within three years all opposition in the south of Wales had been crushed, with new a string of forts built to help enforce the rule of Rome. A number of these were on riverine estuaries, including locations such as Caerhun, Carmarthen, Caernarfon, Loughor, Conwy, Pennal and Neath. Finally, to secure the region even more firmly he permanently redeployed *legio* II *Augusta* from Gloucester to Caerleon on the River Usk where they built the famous legionary fortress and harbour to oversee southern Wales and the Bristol Channel. He similarly tasked *legio* II *Adiutrix* with developing the vexillation fort and harbour at Chester into a full legionary fortress to keep an eye on northern Wales. However, this region continued to be troublesome and was the initial target of our next and greatest soldier governor, Agricola.

Enter Agricola

Arriving back in Britain in the late summer of AD 77, the new governor immediately launched a savage offensive against the Ordovinces in response to their near annihilation of a detachment of Roman cavalry. Within a month he'd hacked his way through to the Isle of Anglesey, once more a centre of native opposition to Rome, surprising the Britons with a lightning assault and completely defeating them. He then consolidated his position, completing what Paulinus had started seventeen years earlier, with Wales finally pacified. Then in AD 78 the new governor turned his attention to the north, spending a year targeting any remaining resistance among the Brigantes to ensure his rear would be secure, with his eye now on the unconquered far north. This campaign included building a ring of new vexillation forts around the newly-incorporated territory up to the Solway Firth-Tyne line (Tacitus, *The Agricola*, 20).

Finally, in AD 79, Agricola launched his first assault across the northern frontier into the Scottish Borders. This campaign followed the same pattern as that of Cerialis against the Brigantes, with two spearheads forging northwards, one on the west coast and one (led by *legio* IX *Hispana*) on the east. As always in these campaigns of conquest in Britain, the *Classis Britannica* was on hand just off the coast of each thrust to fulfil its littoral control, transport and scouting roles, with Moorhead and Stuttard saying that (2012, 103):

> The fleet was to play a vital role throughout the course of the campaign, sailing ahead to reconnoiter harbours, shadowing the troops as they pressed forward on land, shipping supplies up from the south. Just as importantly, it was a useful tool in Agricola's arsenal for psychological warfare, as the sight of Roman galleys plying up and down the…coast of Scotland, using its sea lanes and its anchorages and beaches as if they were their own, struck fear into the Caledonian's hearts.

Agricola's first season north of the border was relatively problem-free, with the remains of a number of marching camps showing the progress of his campaign. At Newstead (Roman *Trimontium*) on the River Tweed near modern Melrose a more substantial fort was also built, near to the site of the capital of the Selgovae tribe. Tacitus says that by the time the campaigning season had ended, the eastern coast spearhead had reached as far north as the River Tay (*The Agricola*, 22). The governor's exploits were also well-regarded back in Rome, with Dio saying the new emperor Titus (who had succeeded his father Vespasian the same year) was given his fifteenth salutation by way of celebration (*Roman History*, 66.20).

Agricola was a seasoned warrior and knew it was imperative not to overstretch his lines of supply, even with the fleet in support. He therefore spent the next campaigning year in AD 80 consolidating his position in the Scottish Borders, the Romans occupying the region up to the Clyde and Forth line and possibly beyond. In this year many of the marching camp sites there were fortified for permanent occupation, and a road system with supply bases built. The principal route later became Dere Street. Military harbours were also constructed, these at Kirkbride, Newton Stewart, Glenluce, Stranraer, Girvan, Ayr and Dumbarton on the west coast, and Camelon on the east. Further north, the key fort, supply base and fortified harbour at Carpow on the Tay may also have been first constructed at this time.

The only region in the Scottish Borders still holding out against the Romans was modern Dumfries and Galloway in the southwest, where the indigenous Novantae had been bypassed. These became the target of Agricola's next campaign in AD 81. Gathering the east-coast units of the *Classis Britannica* together, he launched an amphibious assault with himself in the lead ship (Tacitus, *The Agricola*, 24), either northwards across the Solway Firth from the occupied south coast or westwards across the River Annan in Dumfries and Galloway (some translations of *The Agricola* specifically name the Annan). Once again the combination of land and naval forces proved highly successful, with the Novantae totally defeated.

At this point Tacitus has the governor consider a campaign against Ireland, saying (*The Agricola*, 24):

The side of Britain that faces Ireland was lined with his forces. His motive was rather hope than fear. Ireland, lying between Britain and Spain, and easily accessible also from the Gallic Sea, might serve as a very valuable link between the provinces forming the strongest part of the empire. It is small in comparison with Britain, but larger than the islands of the Mediterranean. In soil and in climate, and in the character and civilization of its inhabitants, it is much like Britain; and its approaches and harbours have become better known from merchants who trade there. A Scots prince, expelled from his home by a rebellion, was welcomed by Agricola, who detained him, nominally as a friend, in the hope of being able to make use of him. I have often heard Agricola say that Ireland could be reduced and held by a single legion with a fair-sized force of auxiliaries: and that it would be easier to hold Britain if it were completely surrounded by Roman armies, so that liberty was banished from its sight.

This is a most interesting passage given it indicates that, just as Britain was a source of trouble when conquering Gaul, so Ireland was for Britain when the empire was trying to conquer Wales and the far north. Certainly it would have been the most likely place to go for refugees escaping the Roman campaigns of conquest in Wales and western Scotland. Further, it may well be that Tacitus is only telling us half of the true story here, and for evidence of that we need to briefly return to Chester. There, the legionary fortress is particularly grand in its design and, covering 25ha in area, larger than any other Roman fortification in Britain dating to the later first century AD excepting perhaps the post Boudiccan Revolt town walls of Colchester. Additionally, remains have been found within its walls of buildings usually associated with a provincial capital, in addition to the usual utilitarian structures of a legionary fortress. This may indicate that at one stage Agricola considered Chester to be the chosen location of the provincial capital of a larger combined province featuring both Britain and Ireland. Given the building work had already started on these unusual buildings within the fortress, perhaps Agricola's plans in that regard were more advanced than Tacitus indicates. Certainly the governor had the means to invade Ireland, with the west-coast fleet immediately available. If this had gathered in Loch Ryan or Luce Bay in Galloway, then it would only have to travel 32km to reach Belfast Lough in today's Northern Ireland. However, such a dramatic intervention would certainly have required imperial approval. Sadly for Agricola the new emperor Domitian refused, even though the governor clearly expected a positive response given the building work in Chester had already begun. The third Flavian ruler had little interest in Britain at this stage, his initial focus being on the development of the *limes Germanicus* series of border fortifications along the Rhine, and securing his position in Rome. Moorhead and Stuttard argue that the decision not to invade Ireland was Agricola's biggest regret during his time as governor in Britain (2012, 103).

Agricola received new orders from Rome at the beginning of AD 82 to focus back on the far north again. This time, as the legionary spearheads advanced well beyond the Clyde and Forth line, they focused on the east coast only given the inhospitable terrain of the Highlands and islands to the west. Tacitus is clearer here than at any other time about the vital role played the *Classis Britannica*, detailing it being used to transport troops from the south to replace casualties, harass the enemy-occupied coast to disrupt economic activity, and maintain tight control of the littoral zone along the coast and down the river systems (*The Agricola*, 25). He also highlights the hazards faced by the fleet in the waters so far north, with its frequent storms and unforgiving tides. We have direct evidence of such dangers back in occupied Britain, with the tombstone of an unnamed *optio* of the regional fleet at Chester. According to the epigraphy on his memorial, he died in a storm off the east coast of Scotland at this time. Tacitus adds that, as the campaign progressed inexorably northwards, the two distinct arms of the Roman military began to share the same fortified camps (*The Agricola*, 26). This is perhaps the best example in our primary sources we have showing the army and fleet working so closely together, whether legionaries, auxilia, or marines and sailors.

To this point most of the native resistance to Agricola's campaigns in the far north had been in the form of guerilla warfare, they withdrawing glen by glen and loch by loch. Now, however, given the success of the governor's combined arms approach, they began to risk open encounters. Tacitus has them directly attacking military installations, and it is in this context we have the last ever historical mention of the famous IXth legion. This references a specific incident when Agricola's legionary spearheads were driving hard through native territory. Tacitus says (*The Agricola*, 27):

The natives of Caledonia turned to armed resistance on a grand scale… They went so far as to attack our forts, and inspired alarm by taking the offensive…But just then Agricola learned the enemy were about to attack in several columns. To avoid encirclement by superior forces familiar with the territory, he likewise divided his own army into three parts and so advanced. As soon as the enemy got to know of this they changed their plans and massed for a night attack on the IXth legion, which seemed to them the weakest. Striking panic into the sleeping marching camp, they struck down the sentries and broke in. The fight was already raging inside the camp when Agricola was warned by his scouts of the enemy's march. Following closely on their tracks, he ordered the speediest of his cavalry and infantry to harass the assailant's rear and then had his whole army join in the battle cry; the standards gleamed in the light of dawn. The Britanni were dismayed at being caught between two fires, while the men of the IXth took heart again: with their lives now safe they could fight for honour. They even effected a sally, and a grim struggle ensued in the narrow passage of the gates. At last the enemy broke under the rival efforts of the two armies, the one striving to make it plain that they had brought relief, the other that they could have done without it.

After this Agricola took no chances, tasking *legio* XX *Valeria Victrix* with building the legionary fortress at Inchtuthil on the north bank of the River Tay in Perth and Kinross. Having stood within its still-visible earthwork fortifications, this is a fine location for what was Rome's most northerly legionary fortress, even if only for a short time. Agricola then built a naval logistics chain of fortified harbours northwards towards the Moray Firth, this matching the well-known marching camp sequence as his legionaries and auxilia penetrated deep into native territory. South to north above the River Tay these naval installations were located at Monifieth, Dun, Aberdeen, and finally Bellie in Moray itself.

This construction programme concluded the fourth northern campaigning season, with Agricola garrisoning his forts and fortified harbours in the far north for the winter and the Britons moving their women, children and elderly to places of safety. Tacitus adds one more interesting detail here, showing the Romans didn't have everything their own way (*The Agricola*, 28). He says that a cohort of Usipi auxiliaries recruited from Rhine Delta mutinied for reasons unknown and, murdering their centurion, stole three *liburnian* biremes. Tacitus enigmatically described the ships as '…a ghostly apparition as they sailed along the coast…' (*The Agricola*, 28) while making their getaway, eventually crossing the North Sea before coming to various kinds of grief on the north German coast due to the ineptitude of the crews.

The Main Engagement

Agricola's fifth and final campaign in the far north took place in AD 83. It marked the culmination of his ambitions to subdue the entire main island of Britain and, given the resistance he had encountered the previous year, he took no chances, fielding the largest force available. This numbered 30,000 men, including all four British legions (at this time II *Adiutrix*, II *Augusta*, IX *Hispana* and XX *Valeria Victrix*, Pollard and Berry, 2012, 194), his auxiliaries (Tacitus specifically mentions 8,000 auxiliary foot and 3,000 cavalry) and the marines of the fleet (Elliott, 2016, 133).

Where Did the Battle Take Place

In this final campaign Agricola's legionary spearheads penetrated further north than ever before, edging along the coast around the Grampian Mountains to reach the Moray Firth, with a sequence of large 44ha marching camps firmly dated to this campaign tracking its progress north (Hodgson, 2014, 41). The most northerly site which has been securely dated is at Auchinhove just south of the Moray Firth itself, this featuring the usual site-type Stracathro gateways associated with Agricola's campaigns. In his excellent guide to the Roman archaeological sites in Scotland, Andrew Tibbs highlights an interesting feature here, saying (2019, 181): 'It is unusually close to two other [more southerly] camps, which are believed to date to the same period: Muiryfold, less than 3.2km away, and Burnfield, which is 8km away.'

Given camps are usually one day's march apart, this indicates that these sites were closely connected, perhaps to allow Agricola to mass his force for a specific reason. There might be one further camp further north than Auchinhove at Bellie near Fochabers in Moray which some believe might be Agricolan. However, its Flavian identification has proved controversial.

Tracing the line of these camps north from the Tay to Auchinhove defines the battlespace where I believe Agricola's meeting engagement with the Britons at Mons Graupius took place. Accepting that, we are then faced with a dilemma given we have no idea where it was. This has led to an intense and ongoing debate as to its exact location. For example, in the nineteenth century the battle site was located at nearly every Roman site a few days march from the east coast above the Tay. Then, with the twentieth century advent of aerial photography and data-based historical analysis, the search became much more specific. Now, the leading candidate site is the Bennachie range of distinctive hills in Aberdeenshire, a red granite massif in the eastern Grampians. This is largely based on etymology, with one interpretation suggesting the Latin Mons (mountain or hill) has been paired by Tacitus with a native word some believe to be Cripius, the Brythonic name for a comb with its distinctive narrow teeth. This suggests a series of peaks, which specifically matches the Bennachie location given the 6.5km-long ridge comprises a series of peaks (Campbell, 2010, 66). Another alternative might be further north around the grouping of marching camps near Auchinhove referenced by Tibbs, explaining their unusually close proximity.

In reality, however, we have no real idea where Mons Graupius was at all due to the lack of any archaeological evidence, except that logic suggests it was along the far northern Agricolan line of camps, and given it took place at the end of the campaign, likely at its north-easterly tip.

The Battle
Wherever the battle of Mons Graupius took place it proved decisive. Given Tacitus gives such a detailed account in *The Agricola*, I chose here to broadly follow his narrative, providing my own interpretation and that of others where more detail is required.

In the first instance, Tacitus describes the response of the natives in the far north as the legionary spearheads marched inexorably northwards from the Tay, eviscerating all before them while the fleet rampaged along the coast. To that point the Britons had been reliant on their usual strategy of guerilla warfare and large-scale ambush to tackle the Romans. Clearly that had failed, and a final stand now had to be made. Tacitus says (*The Agricola*, 29):

> Undismayed by their former defeats, the Barbarians expected no other issue than a total overthrow, or a brave revenge. By treaties of alliance, and by deputations to the several tribal regions, they had drawn together the strength of their nation. Upwards of 30,000 men appeared in arms, and their force was increasing every day. Among the chieftains distinguished by their birth and valour, the most renowned was Calgacus. The multitude gathered around him, eager for action, and burning with uncommon ardour.

Campbell argues the core force Calgacus had at his disposal comprised warriors from the Venicones in Angus, the Taexali in Aberdeenshire and the Vacomagi in Moray, and I agree (2010, 58). Other confederations and tribes in the far north also contributed troops, keen to defend their home territories, and perhaps also looking for plunder. Notably, the size of native British army described by Tacitus broadly matches the size of that being led by Agricola. Further, although Roman military tactics and technology far outstripped that of their opponents, the Britons were fighting in their own terrain and climate. This gave them a degree of synergy in the coming encounter not obvious when one simply compares troop quality. To that end, it was imperative the Romans were led well on the battlefield. Agricola was keenly aware of the fate of Varus' three legions in AD 9 in the Teutoburg Forest when their commanders had failed them in similarly hostile conditions, and was determined not to make the same mistakes.

Tacitus now has Calcagus address his gathered multitude with a rousing speech, delivered in the finest tradition of Latin oratory. The latter is no surprise given this native British 'sermon on the mount' was never given as described, if Calgacus ever existed at all. Instead, it is a literary device used by Tacitus to portray the British leader as a worthy opponent, specifically with an eye on the domestic audience back in Rome. He has Calgacus say the following (*The Agricola*, 30–32):

> Whenever I consider the origin of this war and the necessities of our position, I have a sure confidence that this day, and this union of ours, will be the beginning of freedom to the whole of Britain. To all of us slavery is a thing unknown; there are no lands beyond us, and even the sea is not safe, menaced as we are by a Roman fleet. And thus in war and battle, in which the brave find glory, even the coward will not find

safety. Former contests, in which, with varying fortune, the Romans were resisted, still left in us a last hope of succour, inasmuch as being the most renowned nation of Britain, dwelling in the very heart of the country, and out of sight of the shores of the conquered, we could keep even our eyes unpolluted by the contagion of slavery. To us who dwell on the uttermost confines of the earth and of freedom, this remote sanctuary of Britain's glory has up to this time been a defence. Now, however, the furthest limits of Britain are thrown open, and the unknown always passes for the marvellous. But there are no tribes beyond us, nothing indeed but waves and rocks, and the yet more terrible Romans, from whose oppression escape is vainly sought by obedience and submission. Robbers of the world, having by their universal plunder exhausted the land, they rifle the deep. If the enemy be rich, they are rapacious; if he be poor, they lust for dominion; neither the east nor the west has been able to satisfy them. Alone among men they covet with equal eagerness poverty and riches. To robbery, slaughter, plunder, they give the lying name of empire; they make a solitude and call it peace. Nature has willed that every man's children and kindred should be his dearest objects. Yet these are torn from us by conscriptions to be slaves elsewhere. Our wives and our sisters, even though they may escape violation from the enemy, are dishonoured under the names of friendship and hospitality. Our goods and fortunes they collect for their tribute, our harvests for their granaries. Our very hands and bodies, under the lash and in the midst of insult, are worn down by the toil of clearing forests and morasses. Creatures born to slavery are sold once and for all, and are, moreover, fed by their masters; but Britain is daily purchasing, is daily feeding, her own enslaved people. And as in a household the last comer among the slaves is always the butt of his companions, so we in a world long used to slavery, as the newest and most contemptible, are marked out for destruction. We have neither fruitful plains, nor mines, nor harbours, for the working of which we may be spared. Valour, too, and high spirit in subjects, are offensive to rulers; besides, remoteness and seclusion, while they give safety, provoke suspicion. Since then you cannot hope for quarter, take courage, I beseech you, whether it be safety or renown that you hold most precious. Under a woman's leadership the Brigantes were able to burn a colony, to storm a camp, and had not success ended in supineness, might have thrown off the yoke [I actually have this as a reference to Boudicca and the Iceni]. Let us, then, a fresh and unconquered people, never likely to abuse our freedom, show forthwith at the very first onset what heroes Caledonia has in reserve. Do you suppose that the Romans will be as brave in war as they are licentious in peace? To our strifes and discords they owe their fame, and they turn the errors of an enemy to the renown of their own army, an army which, composed as it is of every variety of nations, is held together by success and will be broken up by disaster. These Gauls and Germans, and, I blush to say, these Britons, who, though they lend their lives to support a stranger's rule, have been its enemies longer than its subjects, you cannot imagine to be bound by fidelity and affection. Fear and terror there certainly are, feeble bonds of attachment; remove them, and those who have ceased to fear will begin to hate. All the incentives to victory are on our side. The Romans have no wives to kindle their courage; no parents to taunt them with flight, and either no country or one far away. Few in number, dismayed by their ignorance, looking around upon a sky, a sea, and forests which are all unfamiliar to them; hemmed in, as it were, and enmeshed, the Gods have delivered them into our hands. Be not frightened by the idle display, by the glitter of gold and of silver, which can neither protect nor wound. In the very ranks of the enemy we shall find our own forces. Britons will acknowledge their own cause; Gauls will remember past freedom; the other Germans will abandon them, as but lately did the Batavi. Behind them there is nothing to dread. The forts are ungarrisoned; the colonia in the hands of aged men; what with disloyal subjects and oppressive rulers, the towns are ill-affected and rife with discord. On the one side you have a general and an army; on the other, tribute, the mines, and all the other penalties of an enslaved people. Whether you endure these forever, or instantly avenge them, this field is yours to decide. Think, therefore, as you advance to battle, at once of your ancestors and of your posterity.

Tacitus has the Britons responding to this anti-imperial call-to-arms with wild '…war songs and savage howlings…' In the Roman writer's narrative, Calgacus then forms up his 30,000 warriors ready for battle, with the hardy and brave pushing to the front (*The Agricola*, 33). Agricola then addresses his own army as it looks on at the deploying Britons, with the Roman leader saying (*The Agricola*, 33–34):

If our present struggle were with nations wholly unknown; if we had to do with an enemy new to our swords, I should call to mind the example of other armies. At present what can I propose so bright and animating as your own exploits? I appeal to your own eyes: behold the men drawn up against you: are they not the same, who last year, under the covert of the night, assaulted the IXth legion, and, upon the first shout of our army, fled before you? A band of rogues who have subsisted hitherto because, of all the Britons, they are the most expeditious runaways. Benumbed with fear they stand motionless on yonder spot, which you will render forever memorable by a glorious victory. Here you may end your labours, and close a scene of 50 years by one great, one glorious day. Let your country see, and let the commonwealth bear witness, if the conquest of Britain has been a lingering work, if the seeds of rebellion have not been crushed, that we at least have done our duty.

Tacitus next has the Roman legionaries and auxiliaries shouting their own acclamation at their general's call to arms, with a vigour to match the Britons. Now the business of battle began, with Tacitus providing one of the most detailed accounts we have of Roman deployment on the battlefield. He says (*The Agricola*, 35):

Agricola restrained the ardour of his troops until he formed his order of battle. The auxiliary infantry, in number about 8,000, occupied the centre. The wings consisted of 3,000 horse. The legions were stationed in the rear, at the head of the entrenchments as a body of reserve to support the ranks, if necessary, but otherwise to remain inactive, that a victory, obtained without the effusion of Roman blood might be of higher value.

There is much detail in this short paragraph, overt or inferred. Notably, this was an unusual deployment for a Roman army in the field. Though it was common for the auxiliaries to engage an enemy before the legionaries were committed, it was not for the legionaries to be deployed en masse at the rear. Tacitus' explanation is that Agricola was preserving his legionaries because they were Roman citizens, while the auxiliaries were not. However, given the legionaries were his best troops, and this was the engagement he believed he would finally defeat British resistance, this does not ring true. A simple assessment of numbers might provide an alternative explanation. Agricola's army for the wider campaign comprised 30,000 men, of which 11,000 at Mons Graupius were auxiliaries. We also know that within the 30,000 were the marines of the fleet that, while not present on the battlefield, had certainly played a key role in the wider campaign. To this whole force we can then add the legionaries of the four legions deployed which, when combined at this stage of the Principate Empire, would number 22,000 men if at full strength. Clearly the numbers here don't add up, with the only explanation being that the legions were badly understrength after a hard campaign. I therefore believe Agricola was hoping his auxiliaries would do the job on their own, as in fact actually happened, given he didn't want to lose one or more of his (perhaps heavily) understrength legions. Here one can again see the long shadow cast by Varus' failure in AD 9. Agricola would only commit his legions if they were really needed. Fortunately for him, as it turned out, they weren't.

Tacitus now turns his attention to the British deployment. Crucially, he indicates Calgacus ensured his warriors were on high ground above the Roman camps below, and held their position there. One should note the degree of control here, this very different to Boudicca's failure to restrain her troops in the Battle of Watling Street. Specifically, Tacitus says (*The Agricola*, 36): 'The Caledonians kept possession of the rising ground, extending their ranks as wide as possible, to present a formidable show of battle. Their first line was ranged just above the plain, the rest in a gradual ascent on the acclivity of the hill.'

He then provides real insight into the tactics of the Britons as the battle began, this matching exactly those described in earlier encounters further south when Caesar, Plautius and Paulinus fought the Britons. Once more we may be dealing with tropes, with Tacitus perhaps duplicating earlier battle reports. However, he certainly had access to his father-in-law's first-hand commentary, together with reports from other Roman eyewitnesses, so I choose to take him at face value. In particular, he says (*The Agricola*, 36):

> The intermediate space between both armies was filled with the charioteers and cavalry of the Britons, rushing to and fro in wild career, and traversing the plain with noise and tumult.

The picture here is of Calgacus' army deployed on a range of steep, mountainous slopes. Agricola's force was deployed below. Both sides comprised around 30,000 men, the Romans perhaps fewer given troops from the overall campaigning force (for example the marines) were committed elsewhere. Ostensibly, this combination of height and greater numbers gave the Britons the advantage. A missile exchange now began, with the Romans having the advantage given their legionary artillery, body shields and high-quality armour. The British foot warriors, with their small shields which Tacitus calls targets, were particularly vulnerable (*The Agricola*, 36). In normal circumstances this should have prompted the Britons to charge down the slope at the Romans. However, they still kept their ground. To force the issue, Agricola now ordered six cohorts of elite auxiliaries forward. Four were of Batavians and two Tungrians, all recruited in the Rhine Delta. These warriors had a fearsome reputation and were soon doing their bloody work, despite the Britons being uphill. Tacitus is particularly graphic here, saying (*The Agricola*, 36):

> The Batavians rushed to the attack with impetuous fury. Incited by their example, the other cohorts advanced with a spirit of emulation, and cut their way with terrible slaughter. Eager in pursuit of victory, they pressed forward with determined fury, leaving behind them numbers wounded, but not slain, and others not so much as hurt.

Tacitus adds here that Calgacus' troops were handicapped by their inferior weapons which were no match for the *lancea* spears and *gladii* stabbing swords of the auxiliaries (*The Agricola*, 36). Indeed, some translations have the auxiliaries here actually thrusting their swords into the faces of the Britons.

Tacitus now brings us back to the British chariots, referencing a mounted engagement. This was on one or both flanks of the auxiliary advance, and happened at the same time. Here the result was a different story, with the Britons initially successful against their mounted opponents. Tacitus says (*The Agricola*, 37):

> The Roman cavalry, in the mean time, was forced to give ground. The Caledonians, in their armed chariots, then rushed at full speed into the thick of the battle, where the infantry were engaged. Their first impression struck a general terror, but their career was soon checked by the inequalities of the ground and the close ranks of the Romans. Pent up in narrow places, the Barbarians crowded upon each other, and were driven or dragged along by their own horses. A scene of confusion followed. Chariots without a guide, and loose ponies, broke from the ranks in wild disorder, and flying every way, as fear and consternation urged, they overwhelmed their own files and trampled down all who came in their way.

Thus we have the British chariots pushing the *equites* backwards to expose the flanks of the foot auxiliaries. Moorhead and Stuttard call this the moment of greatest danger for the Romans (2012, 114). However, the steadfast Agricola showed no sign of panic. He had faith in his auxiliaries, which soon proved well founded given the British chariots were quickly repelled with heavy losses by the Batavians and Tungrians (the rocky terrain also counting against the chariots).

Calgacus now faced disaster. The Roman auxiliaries were butchering his foot in the centre, while his chariots had failed to take advantage of their earlier success against the Roman cavalry. In desperation, he now made a last desperate attempt to turn the day his way, ordering his reserve of foot warriors high up on the slopes to charge downhill. Specifically, they were ordered to wheel into the flank of the Roman auxiliary foot, indicating they were slightly offset from the line of battle below. However, Agricola easily countered by ordering his now rallied *equites*, and his own personal reserve of guard cavalry, to intercept the British foot while on the move. The result was a slaughter.

At that point the Britons broke, with thousands butchered by the Romans as they scrambled to find safety. Over 10,000 perished, with Tacitus describing a dreadful spectacle of carnage and destruction (*The Agricola*, 37). A vigorous Roman pursuit followed, and though some Roman troopers were killed by desperate Britons in the mountains, native resistance was finally broken. Agricola allowed the pursuit to continue until nightfall and then recalled his troops to their marching camps for the night. Tacitus says the Romans lost only 340 men overall, with the army '...elated with success, enriched with plunder, and passing the night in exultation' (Tacitus, *The Agricola*, 38).

His victory secure, Agricola next led his troops on a punitive expedition through the Grampians and the Moray and Buchan Lowlands below the Moray Firth, his scorched-earth policy destroying all economic activity in the region for generations. He then tasked squadrons of the *Classis Britannica* with completing a circumnavigation of Britain, with Tacitus saying (*The Agricola*, 38):

> The Roman fleet now sailed round the furthest shores for the first time, and so established that Britain is an island. At the same time it discovered and overthrew some islands, called the Orkneys, which until then had been unknown. Thule [possibly Iceland] too, was sighted.

The defeat of the natives across the far north now complete, Agricola could claim in his dispatches to Domitian that the entire main island of Britain had now been conquered.

Aftermath and Legacy

To further cement control of the north, a series of forts and fortlets were then built to seal off the various Glens in the Highlands, in much the same way trouble had been contained in the conquest of Wales. Today these are called Glenblocker forts. To celebrate complete victory Domitian, now far more interested in Britain given Agricola's success, ordered the construction of a huge quadrifrons (four-way) monumental arch at Richborough on the east Kent coast to mark the place where the successful Claudian invasion had earlier landed (see Chapter 2). At 25m in height, this was one of the tallest monumental arches in the entire empire. Further, it was clad in highly expensive Carrera marble imported from Italy, marking Richborough out as the imperial gateway into the province from that point. This dazzling white arch was so tall it was visible on the continent on clear days, leading to its re-use at the onset of the Carausian Revolt in AD 286 as a watch tower.

However, Agricola's great success was not to last, with Domitian recalling him sometime between AD 83 and AD 85. When he arrived back in Rome he was initially feted, with the emperor awarding him a statue and triumphal decorations. However, he soon fell from imperial favour and never again held high military or civil office, dying in AD 93. By this time his great achievements in the far north had begun to unravel as Rome gradually lost interest there, perhaps because of the lack of economic potential at the time. Within four years of Agricola's departure the forts cutting off the Highland line had been evacuated and the devastated local population began to trickle back to the fertile lowlands. Then the legionary fortress at Inchtuthil was abandoned before it was fully completed, with *legio* XX *Valeria Victrix* redeploying south to Chester where it replaced *legio* II *Adiutrix* after the latter was redeployed to the Balkans. Similarly, while patrolling in the waters of the far north no doubt continued to maintain control of the littoral zone there, the *Classis Britannica* headed south. Thus as the end of the first century AD approached, the fleet found itself principally operating out of the harbours at Chester on the west coast and South Shields on the east.

Before his departure Agricola had set in place his main physical legacy in Britain, this the 61km Stanegate road (a later name, after 'stone road' in Northumbrian dialect) running from Carlisle (Roman *Luguvalium*) in the west to Corbridge (Roman *Coria*) in the east, through the natural gap formed by the valleys of the rivers Irthing and Tyne. The Stanegate was a substantial military trunk road almost 7m wide, and as Roman troops gradually headed south or elsewhere from the far north, it became the northern border of the province, later to be famously fortified in the AD 120s by Hadrian. However, to the north there remained the unfinished business of conquest. This now troubled the Roman province in the south for the rest of their occupation of Britain, with only the two campaigns of Septimius Severus in AD 209 and AD 210 serious attempts at emulating Agricola.

However, perhaps the biggest legacy of Agricola's campaigns in the far north were political. These were the twin decisions by Domitian to decline Agricola's request to invade Ireland, and then later to give up the far north after the only time the Romans could truly claim to have conquered the whole main island of Britain. From those points, with the territory of both modern Ireland and Scotland outside the imperial domain, history has travelled in a different direction there compared to the Roman occupied lands in the south of the main island of Britain. This has played a key role in defining the political settlement of the British archipelago to this very day.

Chapter 6

The Battle of Carnuntum

Disaster on the Danube, AD 170

T
he Marcomannic Wars fought along the Danube from the later
AD 160s featured a series of conflicts that tested the Roman Danubian
frontier there to breaking point, and often broke it. It was here on the
northern *limes* where in AD 170 the Roman lynchpin fortress at *Carnuntum*
was destroyed, with its garrison wiped out in open battle. This shattering
defeat, which occurred when the attention of the emperor Marcus Aurelius
was elsewhere in the region, allowed thousands of Marcomanni and Quadi
warriors to stream across the border into imperial territory. Soon they were
in Italy, the first Germanic invasion there for 300 years, with panic ensuing in
Rome. Here I set out the Roman disaster at *Carnuntum* in detail, the first time
this key engagement has been narrated in long form to date.

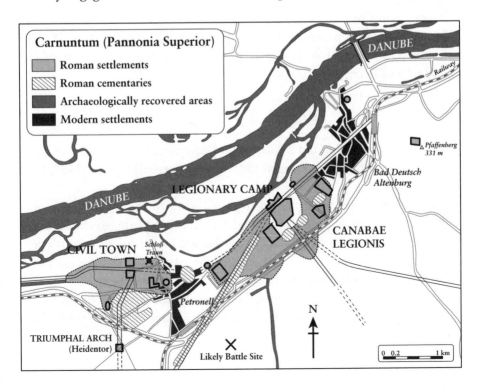

Strategic Build-Up to the Battle

To familiarize the reader with the strategic backdrop to the Battle of Carnuntum, here I first detail the Roman frontier zone along the Danubian frontier during the Principate Empire, and then provide a chronological narrative for the Marcomannic Wars.

The Danubian Frontier

The River Danube is a huge continental waterway, rising in southern Germany and flowing southeastwards 2,850km before draining into the Black Sea. In the Roman period it was a crucial frontier that, along with the Rhine to its west, separated civilization to its south (as the Romans saw it) from 'barbaricum' in the north. This mighty river was therefore a crucial military border zone which, during the Principate Empire, featured nine provinces. West to east, these were:

- Raetia, the province linking the Rhine and Danube.
- Noricum.
- Pannonia Superior.
- Pannonia Inferior.
- Dalmatia.
- Moesia Superior.
- Dacia (a redoubt province standing proud of the Danube, from Trajan's final conquest in AD 106 through to its abandonment by Aurelian in AD 275, Pollard and Berry, 2012, 200).
- Moesia Inferior.
- Thracia.

The Danubian region in the Roman period was particularly complex in terms of wealth and culture, with Cornell and Matthews explaining that (1982, 140):

> The Danubian provinces, taken together, spanned the whole range of Roman civilization, from the settled Celtic tribes of the west and the urbanized seaboard of Dalmatia to the ancient Greek cities of the Black Sea coast. The Thracian regions east of the pass of Succi were Greek-speaking and their cities had Greek names. Meanwhile the 'Latinisation' of Dacia, after an occupation of 170 years, is still actively attested by modern Romanian [the Romance language closest to the vulgar Latin spoken by the Romans].

The key cities of the region included Augsberg (Roman *Augusta Vindelicorum*) which was the provincial capital of Raetia, Wels (Roman *Ovilava*) which was the provincial capital of Noricum, Vienna (Roman *Vindobona*), *Carnuntum* which was the provincial capital of Pannonia Superior (the focus of this chapter, and later where Septimius Severus was proclaimed emperor, Elliott, 2018a, 100), Split (Roman *Aspalathos*) on the Adriatic coast where Diocletian later built has palace when he retired, Budapest (Roman *Aquincum*) which was the provincial capital of Pannonia Inferior, Kostolac (Roman *Viminacium*) which was the provincial capital of Moesia Superior, Roman *Ulpia Traiana Sarmizegetusa* which was the provincial capital of Dacia, Konstantsa (Roman *Tomis*) which was the provincial capital of Moesia Inferior, and Roman *Perinthus* which was the provincial capital of Thracia.

As with the Rhine, the Danubian provinces were defined by the northern *limes* there which ran for much of the river's length. Cornell and Matthews call these the backbone of the empire, with the lengthy fortifications divided into four sections (1982, 140):

- The Rhaetian *limes*, here only the section on the Danube.
- The Noric *limes* in Noricum.
- The Pannonian *limes* in Pannonia Superior and Inferior.
- The Moesian *limes* in Moesia Superior and Inferior, running down to the Black Sea. From AD 106 after Trajan's Dacian conquests until the province was abandoned by Aurelian, this section actually ran far to the north, encompassing the whole Dacian salient, comprising much of modern Romania.

For much of the Principate the Danubian *limes* were home to some of the most experienced legions in the empire. They were based in a string of legionary fortresses along the frontier, ranging from Vienna in the west to *Troesmis* in the east. By the late second century AD the legions here included *legio* III *Italica* in Raetia, *legio* II *Italica* in Noricum, *legio* XIV *Gemina Martia Victrix*, *legio* I *Adiutrix pia fidelis* and later *legio* X *Gemina* in Pannonia Superior, *legio* II *Adiutrix pia fidelis* in Pannonia Inferior, *legio* IV *Flavia felix* and *legio* VII *Claudia pia fidelis* in Moesia Superior, *legio* XIII *Gemina pia fidelis* in Dacia and *legio* I *Italica*, *legio* V *Macedonia* and *legio* XI *Claudia pia fidelis* in Moesia Inferior. As with the Rhine frontier, they were joined by an equivalent number of auxiliaries, while the two regional fleets here were the *Classis Pannonica* on the upper Danube and the *Classis Flavia Moesica* on the lower Danube. The latter also had responsibility for the Black Sea, controlling access from there to the Mediterranean.

These legions faced off against a variety of aggressive northern neighbours. These included the Germanic Marcomanni, Juthungi and Quadi (see Chapter 1 for detail), various Sarmatian tribes including the Iazyges and Roxalani, and remnant Dacians and Bastarnae. All proved tough opponents in the Marcomannic Wars.

The Marcomannic Wars

After the imperial conquests of Trajan, when the Principate empire expanded to its greatest extent, the Roman world experienced a long period of comparative peace during the reigns of Hadrian (excepting the the Third 'bar Kokhba' Jewish Revolt) and Antoninus Pius. This came to a shattering end as soon as Marcus Aurelius and Lucius Verus became joint emperors in AD 161. In the first instance, trouble broke out in the east with the start of the Roman-Parthian War which lasted until AD 165.

However, a far more dangerous conflict then broke out in the mid-AD 160s, with the start of the Marcomannic Wars along the Danube. Now, for the first time since the Cimbrian wars, Italy itself was threatened by 'barbarian' invaders penetrating deep into the imperial centre.

The principal opponents in these wars were the Germanic Marcomanni, Juthungi and Quadi in *Magna Germania*, as the unconquered lands north of the Danube were now known, and their Sarmatian Iazyges allies. All were being driven hard against Rome's Dacian and Danubian frontiers by the westward expansion of the Visigoths and Ostrogoths, the German peoples to their east, who themselves were being driven westwards by the initial expansion of the Huns.

The Marcomanni were descendants of the Suebi who'd fought Julius Caesar in his Gallic campaigns. By the AD 160s they had long migrated away from the borders of Roman Gaul to settle in the region of modern Bohemia. The Juthungi were also of Suebi descent, though resided nearer their original homelands in modern Bavaria, while the Quadi (again with Suebi ancestry) were located further east in modern Moravia. Meanwhile, by this time, the fearsome Iazyges were settled near the Danubian *limes* in the region of modern Hungary and northern Serbia, having travelled there from the Pontic steppe.

The series of conflicts known as the Marcomannic Wars had actually begun slightly earlier, with invasions across the upper reaches of the Rhine and Danube into Germania Superior and Raetia by the Germanic Chatti and Chauci who took advantage of Rome's distraction while campaigning in the east against Parthia. These disruptive incursions lasted from AD 162 to AD 165, with both eventually repulsed. The Marcomannic Wars proper then began in AD 166 when 6,000 Germanic Langobard and Lacringi warriors fought their way over the Danube into Pannonia Superior (Heather, 2009, 96). Though soon defeated by vexillations from *legio* I *Adiutrix pia fidelis* under a *legate* called Candidus and the auxiliary cavalry *ala Ulpia Contariorum* regiment under the Senator Marcus Macrinius Avitus Catonius Vindex, this set a trend that lasted for the next fourteen years.

After these initial incursions, the Romans at first tried to buy off the Germans causing trouble along the Danube. Marcus Iallius Bassus, governor of Pannonia Superior (a noted literary figure and also an adopted member of Marcus Aurelius' family) started negotiations with the eleven most aggressive tribes. A truce was soon agreed with the help of the Marcomanni overking Ballomar, after which any Germans remaining on the south side of the Danube withdrew.

However, no permanent peace deal was reached, and later in AD 166 the frontier was tested again when the Sarmatian Iazyges and their Germanic Vandal allies invaded the province of Dacia in force. Here the frontier defences failed, with the governor Calpurnius Proculus killed leading a hastily assembled army trying to stem the incoming tide of invaders. These then penetrated deep into the provincial interior, with the emperor forced to deploy the veteran *legio* IV *Macedonia* from Moesia Inferior to drive them out of Dacia. An uneasy peace then settled in the region.

Marcus Aurelius and Lucius Verus viewed the ongoing threat from north of the Danube as serious and determined to carry out a major punitive expedition against the Iazyges and their German allies. It is unclear if they intended to conquer new territory, particularly in *Magna Germania* (with the subsequent creation of new provinces), or whether their main aim was a punitive expedition on a grand scale. Whichever, it was not to be in AD 167. A serious outbreak of plague across the Mediterranean put their plans on hold for that year. This was so serious that they were forced to recruit gladiators, bandits and Germans to fill the depleted ranks of the Roman military (*Historia Augusta*, Marcus Aurelius, 21.6).

By AD 168 things had stabilized in Rome and the emperors headed north to *Aquileia* on the northeastern Adriatic coast where they established their forward headquarters. Orders were then dispatched along the northern frontiers to gather an enormous force to campaign across the Danube which they planned to lead in person. This included two newly-raised legions, *legio* II *Italica* and *legio* III *Italica*. Their first targets were marauding Marcomanni, Quadi and Victohali tribesmen who'd taken advantage of the disruption caused by the plague in AD 167 to attack Pannonia Superior. However, as the imperial force approached the key legionary fortress of *Carnuntum* (also headquarters of the *Classis Flavia Pannonica*) the Germans withdrew, giving assurances of their future good conduct. The emperors then returned to *Aquileia* for the winter, leaving the army poised for further campaigning in AD 169. However, the death of Lucius Verus in January that year set back military operations again, with Marcus Aurelius returning to Rome to supervise his funeral.

The now sole emperor returned to the offensive in the autumn of AD 169. His first target were the Iazyges, though the war at first went badly. The Sarmatians struck first, targeting the Roman gold mines at Alburnum in Dacia. The emperor ordered Claudius Fronto, the governor of Moesia Inferior and an imperial favourite, to gather a local force and intercept them. In the ensuing battle the governor was killed and his force scattered. Meanwhile, with the emperor's attention focused on this crisis, several German tribes along the Danube used the opportunity to launch their own raids deep into Roman territory. In the east, these included the Costoboci who, from their Carpathian mountain homelands, struck Thracia with savage ferocity. Rampaging through the province, they soon reached Greece proper where they destroyed the ancient Temple of the Eleusinian Mysteries near Athens.

However, this wasn't the emperor's biggest problem. Across the Danube the one-time mediator Ballomar now seized his chance to launch a strike deep into Pannonia Superior. Gathering his own Marcomanni warriors and Quadi allies, he headed directly for *Carnuntum* to force a decisive meeting engagement. This he got in AD 170 when the Romans suffered their greatest defeat for generations, and of the Marcomannic Wars as a whole.

The Main Engagement

Here I briefly consider the sources for the Battle of Carnuntum, before detailing this key provincial capital and legionary fortress on the Danube. I next provide biographical detail on Ballomar, overking of the Marcomanni and Marcus Aurelius' nemesis in the Marcomannic Wars. Finally, I narrate the battle itself.

Sources

The main written source for much of this period, and the only contemporary source for the Battle of Carnuntum, is Lucian of Samosata. A Hellenized Syrian rhetorician noted for his satirical style of writing, he is also one of the most reliable Roman commentators in terms of historical accuracy.

Lucian was born in Samosota on the banks of the Euphrates, today located in southeastern Turkey. This was formerly the capital of the kingdom of Commagene before it was finally incorporated into the Roman state on a permanent basis by Vespasian in AD 72. As a young man Lucian was apprenticed to his uncle who was a noted sculpture, but when it became clear this wasn't the career for him he ran away to the Ionian coast in western Turkey. There, showing he'd earlier had a fine education, he became a travelling lecturer, eventually visiting schools of education as far afield as Gaul and Spain.

By the age of 30 Lucian had published his first work, and a decade later was enormously popular due to a racy writing style which ridiculed superstition, religious practices and belief in the paranormal. By the AD 160s he was a noted celebrity, and wrote much of his work on the Marcomannic Wars while living a wealthy lifestyle in Athens. Later in life he became senior magistrate in Egypt under Commodus, perhaps even the regional procurator, before disappearing from the historical record.

Lucian wrote over eighty works of literature, and was much copied by later classical historians, hence his importance when narrating the campaigns of Marcus Aurelius on the Danube. The majority of his works in the AD 160s and AD 170s were comic dialogues, featuring two protagonists discussing issues great and small. The most important regarding the Marcomannic Wars, given this provided the setting for much of his output at the time, are *The Liar*, *Dialogues of the Hetaerae*, *Dialogues of the Dead*, *Dialogues of the Gods*, *Menippus*, *Icaro-menippus*, *Zeus Cross-Examined*, *Timon*, *Charon*, *A Voyage to the Lower World*, *The Sale of Creeds*, *The Fisher*, *Zeus Tragoedus*, *The Rooster*, *The Double Indictment* and *The Ship*.

Posthumously, Lucian had a major impact on medieval and more recent Western literature. For example, well-known works overtly inspired by his writings include Thomas More's *Utopia*, William Shakespeare's *Timon of Athens* and Jonathan Swift's *Gulliver's Travels*.

Other key sources for the Marcomannic Wars include Cassius Dio, Herodian and the *Historia Augusta*. However, most of the additional data regarding the Battle of Carnuntum, and conflict in this region at this time, comes from the archaeological record, with this well-known Roman site the subject of excavations and investigation for over a century. In particular, Heather argues this has proved most useful when compensating for the total lack of first-hand commentary in the literary record from the German perspective (2005, 52).

Carnuntum

The Roman site at *Carnuntum* was originally founded as a legionary fortress and headquarters of the *Classis Pannonica* regional fleet in Augustan period, when the first Roman emperor established this crucial province on the southern side of the upper Danube. Pannonia was coterminous with the provinces of Noricum to the west, Moesia to the east, and Italia and Dalmatia to the south. Today, its broad territory sits within western Hungary, western Slovakia, eastern Austria, northern Croatia, northern Serbia, northern Slovenia, and northern Bosnia and Herzegovina. As such it secured the northern approaches to the heart of the empire in Italy, and was frequently the bulwark protecting the imperial centre from southward incursions by predating Germans and Goths keen to plunder the vast wealth there. When this strategy failed, as did happen during the Marcomannic Wars, panic ensued in Rome.

Pannonia proved so important in protecting the imperial interior that, along with Moesia to its west, it was divided into two separate provinces dubbed Superior and Inferior by Trajan when leading his conquest campaigns in Dacia. At this time the legionary fortress of *Carnuntum* also became the provincial capital of Pannonia Superior, with its *canaba* civilian settlement steadily growing from that point into a huge city which, by the time of the Marcomannic Wars, had a population of 50,000. Today the remains of the fortress and city are located on the Danube 40km east of Vienna in Lower Austria, with much visible within the 10km² Carnuntum Archaeological Park. This includes a large monumental arch called the Heidentor (or 'Pagans' Gate'), still standing to its original height immediately south of the civilian settlement and its civilian amphitheatre, the latter also still visible. Meanwhile, nearby in the village of Bad Deutsch-Altenburg, the military amphitheatre adjacent to the fortress is also still visible. There, in 2011, researchers discovered a 1.5ha² gladiator training school compound, the first located found outside of Rome and Pompeii.

The legionary fortress at *Carnuntum* was similar in size to that at York, with fortified gateways in its southwestern, southeastern and northeastern walls. The former gave access to the main trunk roads to Vienna and Sopron (Roman *Scarbantia*), the latter a key Roman *municipium* mercantile town in the region. Meanwhile, the southeastern gate accessed the trunk road heading south past the forts at *Ad Flexum* near modern Mosonmagyaróvár and *Arrabona* near modern Györ, both in Hungary, to Dalmatia and the Adriatic coast. The fortress featured no gateway on its northwestern side given this overlooked the Danube, with the fortified anchorage of the *Classis Pannonica* on the riverbank below. From there the *liburnae*, *myoparo* and *scapha* of the upper Danubian regional fleet operated, and were maintained.

Finally, *Carnuntum* was also famous for a literary reason. This is because it was here, in the *principia* headquarters building in the centre of the legionary fortress, that Marcus Aurelius later completed his *Meditations*. This is a remarkable collection of sombre philosophical observations written down in Greek by the emperor while on campaign on the Danube (Cornell and Matthews, 1982, 103). Given the unpredictable nature of this first conflict in the Marcomannic Wars, one observation is particularly prescient (5.9):

Do not be distressed, do not despond or give up in despair, if now and again practice falls short of precept. Return to the attack after each failure, and be thankful if on the whole you acquit yourself in the majority of cases as a man should.

Moving on to the civilian settlement at *Carnuntum*, Cornell and Matthews explain that the *canaba* (and later the city) was an important trading centre, providing access to *Magna Germania* across the Danube (1982, 142). This made *Carnuntum* not only a key military installation controlling a large section of the upper Danube, but also a fabulously wealthy place of trade, full of merchants and traders. As such, it proved a magnet time and again for predating Germans when conflict broke out in the region.

Ballomar of the Marcomanni
Ballomar, also called Ballomarios in some primary source references, was the overking of the various tribes in the Marcomanni confederation. He was born around AD 140, and died of natural causes around AD 180, within a year of his Roman archrival Marcus Aurelius. Ballomar's name translates as 'Strong Arm', derived from the old German *ballo* meaning limb and *maro* meaning strong or great. He is first mentioned by Cassius Dio in the context of the Roman peace talks with the German tribes in the upper Danubian region in the late AD 160s, when he is referenced brokering a treaty. However, he soon reneged when Roman attention was diverted elsewhere in the region, personally leading his huge army of Marcomanni and Quadi warriors across the Danube in AD 170. His first target was the legionary fortress and civilian settlement at *Carnuntum*, leading directly to the battle there, which I now detail below.

The Battle of Carnuntum
At the time of the Marcomannic Wars Pannonia Superior was home to three legions, these *legio* XIV *Gemina Martia Victrix*, *legio* I *Adiutrix pia fidelis* and later *legio* X *Gemina*. The former was based at *Carnuntum*, *legio* I at Szőny (Roman *Brigetio*) in Hungary and *legio* X at Vienna. The theatre commander for the entire Danubian region was Tiberius Claudius Pompeianus, only just appointed and yet to arrive on the frontier.

Carnuntum's legio XIV was an elite legion with an illustrious career. For example, it was last referenced here playing the key role defeating Boudicca in the Battle of Watling Street (detailed in Chapter 3), and before that participated in Plautius' invasion of Britain (detailed in Chapter 2). After that it was deployed to the Danube by Nero to bolster the defences there, later replacing *legio* XXI *Rapax* in Pannonia during Domitian's reign when the latter was destroyed fighting the Dacians. It then fought throughout Trajan's two Dacian campaigns in the AD 100s, serving with distinction. For a time it was then forward deployed to *Ulpia Traiana Sarmizegetusa*, capital of the new province of Dacia, before finally withdrawing to *Carnuntum* where it was still based when the Marcomannic Wars broke out (Pollard and Berry, 2012, 191).

Before narrating the battle, two key questions need to be addressed. First, why did the Roman commander at *Carnuntum*, likely the *legate* of *legio* XIV *Gemina Martia Victrix*, choose to fight a set piece engagement rather than stay within the safety of the walls of his legionary fortress? Second, why were the Romans so comprehensively defeated?

In the first instance, Ballomar's invasion over the Danube in AD 170 caught the Romans completely by surprise. At the time, the emperor's troubleshooter in the region, Claudius Fronto, had just been killed when his attempt to save the Roman gold mines at Alburnum in Dacia from the marauding Iazyges ended disastrously. Meanwhile, to the southeast the Costoboci were still pillaging their way through Thracia. The eyes and ears of the Roman military along the frontier were provided by *speculatores* and *exploratores* scouts, the latter akin to modern special forces as I have argued in recent work. However, given the jeopardy elsewhere along the Danubian frontier at this time, it seems likely that many of these reconnaissance specialists had been deployed away from the border to help deal with the incursions within imperial territory. Therefore, with Roman attention elsewhere, Ballomar was able to infiltrate his large army across the Danube before the Romans could intercept him. Then, arriving at his first target *Carnuntum*, he found the Romans there completely unprepared for a siege given his surprise assault, with their stock levels low given vital provisions had already been sent to support the Roman military formations in action elsewhere. Therefore, staying within the legionary fortress wasn't an option for the legion's *legate*, who knew a short siege could easily overwhelm the unprepared defenders.

Regarding the scale of the Roman defeat, on paper this seems surprising. We have no way of calculating the size of Ballomar's Marcomanni and Quadi army, though given part of it later penetrated as far south as Italy, it must have been sizeable. The Roman army is detailed in the primary sources comprising around 20,000 troops, which is also the scale of the losses the writers suggest. Of course, Roman authors frequently exaggerated the scale of Roman losses to impress their domestic audience, with for example the 50,000 casualties Cassius Dio says were later lost by Septimius Severus in his AD 209 campaign in Scotland (*Roman History*, 76.13). However, given the scale of the devastation across the region after the Roman defeat at *Carnuntum*, it seems likely to me that a near annihilation of the Roman army there may actually have occurred.

This then begs the question why an elite legion with battle honours to match any other performed so badly?

The answer may lie in the bigger picture across the region. I think it likely much of *legio* XIV was absent when the defeat at *Carnuntum* occurred, with vexillations deployed as theatre reserves elsewhere to bolster ongoing operations against the Iazyges in Dacia and Costoboci in Thracia. Further, the cohorts that did remain in *Carnuntum* were most probably understrength given the recent plague. Any replacements sent would likely have gone to the vexillations deployed elsewhere on active service. Therefore, rather than the legion at *Carnuntum* featuring a full complement of 5,500 men, it numbered far fewer. This meant the bulk of the Roman force in the battle comprised auxiliary foot and horse, whose cohorts would also have been understrength for the same reasons, and also one other troop type. These were allied and mercenary German *foederates*. We know that Marcus Aurelius and Lucius Verus had been forced to recruit Germans to bulk up the regional military establishment after the plague event three years earlier. Clearly they had once more been recruited to reinforce the Danubian frontier defences, including at *Carnuntum*, given the majority of the legionaries were away campaigning against the Iazyges and Costoboci. Based on this analysis and the primary source descriptions, I therefore determine the Roman Army at *Carnuntum* actually comprised only 3,000 legionaries, together with 14,000 auxiliaries and around 3,000 Germans.

Looking at this force, one can now see why it was so vulnerable to attack by Ballomar's Marcomanni and Quadi. Far from being an elite Roman army, this was only a holding force, not much better than the *limitanei* who later protected the borders of the Dominate Empire. Forced into the open through lack of supplies, it now took on a rampaging German army eager to avenge earlier defeats by the Romans. We have little detail in the written record regarding the actual events of the battle, other than references saying the diminished numbers of legionaries from *legio* XIV fought bravely to the end. This may explain why the legion continued to exist after the event, unlike the legions lost fighting with Varus in AD 9. However, the result of the engagement was never in doubt. The Romans and their German allies were quickly overwhelmed, with a massacre ensuing.

For Ballomar, surveying the devastation, one thing was now apparent. The key Roman trunk roads south and west were now undefended, with the imperial heartlands at his mercy. While Roman attention was focused east and south dealing with the Iazyges and Costoboci, he'd turned their western flank in Pannonia.

Aftermath and Legacy

Ballomar lost no time in exploiting his victory, immediately splitting his force into two. One column headed west to ravage Noricum and Raetia, while he led another south himself. This force pillaged its way through southern Pannonia Superior and soon crossed into Italy, sacking the border city of Oderzo (Roman *Opitergium*) on the way. Ballomar then headed directly for the Adriatic coast, where he besieged the key city of *Aquileia*. This sent shock waves through the Roman world of a kind last experienced in the Cimbrian Wars. The emperor, still on the Danube in the north, quickly ordered the Praetorian Prefect Titus Furius Victorinus south to lead a hastily gathered force to repel the Germans. However, his army was promptly defeated and he was killed, the third senior Roman leader to die since the Marcomannic Wars had begun.

Fearing Rome itself now might be under threat, Marcus Aurelius moved quickly to address the situation. He first ordered Pompeianus to Thracia to secure the region after the predations of the Costoboci. Next he ordered up-and-coming field commander Publius Helvius Pertinax, later briefly emperor in AD 193, to take charge of both Dacia and Moesia Superior. Pertinax immediately set to work reordering the economy of Danubian frontier, particularly Dacia which had been devastated by the Iazyges. With taxes from the region's industry, agriculture and population once more flowing into the imperial *fiscus* treasury, new troops were raised and the frontiers and fortifications along the Danube strengthened.

By Spring AD 171 Marcus Aurelius was at last ready to strike back against Ballomar who was still besieging *Aquileia*. With an army of 20,000, including two legions redeployed from Thracia, he attacked the German siege lines. A swift victory followed, with the Marcomanni and Quadi fleeing north. The emperor set off in immediate pursuit, at the same time promoting Pertinax once more, this time to take command of *legio* I *Adiutrix pia fidelis* in Szöny in Pannonia Superior. The two Roman forces now formed a hammer and anvil, catching Ballomar and his surviving warriors as they entered Pannonia Superior. The outcome was a decisive Roman victory, with only Ballomar and a few close followers reaching the safety of the Danube.

The emperor now ordered his theatre commander Pompeianus to carry out a wide-ranging reorganization of the military frontier along the Danube, and also of the defences in northeastern Italy. This included bolstering the *Classis Flavia Moesica* on the lower Danube, and also the building of a new series of fortifications along the border between Pannonia Superior and Italica called the *praetentura Italiae et Alpium*. Meanwhile, Marcus Aurelius ordered Pertinax to deal with the German force still ravaging Noricum and Raetia.

Total success followed, with this second German army also driven beyond the Danube with heavy casualties.

However, the emperor knew the Romans were still in no position to go on the offensive across the Danube. He therefore continued to consolidate his forces along the *limes* there, rebuilding the legionary fortress at *Carnuntum*, and reinforcing the frontier defences elsewhere. Intense diplomatic activity then followed as he attempted to win over as many of the German and Sarmatian tribes as possible before counter-attacking. In particular, peace treaties were signed with the Quadi and the Iazyges, with the Lacringi and Hasdingi Vandals also becoming Roman allies and agreeing to provide warriors for his next campaign.

In the Spring of AD 172 Marcus Aurelius was finally ready, and launched a massive assault across the Danube from Pannonia Superior and Noricum against the Marcomanni and any German and Sarmatian tribes still allied with them. Ballomar's loose confederation was shattered, with the Marcomanni quickly suing for peace. The emperor then took the title 'Germanicus', with coins being minted featuring the term 'Germania Capta'. Pertinax, still leading the *Italica* I legion, was again in the vanguard, though another *legate* gained the greatest fame. This was Marcus Valerius Maximianus who, leading the Pannonia Inferior-based *legio* II *Adiutrix pia fidelis*, killed the chieftain of the German Naristi tribe in single combat. The emperor then granted the *legate* the chieftain's fine stallion as a reward.

The Romans again campaigned north of the Danube in AD 173, this time against the Quadi after they predictably broke their earlier treaty commitments. Victory again followed, though the campaign is best known for the 'miracle of rain' incident recorded on the Column of Marcus Aurelius in Rome. Here, *legio* XII *Fulminata* and perhaps Pertinax with his *legio* I *Adiutrix pia fidelis* had been trapped by a larger force of Quadi and was on the brink of surrendering because of thirst and heat. However, a sudden thunderstorm provided a deluge that refreshed the legionaries and auxilia, while a lightning strike on the Quadi camp sent the Germans fleeing in terror.

Roman military attention now switched to the Rhine frontier. Here, the future emperor Didius Julianus (the brief successor to Pertinax in the 'Year of the Five Emperors') had been the governor of Gallia Belgica since AD 170. This province, once home to some of Julius Caesar's fiercest Gallic opponents, stood just south of the northern border provinces of Germania Inferior and Germania Superior. In AD 173 it suffered a major incursion from the Germanic Chauci. Taking advantage of the Roman tribulations on the Danube, they smashed through the *limes* along the lower Rhine and penetrated deep into the rich farmlands of modern Flanders. The legions in the two German provinces struggled to contain the threat and Didius Julianus was forced to raise a force of local recruits, probably veterans settled in *coloniae*, which he then led to great effect. Soon the Germans had been forced back over the Rhine. The governor then began a programme of fortification along the English Channel coast of his province, before returning to Rome where he took part in a triumph.

With the *limes* along the Rhine now stabilized, in the Spring of AD 174 Marcus Aurelius was now ready to go on the offensive once more. He quickly crossed the Danube with a huge force, targeting any Quadi still holding out against Rome. Over the winter a number of tribes there had deposed the pro-Roman king Furtius and replaced him with his archrival Ariogaesus. Marcus Aurelius refused to recognize the latter and forced him to stand down, sending him to Alexandria in exile. By the end of the year the whole of the Quadi were subjugated, with the leading nobles sending hostages to Rome, warriors being recruited into the ranks of the Roman auxiliaries for assimilation, and Roman garrisons installed in fortified camps throughout their territory.

Marcus Aurelius had one more piece of unfinished business along the Danube, to punish the Iazyges for the death of his friend Fronto in Dacia in AD 169. In AD 175 he again gathered a mighty force and launched an assault from Pannonia Inferior and Dacia deep into their homelands. For this *expeditio sarmatica* the emperor targeted the plain of the River Tizsa in modern Hungary, winning a number of victories after which the leading Iazyges king Zanticus surrendered and a peace treaty was agreed. Captured Roman prisoners were then returned and the Iazyges supplied Rome with 8,000 of their *contos*-lance armed cavalry. Around 5,500 of these were deployed to Britain, where they were based at Ribchester (Roman *Bremetennacum*) in modern Lancashire. The emperor then took the title 'Sarmaticus' and once more minted coins to celebrate victory. This brought to an end the First Marcomannic War.

However, soon the emperor's resolve was tested once more, for early in AD 177 the Quadi reneged on their peace agreements with Rome once more. Ballomar and the Marcomanni soon followed, and so began the Second Marcomannic War. This new insurrection spread rapidly along the upper Danube and soon the Germans had penetrated the *limes* again, raiding deep into imperial territory. Marcus Aurelius reacted swiftly, calling his new campaign the *secunda expeditio germanica*. With his army led by Marcus Valerius Maximianus, the emperor arrived at *Carnuntum* in August AD 178. There the Romans forced a meeting engagement with the Marcomanni who, this time, were comprehensively defeated. The Romans then advanced on the Quadi who were almost wiped out at the Battle of Laugaricio in modern Slovakia. Maximianus' own *legio* II *Adiutrix pia fidelis* fought particularly well here. The few German survivors were then chased back north beyond the Danube, where the Praetorian Prefect

Tarruntenus Paternus then led a punitive campaign against the surviving Quadi in their homeland, which he ravaged.

However, campaigning along the Danube ended dramatically on 17 March AD 180 when Marcus Aurelius died of natural causes in Vienna at the age of 58. He was succeeded by his son Commodus. The new emperor had no interest in continuing his father's campaigns along the Danube. Instead, he was keen to return to Rome to secure his position. Commodus quickly established new peace treaties with the Marcomanni and Quadi, against the advice of his senior military commanders. The terms included that they provide 20,000 warriors to serve in the Roman army, these being distributed to auxiliary units across the empire. Those remaining were partially disarmed and forbidden from attacking their Iazyges, Buri and Vandal neighbours without permission from Rome. Finally, the Germans were also forbidden from settling along a narrow strip on their own northern bank of the Danube, and also on the various large islands along the river's length. Accompanied by Paternus, Commodus then left for the imperial capital in early September AD 180 where he celebrated a solo triumph on the 22 October. Thus ended the Second Marcomannic War, with the so called 'Peace of Commodus'.

However, trouble north of the Danube continued and soon the Iazyges and a German tribe called the Buri (whose homeland was located to the north of the Marcomanni and Quadi, near the headwaters of the Vistula River) rebelled again. Once more the emperor ordered his legions north of the Danube and victories were quickly celebrated by Maximianus once more, and also by the leading Senators Pescennius Niger and Clodius Albinus, both to play key roles in the later 'Year of the Five Emperors' which saw Septimius Severus the ultimate victor. When a lengthy peace finally descended on the region in AD 182, bringing to an end the Third Marcomannic War, Commodus celebrated by taking the title 'Germanicus Maximus'.

Thus ended the most challenging series of conflicts faced by the empire for a century, and given the settlement of many Germans within the empire afterwards one that began a process which was to change the very nature of imperial identity. Soon, German warriors were not just filling the ranks of auxiliary units but joining the legions, while their leaders eventually came to dominate the officer class in the Roman military.

Chapter 7

The Battle of Lugdunum

Severus Secures the Throne, AD 193

O n 19 February AD 197 a titanic clash of arms took place outside Lyon (Roman *Colonia Copia Claudia Augusta Lugdunum*), capital of the Roman province of *Gallia Lugdunensis*. Some call it the biggest battle in Roman history. The protagonists were both North African by origin, the great warrior emperor Septimius Severus and the usurping British governor Clodius Albinus. The engagement was sanguineous in the extreme, with huge casualties on either side. Yet its origins can be traced back to events four years earlier, when Severus himself was still a governor with no evident designs on the purple. Note that here I style the engagement by the name it is most often referenced, *Lugdunum*, rather than its modern name Lyon.

Strategic Build-Up to the Battle

The Battle of Lugdunum is referenced by three primary sources, these Cassius Dio in his *Roman History*, Herodian in his *History of the Roman Empire*, and the anonymous *Historia Augusta*. All begin their tale on New Year's Eve AD 192 when the emperor Commodus was assassinated. This ushered in the 'Year of the Five Emperors'. Severus was governing Pannonia Superior at the time. He fell like a sword of Damocles on Rome after his mentor Pertinax (the first of the five imperial candidates that year) was assassinated by the Praetorian Guard (Elliott, 2020c, 85). By the year's end Severus was the last man standing in the imperial capital, with only two challengers left to his claim on the throne. These were the Syrian governor Pescennius Niger and the British governor Albinus. Prioritising Niger as the bigger threat, Severus proclaimed Albinus his *Caesar* to secure the west. He then fought a year-long campaign in the east against Niger, finally defeating him at the Battle of Issus in May AD 194. Severus then turned his attention to the eastern frontier and the Parthians. However, his plans were curtailed when news reached him that Albinus had usurped in Britain. Herodian is explicit that Severus' earlier appointment of Albinus to be his *Caesar* was a simple ruse to buy time to defeat Niger and secure his eastern frontier (*History of the Roman Empire*, 2.15). Matters came to

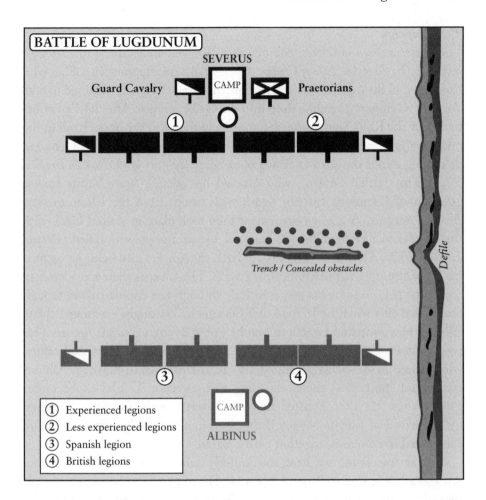

a head in the autumn of AD 196 when word reached Albinus that Severus now felt secure enough to appoint his elder son Caracalla *caesar*, and specifically to be his successor (Elliott, 2018a, 68). The British governor saw the writing on the wall and decided to take the initiative, minting his own coins on which he styled himself a full *augustus*, and then usurping. The move was popular in Britain, with Herodian describing scenes of revelry (*History of the Roman Empire*, 3.7.1). However, soon sobering news reached him that Severus was on his way to stamp the rebellion out, bringing the imperial family including his wife Julia Domna with him (Levick, 2007, 31). Albinus moved quickly, gathering his three British legions and a significant number of the auxiliaries from the province. Together they were ferried by the *Classis Britannica* regional fleet to Gaul. Here Albinus aimed to gather a great army to challenge Severus, and become the emperor himself.

The Campaign

The *Historia Augusta* details Albinus next survived an assassination attempt instigated by Severus (*Life of Clodius Albinus*, 8.3). An experienced soldier who had served in the legions with distinction, the usurper then determined to take the fight to emperor, heading deep into the Gallic interior. After a failed effort to occupy the Rhineland, he headed south and then had the upper hand in the initial engagements against Severan loyalists in southern Gaul, with Herodian describing minor skirmishers taking place there (*History of the Roman Empire*, 3.7.2). This rattled Severus, who ordered his reliable *legate* Virius Lupus, governor of Germania Inferior, south with troops from the Rhine to slow Albinus' advance. A major engagement then took place in central Gaul, with the usurper victorious. Dio says many of Lupus' troops were killed (*Roman History*, 76.2). Albinus then besieged Trier, though the city held out against his hasty attempts to breach its strong walls. The usurper then considered an ambitious plan to force his way into Italy through the Alpine passes, though abandoned this when he learned that Severus had strongly garrisoned them. Albinus now switched targets to one he knew Severus couldn't ignore. This was *Lugdunum* in the southwest, which had been Severus' provincial capital when governor of Gallia Lugdundensis in the AD 180s. On arrival Albinus established his capital there, expelling the governor T. Flavius Secundus Philippianus. He then awaited news of Severus, with his forces bolstered by the arrival of Lucius Novius Rufus, governor of the Spanish province of Hispania Tarraconensis, together with a legion.

It is at this point we hear the unlikely tale of Numerianus, a former schoolteacher in Rome (Birley, 1999, 124). For some reason he was devoted to Severus, unlike much of the Roman political classes who broadly supported Albinus, and now set off for Gaul pretending to be a Senator on official duty. Gathering a small force on the way he then set about harassing Albinus' army camped around *Lugdunum*. Dio says he achieved a degree of success here, killing some of the usurper's cavalry and, more importantly, capturing 70 million *sesterces* (around $210 million in modern money) which he sent to the delighted Severus (*Roman History*, 76.1). The emperor later rewarded him with a fine country estate and a pension for these improbable exploits.

After a short stay in Rome Severus was now ready to advance on Albinus and, sending word to the legions on the Rhine and Danube to join him, chanced a winter passage over the Alpine passes with those troops already with him. He arrived in southwestern Gaul in early AD 197 and headed directly for *Lugdunum*, ready to confront Albinus.

The Armies

The size of the armies at Lugdunum has been much debated in recent years. As commonly translated, Dio is very specific here, saying (*Roman History*, 76.6): 'There were 150,000 thousand soldiers on each side, and both leaders were present in the conflict, since it was a life-and-death struggle between them.'

That would give an enormous total of 300,000 men engaged. Some have questioned this, arguing that Dio actually meant 150,000 overall but that his narrative has since been mistranslated. It is useful here to consider the overall size of the Roman army in the later second century AD. The legions at the time still numbered 5,500 men each, this established as the norm by Augustus. Under Severus they now totalled thirty-three after he formed *legios* I, II and III *Parthica* for his first eastern campaign. This would give a normal establishment of 181,500 legionaries. We can add to this a similar number of supporting auxiliaries and naval *milites* to lift the overall military complement at the time of Severus to over 360,000 men. Now, given Severus had been campaigning in the east when Albinus usurped and may have drawn troops from each region he passed through on his way back to the imperial centre, and that Albinus had similarly added troops from Spain to his three British legions, it is feasible that each had an army of 150,000, though unlikely. The truth is we will never know, but even armies of 75,000 each were still huge by ancient world standards.

What we can infer with a degree of certainty is the composition of the two armies, given one was specifically from the east and one west. As detailed, Severus had been campaigning on the eastern frontier when he learned of Albinus' usurpation. The legions there at his disposal included *legio* XV *Apollinaris* and *legio* XII *Fulminata* in Cappadocia, *legio* IV *Scythica*, *legio* III *Gallica* and *legio* XVI *Flavia Firma* in Syria, *legio* III *Cyrenaica* in Arabia Petraea, and *legio* VI *Ferrata fidelis constans* and *legio* X *Fretensis* in Syria Palaestina (as Judaea was now known). To these we can add his newly-formed three *Parthica* legions. It is highly unlikely Severus would have stripped the entire frontier zone there of his elite troops, so we can expect he instead took vexillations from those not directly engaged on the border, for example those in Syria Palaestina. He also took troops from his three Parthian foundings, perhaps in their entirety.

Travelling east Severus would then have accessed his legions along the Danube, again calling on vexillations if not entire legions to join him. Given his army at the Battle of Lugdunum is referenced by Herodian as being Illyrian (*History of the Roman Empire*, 3.7.3), it seems likely the bulk of his army came from this region. The principal formations there were still the veterans of the earlier Marcomannic Wars, with *legio* III *Italica concurs* in

Raetia, *legio* II *Italica* in Noricum, *legios* X *Gemina* and XIV *Gemina Martia Victrix* in Pannonia Superior (the latter now fully reformed), *legio* II *Adiutrix pia fidelis* in Pannonia inferior, *legio* IV *Flavia felix* and *legio* VII *Claudia pia fidelis* in Moesia Superior, *legio* XIII *Gemina pia fidelis* in Dacia and *legios* I *Italica*, V *Macedonia* and XI *Claudia pia fidelis* in Moesia Inferior. These were some of the crack legions in the whole empire, battle hardened when earlier campaigning with Marcus Aurelius, and latterly with Commodus. Severus also called on troops from the four legions along the Rhine, these being *legios* VIII *Augusta* and XXII *Primogenia pia fidelis* in Germania Inferior, and *legios* I *Minervia pia fidelis* and XXX *Ulpia Victrix* in Germania Superior. As usual, to these legionaries we can add an equivalent number of auxiliaries, these also providing the main mounted component of his army. Finally, we know Severus also took the Praetorian Guard with him, these completely reformed by him with Danubian veterans to twice its original size when he became emperor in AD 193, and the *equites singulares Augusti* imperial guard cavalry who had similarly been increased in size at the same time.

The *Historia Augusta* calls Albinus' army a 'mighty force' (*Life of Clodius Albinus*, 8.4). At its core were the three British legions, *legio* II *Augusta* from Caerleon, *legio* XX *Valeria Victrix* from Chester and *legio* VI *Victrix* from York. All were highly experienced, their legionaries frequently campaigning in the unconquered far north of Britain. As detailed above, when he arrived in Gaul Albinus was then joined by a legion from Spain under Rufus. This overall force of legionaries was again joined by an equivalent number of auxiliary foot and horse, the latter numbering 5,000. Albinus may also have called on the urban cohort stationed at *Lugdunum*, thought to be *cohors* I *Flavia urbana*, where it had earlier been placed by Vespasian to protect the important mint there. The size of Albinus' army is indicated by his first action when arriving in Gaul; he ordered the governors of the four Gallic provinces to urgently provide food and money to support his campaign (Herodian, *History of the Roman Empire*, 3.7.1).

The legionaries of both armies, and the Praetorians of Severus, were equipped and fought in a similar fashion, with armour and weapons common in the high Principate just before Severus began his first reforms of the military. All still carried the *scutum* body shield, wore a substantial helmet (the most common at the time still the Imperial Gallic type) and body armour. The latter would have been either *lorica segmentata* banded and articulated iron armour, *lorica hamata* chainmail or *lorica squamata* scale mail. Better-off equipped legionaries, for example Severus' Praetorians, could also wear additional armour, for example *manicae* arm guards, thigh guards and greaves. Certain troop types in the legions were also differentially equipped to distinguish them on the battlefield.

For example, officers are frequently shown in sculpture wearing iron or bronze muscled cuirasses. Centurions, *aquilifer, imaginifer, signifier* and *vexillarius* standard bearers, and *cornicern* musicians, wore long *lorica hamata* hauberks. For offensive weapons late Principate legionaries still carried a heavy and light *pilum* javelin featuring a long barbed-iron tang, *gladius* sword and *pugio* dagger.

Meanwhile, the auxilia provided most of the cavalry in the Principate, and also a significant proportion of the foot complement. Many of the former were among the most feared warriors in the Roman military, specifically recruited from regions famous at the time for their formidable mounted warriors. In particular, those recruited in Gaul were still known for headhunting. The basic cavalryman at *Lugdunum* was still the *equites* of the first century AD. Their defensive panoply included flat hexagonal or oval shields, a variety of types of iron and bronze helmets (often with neck and cheek guards) and a short *lorica hamata* chainmail hauberk that allowed better movement in the 'four horn' saddle. For offense they were equipped with a *hasta* spear that could be thrown or used as a short lance, and a *spatha* long sword. They were supported by a variety of specialist types. These included specialist shock cavalry, for example *equites contariorum* armed with the *contos* lance, and light cavalry armed with javelins and bows.

Auxilia foot troops were mostly line of battle warriors who fought in a similar manner to the legionaries. They are most frequently shown carrying an elongated oval shield and wearing less sophisticated versions of the legionary helmet, often of bronze rather than iron. Their armour comprised a short *lorica hamata* or *lorica squamata* hauberk. Most foot auxilia were armed with the short *lancea* spear and the *gladius*, though by this time some had begun re-equipping with the long cavalry-style *spatha* sword. Auxilia also provided the majority of the specialist warriors in the armies of Severus and Albinus, including archers, slingers, staff slingers, crossbowmen and javelinmen, though artillery remained the responsibility of the legions.

The Main Engagement

The Battle of Lugdunum was a two-day affair, with the *Historia Augusta* (*Life of Septimius Severus*, 11.1) saying that a precursor engagement took place on 18 February at Tournus (Roman *Tinurtium*), some 40km north of *Lugdunum* on the right bank of the River Saône. Here, Albinus was trying to steer the Severan army away form the usurper's new capital, but failed. Severus had the better of this engagement, despite falling from his horse. Albinus then withdrew to *Lugdunum* where Herodian says the usurper was to remain throughout the battle, leaving his troops to deploy the following day for the main engagement, which was fought outside the city walls (*History of the Roman Empire*, 3.7.2). This is clearly a literary trope used by Herodian to diminish Albinus' reputation after the event, with Dio's more balanced account clear that both leaders fought in the battle with their troops (*Roman History*, 76.6).

As described by both Dio and Herodian, the main battle at *Lugdunum* was a heavy infantry engagement on a grand scale given the lack of cavalry present, particularly in Albinus' army. The clash was specifically a story of two wings, these dividing the battle line in half, rather than it featuring the more traditional clash with a centre and two wings.

On his right Severus deployed his more experienced legions and auxilia, with the less experienced troops on his left, and with the Praetorian Guard and the majority of his cavalry held in reserve under a *legate* called Laetus. Meanwhile Albinus placed the three British legions, these the most loyal to him, on his own right. His left wing comprised the Spanish legionaries, auxilia and the urban cohort.

Severus opened the engagement by ordering his right wing forward. Soon the legionaries were in light *pilum* range, with volley after volley flying between the two lines, the auxilia joining in to throw their *lancea*. Then, as the cohorts closed, the heavier *pila* were thrown at point-blank range, clattering against raised *scuta*. Each legionary now drew his *gladius* and charged to a shuddering impact. The battle now became one of thousands of individual combats, each warrior seeking a killing blow against his opponent. This was civil war and no quarter was given, the fighting savage, with the *gladii* inflicting fearsome wounds. Eventually the experience and morale of Severus' better troops told and Albinus' left flank legionaries and auxilia broke and fled for the safety of *Lugdunum*. Severus' troops pursued, only stopping when they reached the tents of Albinus' camp outside the city walls, which they then comprehensively looted.

The battle on Severus' left wing was far different, and almost cost him his life. Here the experienced II *Augusta*, XX *Valeria Victrix* and VI *Victrix* had carefully prepared their position ahead of the battle. Crucially, they had strewn the ground to their front with concealed field defences. These included shallow trenches 1.5m deep with rows of sharpened stakes in the bottom, pits called *lilies* also with a sharpened stake in the bottom, and bands of *stimuli* wooden blocks embedded in the ground with an iron barb standing proud of the surface (Cassius Dio, *Roman History*, 76.6).

As Severus' left wing advanced, Albinus' legionaries lured them into the trap. Advancing as far as the field defences, they threw their lighter *pila*. Then, as the Severan troops closed, they pretended to withdraw in disorder. Their opponents broke into a full charge, thinking Albinus' right wing was breaking. The inevitable then occurred, with shocked Severan front rankers falling headlong onto the sharpened stakes and iron barbs of the concealed field defences. Propelled by the momentum of the charge, the second and third ranks followed in short order, adding to the carnage. Stunned rear rankers then shuddered to a halt amid shouts from centurions and *optios* trying to regain order. Soon the troops on the Severan left wing began to withdraw, but the speed of the reverse to their front forced those at the very back into a deep defile where many lost their footing. Before long the whole wing was trapped between the field defences to the front and the defile at the back. The British legionaries now crossed their own field defences using pre-laid trackways, reformed on the other side, and charged the mass of disordered Severan foot. Heavy *pila* were hurled as they closed, then *gladii* drawn. Auxilia archers and slingers joined in, a great slaughter following. Severus, watching in horror from the rear, realised the day might be lost if he didn't act immediately, especially as his victorious wing was still looting the enemy camp. He therefore mounted his charger and personally led the Praetorian Guard and *equites singulares Augusti* to rescue his beleaguered left wing. However, things didn't go according to plan and soon these elite troops found themselves drawn into the carnage between the field defences and defile. Dio says the guard were nearly destroyed, with Severus losing his horse again (*Roman History*, 76.6). The wing then broke in full flight, with Herodian adding the three British legions who began chanting their battle hymn to victory as they vigorously pursued (*History of the Roman Empire*, 3.7.3).

Severus now showed battlefield leadership worthy of Caesar himself. Tearing off his riding cloak, he mounted a new horse and led his personal bodyguard into the mass of routers. Slowly and surely many troops began to rally, with Dio saying (*Roman History*, 76.7):

> Severus was hoping that they would be ashamed and turn back or that he himself might perish among them. Some indeed did turn back when they saw him in this attitude…

Eventually the emperor managed to reform a battle line on his left wing, which at last stopped the rampaging British legions who were now exhausted from their pursuit. Then, having regrouped, Severus' troops began to push their opponents back.

With the two wings each fighting a separate battle, *Lugdunum* had to this point many parallels with another decisive encounter of the ancient world, Cynoscephalae. There Philip V's right wing pushed back Titus Quinctius Flaminius's left, and the latter's right the Macedonian left. The parallels now continued, with Laetus and his Severan cavalry reserve spotting an opportunity. The Albinian right wing had advanced far proud of where its own now routed left wing had been deployed, and its own left flank and rear were now exposed. Laetus fell on this in a savage charge, butchering many legionaries in the British legions before they could form a defence. The bloody engagement was soon over, with Severus winning a true Pyrrhic victory given the scale of slaughter on both sides. Addressing these huge losses, Dio says (*Roman History*, 76.7):

> Many, even the victors, deplored the disaster, for the entire plain was seen to be covered with the bodies of men and horses…some of them lay there mutilated by many wounds, as if hacked in pieces, and others though unwounded, were piled in heaps, weapons were scattered about, and blood flowed in streams, even pouring into rivers.

Aftermath and Legacy

Confusion surrounds the fate of the Albinus. Dio says he sought refuge in a house on the River Rhone where he committed suicide (*Roman History*, 76.3), while the *Historia Augusta* has him either stabbing himself or having a slave do so, but surviving (*Life of Clodius Albinus*, 9.3). The usurper, either dead or half alive, was then found by Severus. He was swiftly decapitated, his head sent to Rome and the body ritually desecrated by the emperor who trampled it on his charger. Albinus' family met a similar fate, his sons and mother murdered on Severus' orders, together with any Senators unfortunate enough to have chosen the wrong side. *Lugdunum* itself was sacked and burned, with the Severan dynasty finally secure. It would last until AD 235 when its final emperor, Severus Alexander, was assassinated.

Chapter 8

The Battle of Nisibis

Last Stand of the Parthians, ad 217

The Battle of Nisibis was fought in AD 217 near the modern city of Nusaybin in southeastern Turkey. The protagonists were the Roman eastern army under the recently appointed emperor Macrinus, and the Parthian army of its last king, Artabanus V. The battle was the final culmination of centuries of conflict between these two mighty empires. It lasted a full three days, and ended with both sides suffering huge numbers of casualties. While the Parthians could claim a battlefield victory, within a decade its ruling Arsacid family had been overthrown, to be replaced by the Sassanid Persian Empire founded by Ardashir I.

Before narrating the battle, a short note on names. First, the Parthian king is also sometimes called Artabanus IV. Here, I stick with Artabanus V given this is the name most commonly used by historians today. Meanwhile, another key protagonist in this chapter is Septimius Severus' eldest son Caracalla. Born in *Lugdunum* on 4 April AD 188 when his father was governor of Gallia Lugdunensis, he was actually named Lucius Septimius Bassianus for the first seven years of his life, and then later renamed Marcus Aurelius Antoninus by his father (a clear attempt by Severus to attach himself to the Antonine dynasty). Later still, he was nicknamed Caracalla after a type of Gallic hooded tunic that he was prone to wear and made fashionable. He is sometimes called Antoninus in historical narratives, but here I stick with Caracalla given this is the name most associate with him today.

Strategic Build-Up to the Battle

Here I first detail the Roman eastern frontier where it faced the Parthians and later Sassanid Persians. I then narrate a history of the antagonistic relationship between the Romans and their eastern neighbours through to the Battle of Nisibis in AD 217, providing context for this last engagement between the Romans and Parthians.

The Roman Eastern Frontier

At the height of the Principate Empire in the later second century AD Rome's eastern frontier featured the key barrier provinces of Cappadocia, Syria

BATTLE OF NISIBIS

Parthian forces (legend):
- Parthian baggage train
- Parthian horse archers
- Parthian cataphracts
- Parthian cataphract camels

Roman forces (legend):
- Roman camp
- Roman light infantry
- Roman legionaries
- Roman cavalry
- Roman missile troops

and Arabia Petraea, which all bordered directly onto the Parthian Empire, Syria Palaestina on the Mediterranean coast, and the island of Cyprus in the western Mediterranean.

Cappadocia was the easternmost province of Roman Anatolia and featured the key river-crossing points in the upper Tigris and Euphrates valleys. It was often the launch point for Roman campaigns eastward against Parthia, and later Sassanid Persia. The province's key industry was olive oil production. While the provincial capital was located at Kayseri (Roman *Caesarea*), the most important settlements were the two legionary fortresses and their *canabaes* at Sadak (Roman *Satala*) in the northeast and Malatya (Roman *Melitene*) in the southeast. The former was home to *legio* XV *Apollinaris*, the latter to *legio* XII *Fulminata*. These were the key anchor points of the Cappadocian *limes*, with the Black Sea port of Trabzon the regular home to the *Classis Pontica* regional fleet. The province's military component was completed by a large number of auxiliaries, including many locally recruited mounted bowmen.

Moving south, Syria was also a major bulwark against the Parthians and Sassanid Persians. Founded as a Roman province in 63 BC by Pompey (see Chapter 4), Syria was also highly fertile, sitting as it did on the western arc of the Fertile Crescent. The province was governed from the huge metropolis of *Antioch-on-the-Orontes*, which by the later second century AD had a population of 250,000, making it the third largest city in the entire Roman Empire after Rome and Alexandria. It also featured many other wealthy and often turbulent cities, for example Aleppo (Roman *Beroea*), Hama (Roman *Epiphania*) and Homs (Roman *Emesa*, home of Julia Domna, the wife of Septimius Severus). Severus actually divided the province into two at the beginning of the third century AD after earlier defeating the usurping Syrian governor Pescennius Niger, (as detailed in Chapter 7). These smaller Severan provinces were called Syria Coele in the north and Syria Phoenice in the south, though their existence as separate entities did not long outlast Severus' death in York in February AD 211.

Syria's economic prosperity was based on the wide-scale production of a variety of natural products, these including olive oil and wine, both of which were widely exported from the region throughout the empire. Additionally, the northern Levantine coast was well-known for its purple dye production industry whose key product was a colouring called Tyrian Purple (or Phoenician Red), made from the secretions produced by several species of predatory sea snails of the Muricidae family. Extracting this dye involved tens of thousands of snails and huge amounts of labour, making this one of the most intensive industries to be found anywhere in the empire. Meanwhile, Sidon on the Mediterranean coast was famous for its high-quality glassmaking, linen and wool weaving industries (Cornell and Matthews, 1982, 156).

The key Principate defensive line on this lengthy part of the eastern frontier was the *limes Arabicus*, a southerly extension of the Cappadocian *limes*. It featured a series of forts and smaller fortifications tracking the Mesopotamian border with Parthia (later Sassanid Persia), and the Arabian Peninsula. This was upgraded and expanded towards of the end of the Principate phase of empire by Septimius Severus after his second eastern campaign at the end of the second century AD, when he constructed new fortifications in the Arabian Desert ranging from Basie to Dumata (Elliott, 2018a, 107). Given its importance, this border territory also featured an additional system of defence-in-depth based on (usually loyal) client and allied kingdoms that often formed a buffer between the empire and the Parthians, Sassanid Persians and Arabs. These included Palmyra, Osrhoene, Adiabene and Hatra.

The principal legionary fortresses in Syria were at *Zeugma* (originally the Hellenistic city of *Seleucia-on-the-Euphrates*) in the north, *Raphanea* near the Mediterranean coast and *Danaba* to the south. These were home to the three key legions on the frontier here at the beginning of the third century AD, sequentially *legio* IV *Scythica*, *legio* III *Gallica* and *legio* XVI *Flavia Firma* (Pollard and Berry, 2012, 133). In addition to the usual auxiliary complement, the military presence in the province was completed by the *Classis Syriaca* regional fleet that operated out of the port of *Seleucia Pierra* (Elliott, 2016, 46).

The scale of the Roman military commitment to Syria is very evident in the archaeological record, where D'Amato highlights in particular the huge number of depictions of warriors of various kinds wearing the widest possible array of military equipment and fashion. Providing detail, he says (2017, 37):

> There are vastly too many artworks in the province to list…They show muscled armours in metal and leather with a wide range of different arrangements of cymation [decorated rounded lapels at the base of the cuirass] and pteryges [multi-layered leather strip defences on the upper limbs], and in one case a depiction of a servant lacing a corset at the side. There are helmets of pseudo-Attic and pseudo-Corinthian forms [these probably dress helmets], spears, javelins, gladii and parazonia swords, and Zeus armed with a bipennis [symmetrical, double-headed] axe.

Meanwhile, Arabia Petraea was the opposite of abundant Syria, the province largely a desert inhabited by nomadic and transhumant Arab peoples. For commerce it relied on desert caravans operating through trading centres such as Petra, these the major source of its wealth. Petra was annexed by Trajan during his eastern campaigns (as detailed in Chapter 4), initiating the creation of the province. One legion was based here, *legio* III *Cyrenaica* at Bosra (Roman

Bostra), which was also the provincial capital. From here the legionaries and their supporting auxilia (including camel riding *equites Dromedarii*) had the unforgiving task of manning the southern *limes Arabicus*. Defence-in-depth is also evident here, with the Romans frequently making use of their Ghassanid Arab allies to repel the Lakhmid Arabs who were supporters of the Parthians and later the Sassanid Persians. Legionaries based in this inhospitable province were equipped in the standard fashion for their time, as evidenced by late style Newstead-type *lorica segmentata* vertical fasteners found at the Romano-Nabatean fortress of *Ein Rachel*. However, auxiliary warriors in Roman service here were often equipped in a particularly colloquial style, best suited for the intensely hot and dry conditions. In particular, the camel-riding light cavalry are shown in reliefs such as that at Hadhebt el-Hamra carrying long spears called a *romach* and light throwing javelins called *mizraqs* and *mizraqah*. For defense they carried small 38cm diameter targe-like shields called *deitzaha*, a common Arabian design made from gazelle hide.

Heading west to Syria Palaestina, this was formerly the province of Judaea. Even after the defeat of the Third 'bar Kokhba' Jewish Revolt in AD 136, and Hadrian's subsequent brutal reprisals across the region, the province still featured two legions in the late second century AD. These were *legio* VI *Ferrata fidelis constans* based at *Caparcotna* near Megiddo and *legio* X *Fretensis* based in Jerusalem (by then renamed *Aelia Capitolina*). Given their proximity to Syria proper and Arabia, these were frequently used as a strategic reserve when the eastern frontier was threatened, and to campaign in the east during Roman incursions into Parthia and later Sassanid Persia. Stunning archaeological finds in this region have shown that the legionaries based here were some of the best equipped in the empire, for example being equipped with the same *manicae* banded-iron armed guards often referenced in use with Trajan's legionaries fighting the Dacians and Bastarnae with their vicious two-handed *falx* polearms.

Finally in the region, the province of Cyprus was as far within the empire as it was possible to get. It was originally incorporated into the Republican province of Cilicia, becoming an independent Senatorial province in 22 BC under Augustus. There was little Roman military presence here, though archaeological finds including a socketed *pilum* now on display in the Cyprus Museum in Nicosia, show the occasional deployment of troops equipped for battle. Meanwhile, a *legio* XV *Apollinaris* centurion's signet ring found on the island has been associated with the passage through Cyprus of the future emperor Titus in AD 69 on his way to Judaea (D'Amato, 2017, 37). The provincial capital was located at Paphos (Roman *Nea Paphos*), famous for its 'Tombs of the Kings' Hellenistic and Roman necropolis.

Rome and the Parthians

On a one-for-one basis, the Parthians were the only near-symmetrical threat faced by the Republican and Principate Romans until the arrival of the Sassanid Persians who replaced them in the east. Their armies featured an interesting combination of extremes, comprising fully armoured noble cataphract lancers and lightly-armoured skirmishing horse archers famous for their 'Parthian Shot', the latter their tactic of approaching enemy formations at speed and then loosing arrows over the croup of their mount as they wheeled away. The ratio in Parthian armies between the cataphracts and light cavalry was usually around 10 per cent of the former, using their *contos* lances, and 90 per cent horse archers using their powerful composite bows. Any foot troops in Parthian armies were levy spearmen conscripted in the former Hellenistic cities in the Tigris and Euphrates valleys. Their main function on the battlefield was to provide a rallying point for Parthian mounted troops.

The Parthians were originally a Saka tribe called the Parni, its ruler Arsaces I giving the ruling dynasty its name. They invaded the region later called Parthia in northern Iran in the third century BC. This brought them into conflict with the Graeco-Bactrian kingdom who they quickly defeated, they then turning their attention to the Seleucid Empire where they invaded Media and Mesopotamia under Mithridates I in the mid-second century BC. This began a series of conflicts called the Seleucid-Parthian Wars which lasted from 238 BC to 129 BC, and ultimately played the leading role in bringing the Seleucid Empire down. This eventually drew the Parthians into conflict with the Rome.

As so often later, the Romans and Parthians first came to blows in the context of the kingdom of Armenia. This was originally a satrapy of the Achaemenid Persian Empire. Only superficially affected by Alexander the Great's conquests in the region in the 320s BC, it became semi-autonomous within the sphere of influence of the Seleucid Empire. Then, after the defeat of the Seleucid King Antiochus III at the Battle of Magnesia by the Romans and their Pergamene allies in 190 BC, Artaxias I founded a dynasty there in his name, unifying its various territories and enlarging what became the Armenian kingdom. It then reached the zenith of its power during the reign of Tigranes the Great from 95 BC to 55 BC, briefly becoming the most powerful state in the Roman east, controlling both Mesopotamia and Syria as the Seleucid Empire began its final collapse. However, Tigranes made a fatal error in siding with Mithridates VI of Pontus in the Third Mithridatic War against the Romans, earning the enmity of the Senate. Defeated at the Battle of Tigranocerta by Lucius Licinius Lucullus, Tigranes later fought and lost to Pompey, before finally submitting to Rome. From that time Armenia, sometimes independent and sometimes not, became a buffer state between Rome in the west and the Parthians (and later Sassanid Persians) in the east.

Initial Roman-Parthian relations were cordial. When Pompey was given command of the Roman forces in the region in 66 BC at the height of the Third Mithridatic War, he opened negotiations with the Parthian king Phraates III. An agreement was reached whereby Roman and Parthian troops invaded Armenia in a coordinated campaign the same year. However, unsurprisingly a dispute soon arose, this over the exact placing of the Euphrates frontier between the zones of control of the two superpowers. Pompey then offended Phraates and the Parthian court by refusing to style him 'King of Kings', after which Parthia seized Mesopotamia. Pompey responded in 63 BC by establishing the province of Syria as the new Roman eastern frontier.

There matters rested as the Roman world descended into another round of late Republican civil wars between the *optimates* pro-Senate and *populares* radical political factions (Elliott, 2019, 56). However, in 53 BC the fabulously wealthy *triumvir* Crassus led an invasion of Mesopotamia seeking to build a martial reputation to match that of his fellow *triumvirs* Pompey and Caesar. The result was a catastrophe, his army almost annihilated at the Battle of Carrhae where both he and his son lost their lives fighting a huge Parthian army led by the leading Parthian *spahbed* (general) Surena. Less than a quarter of his men made it back to Syria, with the loss made worse because the Parthians captured a number of *aquila* legionary eagle standards. Such was the level of Roman humiliation that in his recent detailed study Nic Fields calls the battle one of Rome's greatest military disasters (2022, 74). Soon Armenia fell to the Parthian king Orodes II, who then had Surena executed, he paying the price for outshining his ruler. Orodes then supported the leading *Liberators* Gaius Cassius Longinus (best known to posterity as Cassius) and Marcus Junius Brutus (best known as Brutus) against Caesar in their winner-takes-all struggle for control of the Republic (Sheppard, 2020, 48). This proved a shrewd move given the latter's assassination prevented an enormous Roman invasion of Parthia under Caesar to avenge his fellow *triumvir* Crassus' earlier demise.

As Rome now turned on itself in another vicious cycle of late Republican civil wars, Orodes took advantage, raiding the Roman east in 40 BC and 39 BC, before losing to a Roman force under Publius Ventidius Bassus at the Battle of Cyrrhestica in 38 BC. Mark Antony, Caesar's former senior *legate* and now the leading *populares*, next sought fame leading a campaign against the new Parthian king Phraates IV in 36 BC, invading through Cilicia and Armenia. However, his vital siege and baggage train, which had been ordered to take an easier route with the aim of joining him in Parthian territory, was intercepted and destroyed by a large Parthian cavalry force. Antony still advanced against the Parthians, but failed to capture any cities and was forced into a humiliating retreat back to Armenia, with Sheppard calling the ill-fated campaign a '... nightmarish debacle...' given the 100,000 men the Romans had deployed (2020, 56). Here Plutarch provides excellent detail about how effective the mounted bowmen of the Parthians were against Crassus' foot-heavy Roman formations, saying (*Lives*, Crassus, 24.5):

> The Parthians now went back a long way and began to shoot their arrows from all sides at the Romans at once, not with any accurate aim (for the dense formation of the Romans would not suffer an archer to miss even if he wished it), but making vigorous and powerful shots from bows which were large and mighty and curved so as to discharge their missiles with great force. At once, then, the plight of the Romans was a grievous one; for if they kept their ranks, they were wounded in great numbers, and if they tried to come to close quarters with the enemy, they were just as far from effecting anything and suffered just as much. For the Parthians shot as they fled, and next to the Scythians, they do this most effectively; and it is a very clever thing to seek safety while still fighting, and to take away the shame of flight.

From that point, over the next 250 years the Romans and Parthians were more often at war than not. Sometimes the Romans held the upper hand, sometimes the Parthians. In the case of the former, Trajan's highly successful campaigns in the east were a high point, though were later undermined by the Second Jewish Revolt (detailed in Chapter 4). However, later in the second century AD Lucius Verus (co-emperor with Marcus Aurelius) led a huge Roman invasion of Parthia in the Roman-Parthian War of AD 161–AD 165, which (as set out in Chapter 7) was a precursor to the subsequent Marcomannic Wars on the Danube.

This war in the east began when the Parthian king Vologeses III took advantage of the death of Antoninus Pius in AD 161. At the time Armenia was allied to Rome under a client king called Sohaemus. The Parthians promptly deposed him and replaced him with their own puppet ruler. Cassius Dio then says a Roman legion sent from Cappadocia to intervene was annihilated, with its commander Marcus Sedatius Severianus, the governor of Cappadocia, committing suicide (*Roman History*, 71.2).

Vologeses then captured Edessa, capital of the prosperous city-state of Osrhoene, the key Roman client state on the border. Here he deposed its ruler Ma'nu VIII and replaced him with a supporter called Wa'el who promptly started minting coins featuring an image of Vologeses. The Parthians then went on the offensive against the empire proper, invading Cappadocia and Syria. Here they pillaged deep into the interior of both provinces, severely disrupting the regional Roman economy.

Back in Rome the newly-installed diarchy of Marcus Aurelius and Lucius Verus had only just come to power. Neither had much experience of conflict given the lengthy period of comparative peace under Antoninus Pius. Verus was tasked with responding to the Parthian aggression, with the imperial *Consilium Principis* advising he take the best commanders available with him. These were Statius Priscus and Gaius Avidius Cassius, the latter a noted strategist and commander of *legio* III *Gallica* in Syria.

In the first instance, in AD 163 Priscus drove the Parthians out of Cappadocia, and then Armenia. There he reinstalled a pro-Roman ruler. Next, in AD 164 Cassius gathered a huge army in Syria. To secure his rear the Roman general first besieged Edessa, this falling to him when the population massacred the Parthian garrison. Ma'nu VIII was then reinstalled as the ruler of Osrhoene, receiving the epithet Philorhomaios ('Friend of the Romans'). Cassius then launched a savage assault down the Tigris valley where he destroyed the major Hellenistic city of *Seleucia-on-Tigris*. Moving on rapidly, he then captured the Parthian capital of *Ctesiphon*, which he also burned to the ground (Scarre, 1995b, 98). The legions continued their advance, reaching the Parthian heartland in Media by early AD 165. At this point Vologeses sued for peace. This was agreed on the most onerous terms for the Parthians, including the ceding of significant portions of western Mesopotamia to Rome. These lands were incorporated into the provinces of Cappadocia and Syria, with only a plague preventing them being formed into their own new province as originally planned. The joint emperors then celebrated their victory over Vologeses with a huge joint triumph in AD 166, with Verus being awarded the honorific titles *Armeniacus*, *Parthicus Maximus* and *Medicus*.

Septimius Severus was the next Roman emperor to campaign against the Parthians. This was in the context of his accession to power at the point of a sword in the 'Year of the Five Emperors' in AD 193. Here, his first priority as the new emperor was to deal with his rival Pescennius Niger in Syria. By this time Niger had already been proclaimed emperor by his troops in *Antioch-on-the-Orontes*. Once in power in Rome Severus immediately headed east, there fighting a year-long campaign against Niger. He finally defeated him at the Battle of Issus in May AD 194, where he captured his opponent as he attempted to flee to Parthia to take refuge with its new ruler Vologeses V. Niger was beheaded soon after, with Severus making himself wealthy by personally confiscating Niger's estates. Having defeated his rival, Severus then turned his attention to the eastern frontier and the Parthians.

The pretext for his first campaign here actually came in the form of the Roman client states Osrhoene (once more), Adiabene and Hatra, who at the instigation of Parthian agents had used the distraction of Severus' campaign against Niger to massacre the Roman garrisons in the key border fortresses there, then seizing them and ultimately besieging nearby Nisibis, a key border city with Parthia currently under Roman control. They actually claimed allegiance to Severus (their targets had been the troops of Niger, they argued) but gave their game away by keeping the territory they had seized, clearly being encouraged to cause more trouble by Parthia.

War was duly declared and Severus led his first expedition into Mesopotamia, aiming to crack down on the recalcitrant vassal states there but also with his eye on ultimate glory against Parthia. The campaign was a great success and the client states all brought to heal (Osrhoene surrendered straight away, Adiabene was captured and Hatra conceded, although was not captured), with the siege of Nisibis broken. In each case the Parthian agents were handed over and executed. However, Severus' plans to use this platform to continue the campaign into Parthia proper were curtailed when news reached him of his next great challenge, the usurpation of Albinus in Britain. Severus therefore returned to the west at speed, finally defeating Albinus at Lugdunum in AD 197 (as detailed in Chapter 7).

Once peace had been restored in Britain and Gaul, Severus again turned his attention back to the east and Parthia, aiming to secure his name as a great conquering emperor. Arriving back in Rome from Lugdunum, he then headed down the *via Apia* to Brindisi (Roman *Brundisium*) where he and his guard embarked aboard vessels of the *Classis Ravennas* Adriatic regional fleet, soon landing at Yumurtalık (Roman *Aegeae*) in Cilicia from where Severus quickly travelled to Syria. Once in theatre he immediately assaulted the Parthians and the war proved a great success for him, lasting from AD 197 to AD 198. The Parthian capital *Ctesiphon* was again sacked by the Roman legions, and the northern half of Mesopotamia annexed into the empire as a punishment for the client states' earlier land grab after the defeat of Niger. The only negative aspect of the campaign was the emperor's failure to capture the fortress of Hatra again, though he did expand the *limes Arabicus* border defence there.

Ever an emperor keen to impress through public monumentalisation, Severus ensured the Roman public were fully aware of his martial exploits in the east by recording them in great detail on the fine arch he had constructed at the head of the *forum romanum* next to the Senate *curia* house. Here, the highly detailed imagery and epigraphy provides vital insight into the conflicts between the Romans and Parthians at the height of the Principate Empire. In particular, the arch's four largest relief panels show the following:

- Relief 1 on the left *forum*-facing panel shows preparations for the first of the two wars, a battle scene featuring a large number of troops, and the liberation of the besieged city of *Nisibis* in AD 195, with the enemy leader fleeing to the right-hand side. Sadly it has been much worn but is still a useful source of data.
- Relief 2 on the right *forum*-facing panel is also damaged and is thought to show the revolt of a Roman ally, perhaps Osrhoene. In the upper register, we see how Severus later announces the annexation of Osrhoene and *Nisibis*.
- Relief 3 on the left capital-facing panel is better preserved and shows the second campaign, specifically against Parthia at the end of the second century AD. Here we see the Roman attack on Seleucia-on-Tigris, with Parthian troops fleeing left and right. The upper part also shows the citizens of the town surrendering.
- Relief 4 on the right capital-facing panel shows the last battle of the war, namely the siege and sack of *Ctesiphon*, the Parthian capital. A siege engine is shown employed to breach the walls and the city then surrenders. In the upper register we can see how Septimius Severus declares Caracalla as his co-ruler, with Geta named as the crown prince.

Meanwhile, other reliefs on the arch also include images of winged victory flying in the spandrels, four statues of the four seasons, and prisoners of war on the pedestals. Importantly for us we also see how the loot is being transported, these images including representations of the legionaries.

The Main Engagement

Here I first narrate Caracalla's initial invasion of Parthia, and his subsequent assassination which led to the elevation of the Praetorian Prefect Marcus Opellius Macrinus as emperor. I then detail the Battle of Nisibis, the last great clash between the Romans and Parthians.

Caracalla's Invasion of Parthia

After Severus' death in York in February AD 211 his eldest son Caracalla inherited the throne after murdering (or having murdered) his younger brother Geta within a year. He targeted the Parthians at the first opportunity. His chance was presented by the civil war that followed Vologases V's death in AD 208, this between his two sons Vologases VI and Artabanus V. This conflict continued into the AD 210s following Severus' own death, and by AD 214 Caracalla had massed a huge army at Nicomedia after a brief campaign against the Alamanni on the Rhine frontier. This included ten cohorts of the battle-hardened Praetorian Guard, the *equites singulares Augusti* imperial guard cavalry, three full legions, vexillations from five others, and large numbers of supporting auxiliary cavalry and foot, the latter allegedly including an unlikely 16,000 strong pike-armed Hellenistic-style phalanx according to Cassius Dio (*Roman History*, 10.29). This reflected Caracalla's obsession with Alexander the Great, who he clearly hoped to emulate.

From a Roman perspective, the ensuing war was notable for the introduction of a new type of legionary, the *lanciarii* light trooper armed with a quiver of javelins and lighter armour than their front rank line of battle equivalents. Such troops, who seem to have operated like the *velites* of the mid-Republican legions skirmishing forward to deter Parthian mounted bowmen, are attested for the first time in the gravestone epigraphy of troopers from *legio* II *Parthica* in the context of this conflict (Cowan, 2003, 24).

Caracalla's war in the east proved one of the darker episodes in Roman–Parthian relations, with his behaviour increasingly psychotic. In the first instance, in AD 215 he visited Alexandria on the way east to punish the Aristolian School of Philosophy there for the alleged plotting of their founder against his hero Alexander the Great. This was a sure sign of Caracalla's growing mania. While there he also brutally dealt with a revolt, allegedly sparked by his excessive tax demands to fund the Parthian campaign (Kean and Frey, 2005, 118).

With the trouble in Alexandria under control, Caracalla turned his full attention to Parthia. There, by this time Vologases VI and Artabanus V had split the empire in two, with support from the Parthian nobility divided between them. Caracalla arrived in *Antioch-on-the-Orontes* in late AD 215 and immediately began consolidating the frontier zone in advance of his planned offensive. This included awarding colonial status to *Emesa* and *Palmyra*, though Osrhoene in northern Mesopotamia was fully incorporated into the empire after its last king Abgarus IX tried to maintain his kingdom's independence. Caracalla's solution was simple. He lured the Osrhoene king into his palace in *Antioch-on-the-Orontes*, captured him and had him killed. However, the emperor then overplayed his hand trying a similar trick with king Khosrov of Armenia, a Parthian appointee. Though the latter was captured, and would remain imprisoned by the Romans until his death two years later, his country rose in revolt and would remain a problem on the northern flank of the Roman campaign for the rest of the war.

Caracalla now made an even bolder move. Intelligence reached him that Artabanus V, the brother with the most support in the Parthian west, was losing the loyalty of the nobles closest to him. This made him vulnerable to diplomatic intrigue. Caracalla now sent an unprecedented offer to Artabanus, suggesting the Roman emperor marry one of the Persian co-monarch's daughters, uniting their empires. Caracalla was a free agent in that regard, having disposed of his first wife Fulvia Plautilla as soon as his father had died, with Severus having earlier forced him into the marriage. After first demurring, Artabanus accepted, knowing this was the best way to secure the Parthian throne for himself alone.

Delighted, Caracalla set off eastwards with his entire army and soon crossed the Euphrates. A formal rendezvous was then arranged by the Romans for Caracalla to meet his future Parthian wife and father-in-law. This took the form of a lavish reception, with leading members of the Parthian nobility in attendance. However, it proved a deadly trap. At a given moment, Caracalla ordered the Romans present to attack their Parthian guests with concealed weapons. A massacre ensued, with Herodian saying Artabanus only narrowly escaped with the help of his close guard (*History of the Roman Empire*, 4.11.7). Sheppard paints a grim picture of what happened next in Parthia, saying (2020, 63): 'After butchering as much of the Parthian elite as he could catch, and taking much booty and many prisoners, Caracalla debauched his way through the Parthian heartland, pillaging and burning.'

Caracalla's rampage came to a head in late summer AD 216 when the Romans captured the key Parthian religious city of Arbela near the old Assyrian capital Nineveh. This was brutally sacked, with Caracalla ordering the Parthian royal tombs desecrated and the bones of their former kings scattered. With the campaigning season now coming to an end, Caracalla then declared victory and led his army back to Syria with huge amounts of loot (*History of the Roman Empire*, 4.11.8).

However, the emperor had unfinished business in the east. His father Septimius Severus had sacked the Parthian capital *Ctesiphon*, but he hadn't. In fact, he'd failed to force a single major engagement with the Parthians. With his martial honour at stake, he determined to return east. In the spring of AD 217, he invaded Parthia again, and this time with an even bigger army.

Crossing the Euphrates again, Caracalla set up a forward headquarters in Edessa where he began planning his new campaign. While there, he decided to visit the famous Temple of the Moon near Carrhae, planning to say prayers for Crassus. However, on 8 April he met one of the most incongruous ends of any Roman emperor. After stopping briefly to urinate on the roadside, and unwisely sending his bodyguards away so he had some privacy, he was killed by a common soldier called Julius Martialis who stabbed him from behind (Kean and Frey, 2005, 118). Martialis was incensed by Caracalla's refusal to promote him to the post of centurion. Earlier, when word of this grudge had reached the ambitious Macrinus, the Praetorian Prefect had seen an opportunity and encouraged Martialis to act, though even he was probably surprised by how quickly the centurion moved. Unsurprisingly, the prefect quickly had Martialis put to death.

The assassination of Caracalla put the Roman army in a very difficult position. This was because word now reached them that an enraged Artabanus was approaching with an enormous army of his own, determined to avenge Caracalla's treachery at the wedding gathering and the desecration of the royal tombs. Indeed, far from undermining Artabanus, Caracalla's actions had bolstered his support among the Parthian nobility. They now demanded revenge.

The senior Roman officers present panicked and quickly appointed Macrinus emperor given his position as Praetorian Prefect. This was despite it being obvious he'd been behind Caracalla's assassination. Here the *Historia Augusta* is very insightful, having the Roman commanders declare their hatred for the deceased Caracalla (*Life of Opellius Macrinus*, 2.4): 'Anyone as emperor rather than the fratricide [Caracalla], anyone rather than the incestuous one, anyone rather than the filthy one, anyone rather than the slayer of the senate and people.'

Some present did argue Macrinus was unsuitable given he was an equestrian rather than a Senator, but Macrinus was a North African. So were the majority of the high command there, with most earlier appointed by Septimius Severus. Regional support won the day, and Macrinus' position was secure.

The same can't be said for his posthumous reputation. All the primary sources are highly critical of Macrinus, particularly the *Historia Augusta* which portrays him as a classic pantomime villain, saying he was (*Life of Opellius Macrinus*, 2.1): 'Of humble origin, shameless in spirit as well as in countenance, and hated by all, including both civilians and soldiers, he nevertheless proclaimed himself now Severus and now Antoninus.'

Cassius Dio and Herodian are slightly more benign, though not much. They argue he acted against Caracalla through self-preservation given the latter's psychotic behaviour, rather than a desire to become emperor. However, both agree Macrinus was an ineffectual emperor who made a series of dramatic missteps from the beginning of his short reign (Cassius Dio, *Roman History*, 10.31, and Herodian, *History of the Roman Empire*, 4.12.8).

The move to elevate Macrinus was particularly unpopular with the rank and file in the army. Realising this, and knowing battle was likely on the way given the proximity of Artabanus' army, Macrinus now tried to inspire his troops with a stirring address. Here, Herodian has him say (*History of the Roman Empire*, 4.11.9):

You see the barbarian with his whole eastern horde already upon us, and Artabanus seems to have good reason for his enmity. We provoked him by breaking the treaty, and in a time of complete peace we started a war. This is no quarrel about boundaries or river beds; everything is at stake in this dispute in which we face a mighty king fighting for his children and kinsmen who, he believes, have been murdered in violation of solemn oaths.

At least Macrinus was being honest with his troops here. The Parthians were hell bent on revenge and no quarter would be given. However, sadly for the Romans, the new emperor proved to be a poor war leader. Indeed, Harry Sidebottom in his recent biography of his successor Heliogabulus calls him a coward (2022, 70).

Macrinus' first instinct here certainly backs this up. Rather than array his army for battle he tried to placate Artabanus, releasing his Parthian captives to show good faith. Artabanus rejected this out of hand, demanding the Romans relinquish the whole of northern Mesopotamia to the Parthians, rebuild the towns and cities they had destroyed, and pay huge amounts of financial compensation. These terms were unacceptable to the Romans and Macrinus quickly rejected them. Battle would now be joined. Note here all the primary sources say that for some reason Artabanus was unaware Caracalla had been assassinated, believing he was still emperor.

The Battle of Nisibis

The only choice Macrinus now had was the type of battle he would fight. By this point the two armies were camped opposite each other at *Nisibis*, still a key border city under Roman control. Macrinus had three options. First, to lead his army into *Nisibis* and prepare for a Parthian siege, hoping a relief force would arrive from elsewhere in the east. Second, to withdraw west towards *Antioch-on-the-Orontes* where the regional defences would give a greater degree of protection. Finally, to give open battle. The first wasn't an option given *Nisibis* was too small to accommodate his large army. The second wasn't either given he knew his huge column would be harried the whole way by Parthian horse archers. Therefore he prepared for open battle.

We don't have the exact date of the engagement in AD 217, but as dawn broke on the day of the battle both sides deployed ready to fight. The Romans deployed in the classic *triplex acies* formation of three lines, each comprising legionaries in the centre and auxiliaries on the flanks, with *lanciarii* light legionaries and other skirmishes deployed forward of the first line to deter the Parthian horse archers. The legionary artillery were deployed behind the third line to fire over the heads of those to the front. Meanwhile, the auxiliary cavalry were deployed on the flanks.

Opposite, the Parthians deployed in five large divisions, reflecting the feudal structure of their society. Each contained a mass of horse archers around a core of fully armoured cataphract noble lancers. On the flanks they also deployed camel-mounted cataphracts, these aiming to deter the Roman mounted troops opposite (Sheppard, 2020, 64).

The Parthians opened the battle in the early morning, their horse archers whirling in front of the Roman skirmishers, firing volley after volley of arrows. Here the Parthian missile troops outnumbered the Romans, and soon the latter's light troops were driven back through the heavy infantry to the rear. The horse archers now closed with the legionaries and auxilia who locked shields to protect themselves from the barrage. However, the volume of fire eventually told, and here and there gaps began to open in the Roman shield wall. When it did, Parthian cataphracts charged home to try and break the Roman line. The Roman heavy foot countered by throwing showers of spiked caltrops to their front which disrupted the Parthian charge. The Roman line held, just. The Parthians then suffered heavy casualties as their cavalry withdrew.

This set a pattern which continued for the entire first day of the battle, with the Parthians launching several assaults until night fell. All failed. Both sides then withdrew to their camps for the night. The second day was then a complete repeat of the first, with the Parthians charging weak points in the Roman lines but failing to achieve a breakthrough.

However, on the third day Artabanus tried a new stratagem to break the deadlock. He ordered his cavalry to use their greater numbers and superior mobility to outflank the Roman line. The Romans, with superior battlefield training, responded by abandoning the *triplex acies* to deploy into one line of battle, thus extending their frontage to match that of the Parthians. Even then they were still in danger of being encircled, until in a final desperate gambit Macrinus ordered the non-combatant drivers and shield bearers out of the Roman camp to extend their line one last time. The Parthians feared this might be a pre-planned trap, given Caracalla's devious reputation, and so Artabanus finally ordered his army to disengage ready to resume combat the next day. By this time, after three days of combat, Herodian says casualties on both sides were so great that (*History of the Roman Empire*, 4.15.5): '...the entire plain was covered with the dead; bodies were piled up in huge mounds, and the dromedaries especially fell in heaps.'

Macrinus knew he'd had a lucky escape and, in this lull in the fighting, sent word to Artabanus that Caracalla was dead. He then offered substantial compensation if allowed to retire from the field. The Parthian king, his feudal army now restive after a long campaign, agreed. The two sides settled on a price of 200 million *sesterces* to recompense the Parthians, with the Roman army then retiring westwards in good order. However, given the Parthians remained on the field of battle, they claimed one final victory over the Romans.

Aftermath and Legacy

Neither protagonist at the Battle of Nisibis lasted long in power. For Macrinus, the revenge of the Severans was to follow swiftly. As soon as he arrived back in *Antioch-on-the-Orontes* Caracalla's mother Julia Domna and her sister, the fabulously wealthy Julia Maesa, began manoeuvres against him. He quickly found out and banished both, though the ill Julia Domna chose to starve herself to death instead (Kean and Frey, 2005, 119). Julia Maesa did leave for her native Emesa, taking her children Julia Soaemias and Julia Mamaea with her. There they joined the latter's son Heliogabalus who, even though only 14, was the chief priest of the Levantine sun deity of the same name. Once in Emesa, Julia Maesa took advantage of a visit by some legionaries of the nearby Raphanea-based *legio* III *Gallica* to convince them her grandson was actually the illegitimate son of Caracalla, and so the true heir to the throne. The soldiers proclaimed him emperor there and then.

Things now moved quickly against Macrinus. An attempt to defeat Heliogabalus at Raphanea failed. This led to an engagement outside *Antioch-on-the-Orontes* on 8 June AD 218 where Macrinus fled the field and headed for Rome. However, he was soon captured in *Chalcedon* in Bithynia before he could cross to Europe. Meanwhile, before fleeing he'd sent his son Diadumenianus (recently made his co-emperor) to the care of Artabanus in Parthia. However, the boy was captured in transit at *Zeugma* and executed in late June. When Macrinus heard the terrible news he tried to escape captivity, but was injured and then executed in Cappadocia. His head was sent to Elagabalus in Antioch, where it joined that of his son.

Artabanus fell next. While he'd been campaigning against Caracalla and Macrinus, one of the most powerful clans in the Parthian Empire had begun to work against him. This was the House of Sassan in modern Iran. By AD 224 its leader Ardashir I felt strong enough to usurp, and soon Artabanus was overthrown, ushering in the Sassanid Persian Empire. This proved a truly symmetrical threat to Rome, one that could match the legions in any theatre of war on a one-for-one basis.

Ardashir I's usurpation set the scene for centuries of conflict between Rome and Sassanid Persia, with him invading the Roman east at the first opportunity to secure the support of the Parthian nobility now needed to keep him in power. This set in place a pattern of offensive and counter offensive by each superpower which continued until the Arab Conquest of Sassanid Persia, and much of the Byzantine Empire (as the eastern Roman Empire was by then known), in the seventh century AD.

Conclusion

In this book I have detailed the eight battles which I think were the key engagements in the Principate Roman Empire, based on their immediate impact or their legacy. Other candidate encounters were also seriously considered, for example in the Cantabrian Wars at the beginning of Augustus' reign when the first Roman emperor conquered northern Spain, Trajan's two campaigns of conquest against the Dacians at the beginning of the second century AD, and Aurelian's reconquest of Postumus' Gallic Empire in the west and defeat of Palmyra in the east in the AD 270s. All deserve to be set out in long form, but sadly here didn't make my final list due to lack of space.

What is apparent having researched each engagement are the repeating patterns evident in all three periods of Roman history, namely the Republic, and the Principate and Dominate phases of empire. For example, each featured a defeat so cataclysmic it changed the nature of the Roman military. In the Republican period, while some argue this was the Battle of Cannae in 216 BC at the height of the Second Punic War, I believe it was the shattering loss at the Battle of Allia in 390 BC when the hoplite-based Tullian legions of Rome were overrun by the Senones Gauls led by Brennus. This led to the subsequent Gallic sack of Rome, an event which resonated through the entirety of Roman history from that point. Similarly, in the Principate, the AD 9 Varian Disaster was a scarring event that shocked Rome to the core. In the Dominate, we then have the Battle of Adrianople in AD 378 when the eastern emperor Valens and much of his army perished fighting the Gothic army of Fritigern. This was an event so cataclysmic it destroyed in a day the integrity of the Roman military establishment to the extent it never recovered.

However, each phase also included a victory so great it resonated through the Roman world at the time, and down the years afterwards. For the Republic, this was Publius Cornelius Scipio Africanus' defeat of Hannibal at Zama in North Africa in 202 BC which broke Carthaginian resistance at the end of the Second Punic War and handed Rome control of the whole western Mediterranean. For the Principate, my candidate is Paulinus' victory over Boudicca in the Battle of Watling Street in AD 60/61, which I detail in this book. This may seem surprising given Britannia was an obscure Roman province at best, the wild northwest of empire in fact. However, this was such a textbook victory against the odds, even taking into account the pro-Roman nature of the primary sources, that it served as an example from that point of how to defeat an opponent when faced with overwhelming odds. Meanwhile, for the Dominate I choose Flavius Aetius' victory over Attila the Hun at the Battle of the Catalaunian Plains in AD 451. Here, not only did he halt Hunnic expansion westwards into Gaul, but had to wrangle control of an army bristling with problematic German allies in order to do so.

All of these engagements, and the other Principate examples covered in this book, reflect two of the key traits that helped ensure the Roman Empire lasted as long as it did. First, the ability to successfully assimilate their opponent's best military tactics and technology. In the regard, the Roman military establishment changed time and again, especially after dramatic defeats, to introduce new troops types, equipment and organization as required. Second, Roman society's unusual propensity for true 'grit', with its seeming inability to accept defeat in any form, and almost always come back from defeat to achieve ultimate victory. In the Principate, only rarely was this not the case, for example after the annihilation of Varus' army in the Teutoburg Forest, after which the Romans forever abandoned any plans for a new province in Germania.

Finally here, all of the battles covered in this book feature a number of common themes that can be drawn together to show the Roman military establishment at its best, even in defeat. First, battlefield leadership. Here I extend the term to include not only battlefield management at the tactical level, but also the strategic given in all of these engagements, when the Romans controlled the wider battlespace, they went on to win. Think of Paulinus' exemplary choice of battlefield when faced with Boudicca's huge force in AD 60/61. Next, the role of the command team advising the overall army leader. One can only speculate how Varus, surrounded with campaign veterans, clearly ignored good advice at every step, while Agricola wisely acknowledged good counsel as he approached the very edge of the Roman known world. Meanwhile, another common theme concerns the role of the Roman auxilia. Often overlooked given the usual focus on legionaries, auxiliaries always played a key role in Roman engagements during the Principate. There is no finer example than Mons Graupius in AD 83 when our primary sources say they did all of the fighting as Agricola defeated Calgacus, with the legionaries looking on. Another theme evident in many of these engagements is the role played by maritime forces. More often than not, Roman campaigns made maximum use of the coast and rivers to provide logistics support for their legionary and auxilia spearheads. When they did, they were usually successful. Again, think of Agricola campaigning in the true heart of darkness, as the Romans viewed it, in the far north of Britain. Developing this theme, mastery of logistics more broadly gave the Romans an advantage over all of their opponents, even the Parthians in the east. Finally, Roman engineering skill was also a common theme in all of the battles covered here, with the siege and assault of Masada providing no better example.

I hope the reader has enjoyed reading my selection of great battles of early imperial Rome, and that my narration has inspired others to look again at battles well-known, or to seek out other engagements less so.

Appendix

The Principate Roman Military

The Roman military in the Principate phase of empire was pre-eminent in a world where at that time it lacked a true symmetrical threat until the advent of the Sassanid Persians in the early third century AD, excepting perhaps their Parthian predecessors. Most often on campaign and in battle it won. This is the Roman military most recognisable to the general public. Think of legionaries resplendent in torso-covering *scutum* shields, fine *lorica segmentata* banded iron armour and bright-crested imperial Gallic helmets, their *gladii* swords at the ready.

Here in this appendix, to inform the reader, I set out the Principate Roman military in detail. First I consider the legionary from the time of Augustus as the empire began through to the accession of Diocletian in AD 284. I then focus on a brand new institution in the Roman military, the auxilia. Next I detail Roman naval power in the Principate phase of empire, before closing the appendix with a review of one of the empire's most enigmatic institutions, the Praetorian Guard.

The Principate Legionary

Augustus carried out the first Principate reformation of the Roman military. Given the enormous military establishment he inherited at the end of the last round of Republican civil wars, this was very extensive and designed to reduce this hugely expensive complement to manageable numbers. The reforms included the legions, their supporting troops (most, from this time onwards, becoming the full-time auxilia) and his fleet.

His first move with the legions was to tackle the huge number he now had scattered around his new empire, these numbering an improbable sixty. Over a five-year period he reduced this total to twenty-eight, it then falling to twenty-five after Varus' losses in Germany in AD 9. Subsequent emperors increased the number again, with the total hovering around thirty for the next 250 years, for example the twenty-nine in existence at the time of the accession of Marcus Aurelius and Lucius Verus in AD 161. The total only rose above thirty during the Severan dynasty after Septimius Severus created *legio* I *Parthica*, *legio* II

Parthica and *legio* III *Parthica* for his eastern campaigns, bringing the total to thirty-three (see Chapter 7).

The Principate legions after the Augustan reforms numbered 5,500 men, organised into ten cohorts. Of these, the first had five centuries of 160 men (*legio* II *Parthica*'s first cohort had six such centuries), with the other cohorts having six centuries of eighty men. Each century was then broken down into ten eight-man sections called *contubernia*, whose men shared a tent when on campaign and two barrack-block rooms when in their legionary fortress. Additionally, the legions also featured 120 auxiliary cavalry, these acting as dispatch riders and scouts. We know specifically of one such individual who actually served in this latter role in *legio* IX *Hispana*. This is Quintus Cornelius whose now-lost tombstone was found around 1800 on the south side of the churchyard of St Peter-at-Gowts church in Lincoln. His inscription (RIB 254) reads:

> Quintus Cornelius, son of Quintus, of the Claudian voting-tribe, trooper of *legio* IX from the century of Cassius Martialis: aged 40 years, of 19 year's service, lies buried here.

The numbering and naming of the legions seems confusing to us today, reflecting their being raised by different Republican leaders (especially in the civil wars of the first century BC) and emperors, and at different times. Therefore many shared the same legion number (always permanent) but had different names, for example there being five third legions. Others shared the same name but had different numbering, for example Septimius Severus' three Parthian legions. The longevity of this numbering, and the clear differential in the naming, suggests that the strong sense of identity of the Republican Marian legions was certainly carried over into their Principate counterparts.

In that regard, the standards carried by the legions were very important and had expanded in number by the time of the Principate into a formal complement comprising four different types. First and most important was the *aquila* eagle standard first introduced into the late Republican legions by Marius and carried by the *aquilifer*. The eagle by this time was made entirely of gold, and only left camp when the entire legion was on the move. It was the loss of three of these standards in the Varian Disaster in AD 9 that so vexed Augustus. Another standard, the *imago*, featured an image of the emperor and was carried by the *imaginifer*, while *signa* standards were allocated to each individual century and featured the legion's battle honours. These were carried by the *signifier*. Flag-based standards were also used, called *vexilla*, one of which showed the name of the legion, while others of the same type were allocated to legionary detachments, hence their naming as *vexillations*. The *vexilla* were carried by *vexillarii*. These various standards were joined in their signalling role in the legions by the *cornicern* musician who played the *cornu*. The latter always marched at the head of the centuries, with the *signifer* or other appropriate standard bearer.

Principate legionaries could be volunteers or conscripted, depending on the circumstances, although by the time of the diarchy of Marcus Aurelius and Lucius Verus they were increasingly enrolled as conscripts given the losses suffered first in the Roman-Parthian War and later the Marcomannic Wars (see Chapter 6). Such conscripted recruitment was usually on a regional basis, as with their foundings *legio* II *Italica* and *legio* III *Italica*, who were recruited in Italy. Those recruited by either means were exclusively Roman citizens for most of the Principate, originally being all Italian at the end of the Republic, although increasingly they came from Gaul and Spain as citizenship spread, and later came from North Africa and the eastern Mediterranean. The recruiting base for legionaries then increased even further with the Edict of Caracalla in AD 212, as this made every freeman living in the empire a citizen. Meanwhile, throughout the Principate phase of Empire there was a height requirement for the legionary, this being 1.8m.

Augustus greatly increased the term of service for the legionaries in his reforms from the six years of the late Republic to twenty years, this being designed to maintain a stable base of highly experienced troops in the legions. The last four years were served as a veteran excused fatigues and guard duty, such troops were called *vexillum veteranorum*. This length of service was then later extended by Augustus to twenty-five years, with five as a veteran, a term which lasted well into the Dominate phase of empire. The increase was due to a shortage of recruits (Augustus being too successful when slimming down the number of legions), and because of the strain placed on the imperial *fiscus* treasury to pay the *praemia* retirement gratuity for retiring legionaries given the very large number of troops Augustus inherited.

Such gratuities could now be money (3,000 *denarii* in the late first century BC, this rising to 5,000 *denarii* by the time of Septimius Severus), or land as in the later Republic. In the latter case this was now in the form of *centuriated* land parcels designed to set the retiree up as a farmer, or in *colonia* settlements as in the later Republic. Such retired legionaries often settled near to their former legionary bases, these settlements then developing into *coloniae* towns for example with Gloucester (Roman *Glevum*).

In terms of pay, the Augustan legionary received the same 225 *denarii* as introduced by Caesar, from which deductions were formally made for arms, clothing and food. This was increased to 300 *denarii* by Domitian, a level it remained at until the reign of Septimius Severus who increased it to 450 *denarii*. His son Caracalla increased legionary pay even more, by a further 50 per cent, following his father's advice to keep the soldiery happy above all else. This basic pay was also often increased through donatives such as the 75 *denarii* left by Augustus to all of his legionaries in his will. Even at its most basic level this was a good salary for a Roman citizen, and in an age before popular banking the legionaries often handed their savings to their unit standard bearers, a duty which placed a huge amount of trust upon them. We have a direct example of one such a standard bearer performing this role. This is Rufinus, a *signifer* with *legio* IX *Hispana*, whose tombstone was found in York. His image on the monument shows him holding a *codex ansantus* case of writing tablets in his left hand, there to record his fellow legionaries accounts.

Meanwhile, to provide some context here as to the impact this legionary and other military expenditure had on the imperial *fiscus* treasury, in the second century AD the overall annual cost of the Roman military was 150 million *denarii* (this comprising the salaries and retirement gratuities for legionaries, auxilia and the *miletes* of the regional fleets).

The diet of the Principate legionary was very similar to that of his later Republican predecessor, though by this time more care was taken when on campaign to ensure the security of their grain supply. This is well-evidenced by the Scottish campaigns of Septimius Severus in Scotland where he expanded the size of the granaries at the key naval supply base at South Shields (Roman *Arbeia*) by a factor of ten.

Meanwhile, religion continued to play a major role in the daily lives of the Principate legionary, with the obligation to worship the Gods of the Roman pantheon (as in the Republic) now joined by the even more important requirement to worship the imperial cult of the sitting emperor. Additionally, the worship of certain Gods that had a specific association with the Roman military now also appeared. These were often eastern in origin and included Mithras, Bacchus and Isis. The worship of all of these Gods, and also the dates of the traditional festivals of Rome (together with the accession days and birthdays of emperors), structured the religious year for the Principate legionary.

Elsewhere in the Principate legionary's daily life, he was officially unable to marry until he retired, though legionaries often contracted technically illegal marriages. Septimius Severus changed this, granting the soldiers their right to marry and at the same time giving the formerly illegal spouses and offspring legal rights for the first time.

In terms of command structure, the legions from the early Principate were led by a Senatorial-level *legatus legionis*. His second-in-command was also of Senatorial-level, called the *tribunus laticlavius*, a younger man gaining the experience needed to command their own legion in the future. Third in command was the *praefectus castrorum* (camp prefect), a seasoned former centurion responsible for administration and logistics. Below this level there were five younger equestrian-level tribunes, called the *tribuni angusticlavia*, these being allocated tasks and responsibilities as necessary. The actual control of each cohort in the legion remained the responsibility of the centurions, as with the late Republican legions.

Equipment of the Principate Legionary

As with the late Republican legionary, those of the Principate were for the most part specialist heavy infantry whose arms and armour were always geared towards defeating their opponents through the shock of impact and discipline.

In terms of his defensive panoply, for a shield the Principate legionary was still equipped with the curved, rectangular *scutum* (though squarer in design than those of their Republican counterparts). As before it was used as an offensive weapon in its own right, and in defence allowed the legionaries to adopt a number of defensive formations including the *testudo*. This featured interlocking shields providing full cover on all sides, including from above. Other formations that made great use of the shield included the *orbis* to provide all-round defence and the *cuneus* wedge formation used to puncture an opponent's battle line (as used by Paulinus when defeating Boudicca, see Chapter 3).

In terms of armour the legionaries of the Principate wore a variety of types of full body armour. The most commonly depicted in contemporary culture and found in the archaeological record is the famous *lorica segmentata*, constructed of articulated iron plates and hoops. The origins of *lorica segmentata* are unclear though it may have originally been a form of gladiator armour. The first types emerge in the archaeological record at the end of the first century BC when it began to replace *lorica hamata* as the main type worn by the legionary, and from that point the armour evolved through three specific versions, these being (all named after the location where examples were found):

- The Dangestetten-Kalkriese-Vindonissa type, those found dating to between 9 BC to AD 43.
- The Corbridge-Carnumtum type, those found dating to between AD 69 to AD 100.
- The Newstead type, those found dating to between AD 164 to AD 180.

Each successive version was less complicated than that which preceded it, for example that found in the *principia* of the vexillation fort at Newstead in the

Scottish Borders in 1905 featuring rivets to replace earlier bronze hinges, a single large girdle-plate to replace the two previous ones, and hooks to replace earlier and more complicated belt-buckle fastenings.

Other types of armour continued to be worn, including *lorica hamata* that stayed in use throughout the Principate, and came back into full favour in the third century AD. A further variant was *lorica squamata* scale mail (cheaper than chainmail but inferior in flexibility and protection) made from small bronze or iron interlocking scales, while in the provinces even more exotic types were to be found, for example a suit of crocodile-skin armour found in a third century AD context in Manfalut, Egypt, and now housed in the British Museum. It is not clear in such cases if the function of the armour was more religious than military, in this instance perhaps referencing a military crocodile cult associated with the Goddess Isis.

Additionally, when fighting certain types of opponent (such as the Bastarnae using the two-handed *falx* slashing weapon) extra armour was fitted including articulated iron *manicae* arm guards, thigh guards and greaves. Specific troop types within the Principate legions were also often differentially equipped with armour when compared to the rank and file legionaries to mark them apart, with officers frequently shown wearing iron and bronze muscled cuirasses and centurions and *signifers* wearing chainmail (even when the majority of legionaries were wearing *lorica segmentata*).

Finally in terms of defensive military equipment, the helmet of the legionary also evolved throughout the Principate. At the time Augustus became emperor the Coolus and Port types of the late Republic were still the most common. However, the latter soon developed into the much more substantial classic imperial Gallic helmet. In particular this featured a much larger neck guard. A final imperial type originated in Italy, hence it being called imperial Italic. This was a bronze compromise between the new designs of Celtic origin and the more traditional Roman types of the late Republic. All of these helmets featured prominent cheek guards (again of Celtic provenance), neck guards and often a reinforcing strip on the front of the cap to deflect downward sword slashes. Ear guards were added from the AD 50s.

The Principate legionary also still carried his two *pilum* weighted javelins, again one light for use in the approach and one heavy for use immediately prior to impact. However, the principal weapon was still the *gladius*, worn as before on the right-hand side for rank and file troopers. When Augustus took office the main type was still the *gladius Hispaniensis*. This developed during his reign into the Mainz-type *gladius* that was broader and shorter, featuring a longer stabbing point. A further development, adopted towards the close of the first century AD, was the Pompeii-type *gladius*, this being slightly shorter than the Mainz type with a squatter, triangular stabbing point. All of these swords were still used in the same cut-and-thrust fencing style of the late Republic, this continuing to dominate Roman fighting techniques even when the length of the swords began to increase again in the later second century AD. The weapons complement was completed by the *pugio* dagger. Both this and the *gladius* were suspended from two individual belts that crossed over front and back.

This traditional Principate legionary panoply was beginning to change by the late second/early third centuries AD. This was largely a response to a change in the nature of their opponents. Previously, the legions had most often faced a similar infantry-heavy force (excepting the Parthians in the east), but were now tackling a multitude of threats, many of a differing nature that required a more flexible response. In particular, the heavily armoured charging lancers of the Sarmatian tribes faced by the Romans in the Marcomannic Wars made a strong impression.

This change is shown in real time on four of the monuments set up in Rome by four great warrior emperors – Trajan's Column, the Column of Marcus Aurelius and the Arches of Septimius Severus and Constantine. The latter is particularly important given it is in effect a time machine, built in AD 315 in the Dominate phase of empire to celebrate Constantine's victory over Maxentius at the Battle of Milvian Bridge in AD 312. At the time the imperial *fiscus* was running low, as it had been used by Maxentius to fund his failed defence of Rome. Therefore, the architects of the new arch sourced panels from existing monuments to complement its new and contemporary depictions of his martial success. These included four panels called the Great Trajanic Frieze which comprised slabs from a monument to celebrate victory in Trajan's two Dacian campaigns, and similar panels from a lost Arch of Marcus Aurelius to celebrate his successes in the Marcomannic Wars.

The change in the equipment of the later Principate legionary was initially evident in his weaponry. First, from the reign of Septimius Severus the longer cavalry-style *spatha* sword began to replace the shorter *gladius* for all Roman foot soldiers. This weapon was up to 80cm in length, although some of 1m-length have been identified. The new sword was suspended from a baldric on a Sarmatian-type scabbard slide, and came to dominate Roman military equipment in the west until the empire's end there, continuing in use in the east afterwards. It seems likely the adoption of this weapon had its origins in the need for more reach to tackle armoured mounted opponents.

A similar change is also evident in the use of the *pila*, which were gradually replaced by a thrusting spear of between 2 and 2.7m in length in the same time period. This change is visible actually taking place on the four monuments detailed above. Thus on Trajan's Column, the Column of Marcus Aurelius and the reused panels on the Arch of Constantine, legionaries are shown in classic *lorica segmentata* armour mostly armed with *pila*, while on the Arch of Septimius Severus and on the contemporary panels of the Arch of Constantine they have been replaced by spears. This was again a response to the experiences fighting mounted opponents more frequently, as with the longer sword. A legionary spear wall made much more sense engaging such opponents than the use of *pilum* impact weapons, with one such legionary phalanx actually depicted on a panel on the Arch of Septimius Severus, there countering Parthian cataphracts.

Moving to the defensive panoply, this change is also evident with the shield. In the later second century AD the traditional *scutum* began to be replaced by a large flat (and sometimes slightly dished) oval body shield, confusingly still called a *scutum*. This new design was of simple plank construction, with stitched-on rawhide, and was strengthened with iron bars. The two types appear to have been used side by side for some time, with examples of both found at the fortified frontier-trading town of Dura-Europos in Syria dating to AD 256. This transition is also very evident on the four monuments detailed above, with many of the large round shields featuring on the Severan arch, and even more on the contemporary panels of the Arch of Constantine. Once again this change seems to have been associated with the type of opponent more commonly faced by the Romans, the round shield perhaps more suited to dealing with a mounted threat. It certainly gave greater freedom of movement for the new swords and spears coming into use with their greater reach, and would also have been cheaper to produce.

Not surprisingly, a change is also evident in the body armour of the legionary as the Principate approached its end. Thus on Trajan's Column and the Column of Marcus Aurelius most are wearing *lorica segmentata*, as they are on the reused panels on the Arch of Constantine. However, on the Arch of Septimius Severus there is a much higher proportion wearing *lorica hamata* and *lorica squamata*, this proportion increasing yet again on the contemporary panels of the Arch of Constantine.

Meanwhile, as the Principate progressed, legionary helmets also became increasingly substantial, with the Italic imperial type disappearing entirely by the early third century AD. The Gallic imperial style did continue in use, but was increasingly supplemented by heavier, single bowl designs reinforced by crosspieces and fitted with deep napes, leaving only a minimal T-shaped face opening. These helmets provided exceptional levels of protection. A final change in this time period was the appearance a new type of legionary. This was the *lanciarii* light trooper armed with a quiver of javelins and lighter armour than their front rank line of battle equivalents, (as detailed in Chapter 8).

Roman legionaries also provided the battlefield and siege artillery component of Roman armies when on campaign. Such weapons included light *scorpio* dart-throwers and the larger *ballista*, the latter firing large bolts and shaped stones. When at full strength, each cohort fielded one of the latter and each century one of the former. This gave an impressive total of ten *ballistae* and fifty-nine *scorpiones*. A final development with regard to Principate legionary artillery was a move to replace the *ballista* with *onager* catapults, the latter larger and better suited to siege warfare, from around AD 250.

Finally, regarding the Principate legions of Rome in the period covered by this book, the below table details all known such formations for reference:

Legion	When Founded	Destroyed/ disbanded
legio I *Germanica*	Later Republic	Disbanded AD 70 after Civilis Revolt
legio I *Adiutrix pia fidelis*	Provisionally recruited by Nero, then made a regular legion by Galba	
legio I *Italica*	Under Nero	
legio I *Macriana*	Under Nero	Civil war legion, disbanded AD 69/70
legio I *Flavia Minervia pia fidelis*	Under Domitian	
legio I *Parthica*	Under Septimius Severus	
legio II *Augusta*	Later Republic/under Augustus	
legio II *Adiutrix pia fidelis*	Under Nero	
legio II *Italica*	Under Marcus Aurelius	
legio II *Parthica*	Under Septimius Severus	
legio II *Traiana fortis*	Under Trajan	
legio III *Augusta pia fidelis*	Later Republic/under Augustus	
legio III *Cyrenaica*	Later Republic	
legio III *Gallica*	Under Caesar	
legio III *Italica concors*	Under Marcus Aurelius	
legio III *Parthica*	Under Septimius Severus	
legio IIII *Flavia felix*	Under Vespasian	
legio IIII *Macedonica*	Under Caesar	Disbanded AD 70
legio IIII *Scythica*	Under Mark Antony	
legio V *Alaudae*	Under Caesar	Destroyed under Domitian

Legion	When Founded	Destroyed/ disbanded
legio V Macedonica	Later Republic	
legio VI Ferrata fidelis constans	Under Caesar	
legio VI Victrix	Later Republic	
legio VII Claudia pia fidelis	Under Caesar	
legio VII Gemina	Under Galba	
legio VIII Augusta	Later Republic	
legio IX Hispana	Later Republic	Disappears in the early second century AD
legio X Fretensis	Later Republic	
legio X Gemina	Under Caesar	
legio XI Claudia pia fidelis	Later Republic	
legio XII Fulminata	Under Caesar	
legio XIII Gemina pia fidelis	Later Republic	
legio XIV Gemina Martia Victrix	Later Republic	
legio XV Apollinaris	Under Augustus	
legio XV Primigenia	Under Caligula	Disbanded AD 70
legio XVI Flavia Firma	Under Vespasian	
legio XVI Gallica	Under Augustus	Disbanded AD 70
legio XVII	Under Augustus	Destroyed in AD 9 in Germany (see Chapter 1)
legio XVIII	Under Augustus	Destroyed in AD 9 in Germany (see Chapter 1)
legio XIX	Under Augustus	Destroyed in AD 9 in Germany (see Chapter 1)
legio XX Valeria Victrix	Under Augustus	
legio XXI Rapax	Under Augustus	Possibly destroyed under Domitian
legio XXII Deiotariana	Under Augustus	Possibly destroyed under Hadrian
legio XXII Primigenia pia fidelis	Under Caligula	
legio XXX Ulpia Victrix	Under Trajan	

After Goldsworthy, A., *The Complete Roman Army* (London: Thames & Hudson, 2003).

The Auxilia

Legionaries were not the only soldiers in the Roman military during the Principate phase of Empire. Earlier, Republican Roman armies had always used mercenary and allied auxiliary troops to support the legions. These were recruited to fulfil a wide variety of supporting roles on the battlefield, fighting under their own officers and in their own native formations.

However, this all changed as part of the Augustan reforms of the military. In addition to his rationalization of the legions, the first emperor also formalised the supporting troops in the Roman military establishment, and from this time they were called auxiliaries (or auxilia in shortened form, as used in this book). These were now regular troops and featured both cavalry and infantry, recruited from *peregrini* non-Italian freemen, often from recently conquered new provinces as the new empire expanded. The number of auxilia quickly grew, with Tacitus (*The Annals*, 4.5) saying that by AD 25 there were as many in the Roman army as legionaries, the latter number at that time around 175,000.

Though auxilia were full line of battle troops, they were the junior partners to their legionary counterparts. Foot troops were paid 100 *denarii* per annum from the later first century AD, with cavalry paid 200 *denarii* (those based on the wing of a battle formation being paid 333 *denarii*). Terms of service were similar to those of the legionaries, with auxiliaries normally serving twenty-five years. Upon retirement the trooper was given a citizenship diploma that granted Roman citizenship to himself and his heirs, the right of legal marriage to a non-citizen woman, and citizenship for existing children.

The auxilia provided most of the cavalry and much of the foot complement of Roman armies. Auxiliary cavalry were organised into *quingenary alae* of 512 men or *milliary alae* of 768. Each was commanded by a *praefectus alae*. As detailed in Chapter 7, the basic cavalrymen were called *equites*, their defensive panoply featuring flat oval or hexagonal shields, short *lorica hamata* chainmail hauberks and bronze and iron helmets. For offensive weaponry they carried a *hasta* spear and a *spatha* long sword. Many *equites* armed in this way were among the most feared units in the Principate military, they specifically recruited from regions famous at the time for their formidable mounted warriors. A good example are the auxiliary cavalry of Gallic origin who were known for their predilection for trophy headhunting.

In the early Principate the *equites* were supported by a variety of different types of light cavalry fighting in the style of their native region. Examples included Moorish *symmachiarii* javelin-armed skirmishers, and eastern horse archers. By the later second century AD such specialist light cavalry had been fully integrated into the Roman military establishment. Examples included javelin-armed *equites illyriciani* and bow-armed *equites sagittarii*. Specialist shock cavalry had also begun to appear by this time, initially in the form of *numeri* temporary units of indigenous troops recruited in the east, often called *contarii* referencing their long *contos* lances. A fine example is found in Britain where in AD 175 Marcus Aurelius sent 5,500 of the 8,000 Iazyges lancers supplied to the Roman military as part of a peace treaty with the Sarmatians during the Marcomannic Wars (see Chapter 6).

As the later Principate progressed such shock cavalry were quickly formalised into full auxiliary *ala*, for example the lancers as *equites contariorum* and heavily armoured cataphracts as *equites cataphractarii*. The latter were based on the Parthian cataphracts Rome often encountered in the east and were again armed with the *contos*, wearing a suit of scale armour called *lorica plumata* which covered the entire body, with a substantial helmet with gilded face plate. Their horses were often similarly fully armoured.

In terms of auxilia foot troops, although these were the junior partners to their legionary counterparts, they were still among the best soldiers of the ancient world. Auxilia infantry formations in the Principate were based on a single *quingenary* cohort of 480 troops, or a double-sized *milliary* cohort of 800 troops. These cohorts (both the small and large) were divided into centuries of between 80 and 100 men, these under the command of a centurion, clearly replicating the similar structure in a legionary formation. However, the centurions, unlike the auxiliary troopers, were sometimes Roman citizens appointed from the legions. Others were drawn direct from the rank and file of the auxiliary unit. Above this level their cohort was commanded by an equestrian, a *praefectus* for a *quingenary* unit and a tribune for a *milliary* unit.

Auxilia foot fought in both close and loose formation, the latter making them especially useful in difficult terrain. When in close order auxiliary foot troops were line of battle troops who fought in a similar manner to the legionaries. The auxiliary shield throughout the Principate was usually an elongated oval plank design covering the torso and featuring a central iron or bronze boss, the shield smaller in size than the legionary *scutum*. In terms of armour auxilia are most frequently shown wearing *lorica hamata* chainmail or *lorica squamata* scale mail hauberks, these shorter and less sophisticated than those worn by their legionary counterparts. Auxilia helmets were also less sophisticated, often-cheaper bronze versions of those worn by the legionaries. They were armed with the short, throwable *lancea* spear rather than *pila*, and a sword similar to the legionary *gladius*, this later replaced by the longer cavalry-style *spatha* as with the legionaries. The auxilia also provided the majority of the specialist warriors in Roman military formations, for example archers, slingers, staff slingers and javelinmen.

The former, called *auxilia sagittarii* and organized into *cohortes sagittariorum*, were a particularly important component of Roman armies and wore distinctive uniforms that distinguished whether they had been recruited in the west or east. Those from the east, where they had to contend with Parthian and other eastern horse archers, often had better protection than their line of battle auxilia counterparts, wearing long *lorica squamata* coats of scale mail and conical iron helmets. Such troops are well represented in relief on Trajan's Column.

Roman archers fought using a composite bow based on those of the horsemen of the Asian steppe, made from laminated layers of wood, bone, horn and sinew. This gave the weapon much greater penetrating power than the self-bow used by less sophisticated opponents. Further, notched stiffeners at each end of the bow, and its handgrip, gave the bowstring greater leverage. This kept the weapon from bucking when fired, which increased accuracy.

Roman arrows also featured sophisticated technology, with different arrowheads used depending on the opponent engaged. Against unarmoured enemies, for example the majority of German and Gothic foot troops, a broad arrowhead was used to maximize damage to the opponent's body. Meanwhile, against more heavily armoured troops such as Sarmatian lancers and Parthian cataphracts, a much narrower bodkin-point arrowhead was used, this causing less damage but able to penetrate armour. Other specialist arrowheads included those designed for use in a siege which featured an iron basket behind the arrow tip, this designed to carry lit inflammable material.

Roman arrow shafts were made of wood, reed or cane depending on where they were manufactured. The arrowhead was set in place with a wooden pile to ensure the arrowhead didn't shatter on impact. The arrows were carried in a *pharetra* quiver held between the shoulder blades by leather straps. Auxiliary archers also had bracers on their left wrists to protect them from the kick of the bowstring when firing. They also had either leather finger guards or a metal thumb ring to enable them to pull the bowstring rapidly. For self-defence they carried a standard auxiliary sword.

Auxilia units could also be fielded in combined formations that featured both infantry and mounted troops, their organisation being less well-understood. Such infantry cohorts, cavalry *alae* and combined units were very flexible and could easily be moved around the empire as needed in the same manner as vexillations of legionaries.

For reference, the below table details the known auxiliary cohorts and *alae* of the mid-Principate empire:

Unit Location Date

Unit	Location	Date
Brittones Aurelianensis	*Upper Germany*	*AD 200*
Cohors Sagittariorum	*Hispania Baetica*	*Later second century AD*
Cohors I Aelia Brittonum milliaria	*Noricum*	*Later second century AD*
Cohors I Aelia Dacorum millaria	*Britannia and Noricum*	*Later second century AD*
Cohors I Dardanorum Aurelia	*Dalmatia*	*Later second century AD*
Cohors I Delmatorum	*Dalmatia*	*Later second century AD*
Cohors I Frisavonum	*Britannia*	*Later second century AD*
Cohors I Hemesenorum eq. mil. Sagittaria CR	*Pannonia Inferior*	*Later second century AD*
Cohors I Pasinatum Aurelia Nova	*Dalmatia*	*Later second century AD*
Cohors I Sacorum Aurelia Nova	*Dalmatia*	*Later second century AD*
Cohors I Septima Belgarum	*Upper Germany*	*AD 200*
Cohors I Tungrorum mil.	*Britannia*	*Second century AD*
Cohors I Ulpia Tiaiana Cugernorum CR	*Britannia*	*Second century AD*
Cohors I Ulpia Traiana Campestris Voluntariorum	*Dalmatia*	*Second century AD*
Cohors II Aforum Flavia	*Mauretania*	*Late second century AD*
Cohors II Astorum Equitata	*Britannia*	*Second century AD*
Cohors II Dacorum Aurelia	*Pannonia Inferior*	*Late second century AD*
Cohors II Gallorum Equitata	*Britannia*	*Second century AD*
Cohors II Tungrorum mil.	*Britannia*	*Second century AD*
Cohors III Aquitanorum equitata CR	*Upper Germany*	*Late second century AD*
Cohors III Gallorum	*Hispania Baetica*	*Late second century AD*
Cohors III Nerviorum CR	*Britannia, Hispania Baetica*	*Late second century AD*
Cohors III Breucorum	*Britannia*	*Second century AD*
Cohors III Tungrorum mil.	*Mauretania*	*Late second century AD*
Cohors IV Gallorum	*Gallia Lugdunensis*	*Late second century AD*
Cohors IV Tungorum mil.	*Lower Germany*	*Second century AD*
Cohors V Baetica	*Hispania Baetica*	*Late second century AD*
Cohors VI Raetorum	*Britannia*	*Late second century AD*
Cohors VII Delmatorum eq.	*Mauretania*	*Late second century AD*
Ara Colonia Ulpia Traiana	*Lower Germany*	*Late second century AD*

Ala Asturum	*Gallia Lugdunensis*	*Second century AD*
Ala (Gallorum) Placentia	*Britannia*	*Late second century AD*
Ala (Hispanorum) Vettonum CR	*Britannia*	*Second century AD*
Ala Noricorum	*Lower Germany*	*Late second century AD*
Ala (Gallorum) Sebosiana	*Britannia*	*Second century AD*
Ala I (Hispanorum) Aravacorum	*Pannonia*	*Late second century AD*
Ala I Asturum	*Britannia*	*Second century AD*
Ala I Britannica	*Mauretania*	*Late second century AD*
Ala I Caninafatium	*Pannonia*	*Late second century AD*
Ala I Contaforium	*Pannonia*	*Late second century AD*
Ala I Ituraeorum	*Pannonia*	*Late second century AD*
Ala I (Pannoniorum) Sebosiana	*Britannia*	*Second century AD*
Ala I (Pannoniorum) Tampiana	*Britannia*	*Later second century AD*
Ala II Asturum	*Britannia*	*Second century AD*
Ala II Pannoniorum	*Pannonia*	*Second century AD*

After D'Amato, R., *Roman Army Units in the Western Provinces (1)* (Oxford: Osprey Publishing, 2016).

The Regional Fleets

The regional navies of the Principate Empire were also the result of the military reforms of Augustus. Before this date the fleets of the Republic were ad hoc in nature, designed to fight symmetrical engagements against opponents including Carthage, the Hellenistic kingdoms and Roman civil war rivals across the Mediterranean. Augustus rationalized this system, recreating the various fleets he inherited into regional navies that reflected the Empire's expanding geographical reach. By the end of the first century AD there were ten such fleets, each with a specific area of territorial responsibility. These are detailed in the below table which also shows the annual stipend of each fleet's *praefectus classis* admiral, reflecting its status.

Fleet	Annual Stipend
Classis Ravenna	*300,000 sesterces*
Classis Misenensis	*200,000 sesterces*
Classis Britannica	*100,000 sesterces*

Fleet	Annual Stipend
Classis Germanica	*100,000 sesterces*
Classis Flavia Pannonica	*60,000 sesterces*
Classis Flavia Moesica	*60,000 sesterces*
Classis Pontica	*60,000 sesterces*
Classis Syriaca	*60,000 sesterces*
Classis Nova Lybica	*60,000 sesterces*
Classis Alexandrina	*60,000 sesterces*

After Ellis Jones, J., *The Maritime Landscape of Roman Britain* (Oxford: BAR/Archaeological and Historical Associates Ltd, 2012).

The *Classis Britannica* in Britain provides a good example of one of the larger Principate regional fleets. This featured 900 ships and 7,000 crew, including sailors, marines and support personnel. Each regional fleet had an origin specific to its region of operations, with that in Britain dating to the original 900 vessels built by Caligula for his abortive AD 40 invasion. These were later used by Claudius for his AD 43 invasion, (as detailed in Chapter 2).

All regional fleets performed both military and civilian roles. In the former context the *Classis Britannica* had responsibility for the North Sea, English Channel, Atlantic approaches, Bristol Channel and Irish Sea, the east and west coasts of the main island of Britain, the river systems of Britain and the continental coast up to the Rhine Delta. The latter reflected the way the Romans viewed *Oceanus* separating Britain from the continent, not as a barrier as we do today in the context of recent military history, but as a point of connectivity linking Britannia physically with the rest of the Empire. This is reflected in the fact that the *Classis Britannica*'s headquarters were in Boulogne-Sur-Mer in northwestern Gaul. Meanwhile, in its civilian activities the *Classis Britannica* was used in a variety of roles. This included administration, engineering and construction, and running industry and agriculture.

The principal warship of the *Classis Britannica* was the small and mobile *liburnian* bireme galley, a vessel type used in all the regional fleets of the Principate Empire. These had replaced the large polyreme galleys of the Republican civil wars by the end of the first century BC given the lack of any symmetrical enemy threat at sea in either the Mediterranean or northern waters from that time. The name originates from the Liburni tribe in Dalmatia whose fast biremes were renowned in the Roman world for their feats of piracy. Such ships are the most common type depicted on Trajan's Column in the context of the conquest of Dacia. The commonality of *liburnae*, certainly in northern waters, is testified by an analysis of Roman ship fittings found at Richborough using data from the 1922–1938 excavations that shows such vessels were the most common type present.

The *libernae* of the regional fleets carried the same suite of weapons as their Republican polyreme forbears. In naval engagements the principal weapon was a large bronze or iron ram designed to punch a hole in an opposing vessel's hull below the waterline, or alternatively to run down the length of a target vessel aiming to disable it by destroying the oars (and oarsmen) on the given side. Meanwhile artillery was also a common feature on regional fleet *libernae*, these either bolt shooting or stone-throwing *ballista*, or larger stone-throwing *onagers*. These weapons could be used in direct ship-to-ship engagements with standard ammunition, or more problematically with ammunition set alight designed to set their opponents afire. Additionally, the sickle-shaped hooks on the end of long poles detailed by Caesar that were used to cut the rigging of enemy vessels were also still in use, while another late Republican innovation called the *harpax* (harpoon) also featured. This was a simple grapnel attached to a 2.3m shaft trailing a line. It was designed to be fired from a *ballista*. Metal strips were often attached to the line to prevent it being cut, and once ensnared the opposing vessel was then reeled in and the opponent boarded. The mid-Republican *corvus* was also still in use, though not all *libernae* were equipped with it.

A final point of interest here regarding the *liburnae* of the regional fleets is that they seem to have been individually named. An example is provided by the grave stele of a junior officer of the *Classis Ravennate* that describes him as the captain of the *liburna Aurata* (the latter meaning golden).

In terms of other vessel types, and using the *Classis Britannica* again for our examples, we know of at least one larger trireme that served in the fleet based on an inscription from Boulogne that mentions such a vessel in the service of the regional fleet. However, for the most part the vessels carrying out the majority of military activity in the waters around Britain remained the *liburnae* throughout the Principate. They were supported, especially around the coastal littoral and along river systems, by a variety of *myoparo* cutters and *scapha* skiffs. Meanwhile merchant vessels based on Romano-Celtic designs with high freeboards and shallow drafts provided much of the fleet's maritime transport capability.

Each regional fleet was commanded by an equestrian-level *praefectus classis* fleet admiral appointed directly by the emperor. He reported to a province's procurator rather than governor given each fleet's civilian activities, though clearly he fell under the latter's command when on military duty. Over time the position of *praefectus classis* grew into a very senior position on the equestrian career path, with the commanders of the *Classis Ravennate* and

Classis Misinensis having the same status as the head of the Praetorian Guard in Rome. However, the most successful *praefectus classis* was Publius Helvius Pertinax, the one-time commander of the *Classis Germanica* in the later second century AD who became the first emperor in the 'Year of the Five Emperors' in AD 193, before his assassination by the Praetorian Guard.

The *praefectus classis* of the first regional fleets was initially a former legionary tribune, and later a *legate*. It is clear from epigraphic data that it was common for the fleet admirals to switch between legionary and *classis* command, and indeed between both and senior civilian positions. Later, after Claudius' integration of the civil and military branches of the imperial administration, the post of *praefectus classis* was opened up to freedmen of the imperial household. This changed back after the 'Year of Four Emperors' in AD 69 when sea power was one of the keys to the eventual victory of Vespasian, and after this time the post reverted back to being an equestrian only position. One can judge from the table above listing the pay of the *praefectus classis* of each of the regional fleets their order of seniority. Additionally as the Principate phase of empire progressed new titles also began to be added to those of the *praefectus classis*, further indicating levels of importance. Thus the commanders of the two senior fleets received the title of *praetoria* to add to the *praefectus* for their commanders, leading to the titles *praefectus classis praetorii Ravennate* and *praefectus classis praetorii Misinensis*. Similarly the commanders of the Pannonian and Moesian regional navies gained the title *flavia*, while the commanders of the German and Egyptian regional fleets were later called *Augusta*. We don't know of any added title for the commander of the *Classis Britannica*, but analogy may shed some light here given that the procurator in Britain also carried the title *Augusta*.

Using the *Classis Britannica* again as our example, through epigraphy we know of specific individuals who held the post of *praefectus classis* in this regional fleet. These included Q. Baienus Blassianus, named in the role in an inscription from Ostia, Lucius Aufidius Pantera who is named on an altar found re-used in the later third century AD Saxon Shore fort at Lympne, and Marcus Maenius Agrippa who appears on an inscription from Camerinum in Umbria.

As part of his headquarters operation the *praefectus classis* had a specialist staff. This included a *subpraefectus* executive officer and aide-de-camp, *cornicularius* chief of staff, *actuarii* clerks, *scribae* scribes and seconded *dupliarii* ratings attached from the fleet. Below the headquarters staff the fleets relied heavily on Hellenistic nomenclature in terms of command structure. The commander of a squadron of ships was called a *navarchus* (the most senior the *navarchus principes*), and the captain of an individual vessel a *trierarchus*. Aboard ship the *trierarchus*' executive team included a *gubernator* senior officer responsible for the steering oars, a *proretus* second lieutenant and the *pausarius* rowing master. Other junior officers included the *secutor* master at arms, *nauphylax* officers of the watch and specialists including the *velarii* with responsibility for the sails and *fabri* ships' carpenters.

Below this level the ships company was based on the military organization of their land-based counterparts, with the basic unit called a century. This reflected the preference for close action when engaged in naval combat. The century was commanded by a centurion, who was assisted by an *optio* second-in-command, a *suboptio* junior assistant, a *bucinator* bugler or *cornicern* horn player, and finally an *armorum custos* armourer. The rest of the ship's complement was comprised of marines (*ballistarii* artillery crew, *sagittarii* archers and *propugnatores* deck soldiers), *velarius* sailors, and plenty of *remiges* oarsmen. The latter were always professional rather than the slaves often depicted in popular culture, the whole company being styled *milites* (soldiers, the singular being *miles*) as opposed to *nautae* sailors. This again reflected the Roman preference for maritime close action.

In the Principate, service as a naval *milite* was regarded in the same way as being an auxilia. Those in the *Classis Britannica* were often recruited from the former tribes of the coastal regions in northwestern Gaul. Terms of service for all ranks was twenty-six years, a year longer than their auxiliary counterparts, the reward on completion being Roman citizenship. We have unique insight into this in the form of a recent archaeological discovery. This was the finding of the copper-alloy military diploma of one Tigernos, a sailor of the *Classis Germanica*, granting his citizenship after completing his service. Interestingly, he may prove to be Britain's first named sailor as, despite his service on the Rhine, the diploma was found broken into eight pieces at the Roman fort in Lanchester (Roman *Longovicium*), County Durham.

Each naval *miles* received three gold pieces or 75 *denarii* upon enlistment, with their basic annual pay at the beginning of the Principate being 100 *denarii* for the lower ranks. Crewmembers given greater responsibilities were paid an additional bonus on top, with those paid one-and-a-half times the basic salary called *sesquiplicarii* and those paid double called *duplicarii*. From this annual salary, as with their land-based equivalents, the *milites* would have had deducted a certain amount to cover the cost of arms, equipment and food, and an additional amount which would be paid into the squadron's savings bank for their retirement fund.

Clothing for the naval *milites* differed between the regional fleets. This reflected differing climatic and operational conditions. Again using the *Classis Britannica* as an example, an essential item of clothing in the northern waters would have been the *birrus* rain-proofed hooded cloak. Other key items of clothing for the *milites* of this regional fleet would have been the *pilos* conical felt hat, belted tunic with trousers, and sandals or felt stockings with low-cut leather boots rather than *caligae*. The short *sagum* cloak was worn when on formal duty.

For weaponry the marines of the regional fleets' navies were armed in a similar manner to the land-based auxilia. Principal missile weapons, in addition to artillery, included bows, slings, javelins and darts. For hand-to-hand work the marines also carried boarding pikes, the *hasta navalis* naval spear, various types of sword and the *dolabra* boarding axe.

The Praetorian Guard

The Praetorian Guard was an elite Roman military unit, permanently based in Rome at their *Castra Praetoria* barracks built on the eastern slopes of the Quirinal Hill outside the Servian Walls. From here they served as the personal bodyguard of the Roman emperors.

The guard had its origins in the Roman Republic. Various commanders of the time were well-known for assigning crack troops to be their personal bodyguards, for example Sulla and Mark Antony. Caesar himself used his own legion, *legio* X *equestris*, as his personal guard. However, the term Praetorian in the later Republic specifically related to a small escort for high-ranking officials including leading Senators, governors, *proconsuls* and procurators.

It was the first emperor Augustus who actually created the select force he styled the Praetorian Guard for his own personal protection, sometime after 27 BC. This comprised nine cohorts of 500 men each, these later being increased to 1,000 men. He also added a small number of *equitatae* Praetorian cavalry, these being later replaced by the *equites singulares Augusti* Imperial Guard Cavalry. Claudius increased the number of foot guard cohorts to twelve, and Vitellius (April to September AD 69) increased this again to sixteen in AD 69 during the 'Year of the Four Emperors' after disbanding the original nine. However, the ultimate victor Vespasian decreased this to nine again.

Praetorian Guard cohorts rotated duty in the imperial palace on the Palatine Hill, with three on guard at any one time. As with the legions, the Praetorian Guard cohorts also included specialists who were able to perform a wide variety of tasks when on campaign. A good example can be found on the tombstone of guardsman Caius Caristicus Redemtus from Brescel (Roman *Brixellus*) in Cisalpine Gaul who is described as a *plumba(rius) ordina(rius/yus)* centurion-ranked lead worker.

The Praetorian guardsmen were well-rewarded for their loyalty to the emperor. Augustus ensured the Senate passed a law allowing him to pay them at least twice a legionary's salary. This was increased again by Domitian and later by Septimius Severus. They also had better terms of service, this only sixteen years compared to the legionaries' twenty-five. On retirement they were paid a huge gratuity of 20,000 *sestertii*, though given the many benefits of being a guardsman many re-enlisted. Such troopers were known as *evocatii Augusti*.

Early guardsmen, particularly in the reigns of Augustus and Tiberius, were recruited from existing legions and were experienced warriors, though as the Principate progressed this changed and they were increasingly recruited straight into the guard from civilian life. These later Principate guardsmen developed a reputation for being more interested in fine living than soldiering, and interfering in imperial succession, and when Septimius Severus became the ultimate victor of the 'Year of the Five Emperors' in AD 193 he immediately disbanded them and replaced them with his own Danubian veterans, doubling the size of the guard at the same time (also doubling the size of the *equites singulares Augusti*). At all times the guard only left Rome when on campaign with the emperor, which was more common at the beginning and end of the Principate.

The Praetorian Guard were the only soldiers allowed in the *pomerium* sacred centre of ancient Rome while bearing arms. This put them in a powerful position, particularly at times of imperial succession when they often played the decisive role if the throne was contested. The ultimate and most shaming example was when they held an auction for the throne in March AD 193 at the *Castra Praetoria* after a party of 300 guardsmen assassinated Pertinax whom they had elevated to the throne on New Year's Day that year, his crime being to refuse to pay them a huge donative given the *fiscus* treasury at the time was almost bankrupt. Two candidates, the city prefect (and confusingly Pertinax's father-in-law) Titus Flavius Claudius Sulpicianus and the ambitious leading Senator Didius Julianus bid against each other, the former within the camp and the latter standing on its walls. Ultimately the latter outbid the former, but was soon deposed and later killed, with Septimius Severus arriving in Rome to seize the throne, avenge the death of his former mentor Pertinax and reform the guard as detailed.

Praetorians also had other responsibilities in the imperial capital, including crowd control during the games in the Colosseum and elsewhere. Here they sometimes went a step further, participating in wild beast hunts and similar as part of the entertainment, as under the mad and bad Commodus (AD 180–AD 193), himself a frequent participant in the arena.

The Praetorian Guard was commanded by two Praetorian Prefects, the first office holders being Quintus Ostorius Scapula and Publius Salvius Aper from 2 BC. From the reign of Vespasian these prefects were always equestrians, the appointment a serious career advancement. Many chose to monumentalize their success through public building works. A fine example can be seen today in Ostia Antica, the former port of ancient Rome. Here the *forum* bath complex was built at the expense of the prefect Marcus Gavius Maximus.

When on campaign with the emperor, foot guardsmen were equipped in the same way as the better armed legionaries of the day. At the height of the Principate this would have been with *pilum, gladius, pugio, scutum* (this often featuring an image of winged victory, scorpions and crescents) and *lorica segmentata*, though in the case of the latter *lorica squamata* scale mail had begun to feature on images of guardsmen in contemporary sculpture. By the mid-third century AD this was the predominant type of Praetorian armour. One point of the difference in the defensive panoply when compared to standard legionaries was the helmet, with particularly fine examples being worn. These included exquisitely detailed imperial Gallic types, as seen on a number of guardsman on Trajan's Column, and also designs referencing the classical past. In that regard, Greek Attic helmets were a common type worn by Praetorians. The base uniform colour was red, with large white helmet plumes (red in the case of centurions and officers). When in Rome on escort duty, smaller oval shields and *lancea* light spears were carried, with the suit of armour replaced by a fine quality light toga.

The Praetorian Guard remained a potential source of instability in the imperial capital, even after the changes made by Septimius Severus, and was finally abolished by Constantine I (AD 306 to AD 324) in AD 312 after the defeat of his rival Maxentius (AD 306 to AD 312) at the Battle of the Milvian Bridge. The victor then declared a *damnatio memoriae* against them, officially removing the guard from imperial history, with the *Castra Praetoria* being publicly dismantled.

Bibliography

Ancient Sources

Apuleius, *The Golden Ass*, trans. P.G. Walsh (Oxford: Oxford World Classics, 2008)

Aurelius, Marcus, *Meditations*, trans. M. Staniforth (London: Penguin, 1964)

Caesar, Julius, *The Conquest of Gaul*, trans. S.A. Handford (London: Penguin, 1951)

Cato, Marcus, *De Agri Cultura*, trans. H.B. Ash and W.D. Hooper (Harvard: Loeb Classical Library, 1934)

Claudian, *Works*, trans. M. Platnauer (Harvard: Loeb Classical Library, 1989)

Dio, Cassius, *Roman History*, trans. E. Cary (Harvard: Loeb Classical Library, 1925)

Eusebius, *Ecclesiastical History: Complete and Unabridged*, trans. C.F. Crusé (Oregon: Merchant Books, 2011)

Eusebius, *De Vita Constanti*, trans. C.F. Crusé (Oregon: Merchant Books, 2011)

Eutropius, Flavius, *Historiae Romanae Breviarium*, trans. H.W. Bird (Liverpool: Liverpool University Press, 1993)

Florus, Julius, *Epitome of Roman History*, trans. D. Koryczan (Independently Published, 2017)

Flaccus, Quintus Horatius (Horace), *The Complete Odes and Epodes*, trans. D. West (Oxford: Oxford Paperbacks, 2008)

Frontinus, Sextus Julius, *Strategemata*, trans. C.E. Bennett (Portsmouth, New Hampshire: Heinemann, 1969)

Gaius, *Institutiones*, trans. F. De Zulueta (Oxford: Oxford University Press, 1946)

Gildas, *De Excidio et Conquestu Britanniae*, trans. H.A. Williams (Moscow: Dodo Press, 2010)

Herodian, *History of the Roman Empire*, trans. C.R. Whittaker (Harvard: Loeb Classical Library, 1989)

Historia Augusta, trans. D. Magie (Harvard, Loeb Classical Library, 1921)

The Holy Bible, King James Version

Homer, *The Iliad*, trans. E.V. Rieu (London: Penguin Classics, 1950)

Josephus, Flavius, *The Antiquities of the Jews*, trans. W. Whiston (Saint Paul, Minnesota: Wilder Publications, 2018)

Josephus, Flavius, *The Jewish War*, trans. M.E. Smallwood (London: Penguin Classics, 1981)

Justinian, *The Digest of Justinian*, trans. A. Watson (Philadelphia: University of Pennsylvania, 1997)

Libanius, *The Julianic Orations*, trans. A.F. Norman (Harvard: Loeb Classical Library, 1989)

Livy, *The History of Rome*, trans. B.O. Foster (Cambridge, MA: Harvard University Press/Loeb Classical Library, 1989)

Marcellinus, Ammianus, *The Later Roman Empire*, trans. W. Hamilton (London: Penguin, 1986)

Orosius, Paulus, *Seven Books of History against the Pagans*, trans. R.I. Woodworth (New York: Columbia University, 1936)

Paterculus, Velleius, *Roman History*, ed. A.J. Woodman (Cambridge: Cambridge Classical Texts, 1977)

Pausanias, *Guide to Greece: Central Greece*, trans. P. Levi (London: Penguin Classics, 1979)

Pliny the Elder, *Natural History*, trans. H. Rackham (Harvard: Harvard University Press, 1940)

Pliny the Younger, *Epistularum Libri Decem*, ed. R.A.B. Mynors (Oxford: Oxford Classical Texts/Clarendon Press, 1963)

Plutarch, *Lives of the Noble Grecians and Romans*, ed. A.H. Clough (Oxford: Benediction Classics, 2013)

Polybius, *The Rise of the Roman Empire*, trans. I. Scott-Kilvert (London: Penguin Classics, 1979)

Quintilian, *Institutes of Oratory*, J. Selby Watson (Scotts Valley, California: Create Space Independent Publishing Platform, 2015)

Second Maccabees, T. Horn (Crane, Michigan: Defender Publishing LLC, 2012)

Siculus, Diodorus, *Library of History*, trans. C.H. Oldfather (Harvard: Loeb Classical Library, 1939)

Statius, *Silvae*, B.R. Nagle (Bloomington: Indiana University Press, 2004)

Strabo, *The Geography of Strabo*, trans. D.W. Roller (Cambridge: Cambridge University Press, 2014)

Suetonius, *The Twelve Caesars*, trans. R. Graves (London: Penguin Books, 1957)

Tacitus, Cornelius, *The Agricola*, trans. H. Mattingly (London: Penguin Books, 1970)

Tacitus, Cornelius, *The Annals*, trans. M. Grant (London: Penguin Classics, 2003)

Tacitus, Cornelius, *The Histories*, trans. W.H. Fyfe (Oxford: Oxford Paperbacks, 2008)

Tibullus, Albius, *Catullus, Tibullus and Pervigilium Veneris*, trans. F.W. Cornish, J.P. Postgate and J.W. Mackail (Harvard: Loeb Classical Library, 1989)

Victor, Aurelius, *De Caesaribus*, trans. H.W. Bird (Liverpool: Liverpool University Press, 1994)

Zosimus, *New History*, trans. R.T. Ridley (Leiden: Brill, 1982)

Modern Sources

Allen, S., *Celtic Warrior 300 BC–AD 100* (Oxford: Osprey Publishing, 2001)

Avery, A., *The Story of York* (Pickering: Blackthorn Press, 2007)

Barker, P., *The Armies and Enemies of Imperial Rome* (Cambridge: Wargames Research Group, 1981)

de la Bédoyère, G., *Praetorian: The Rise and Fall of Rome's Imperial Bodyguard* (New Haven: Yale University Press, 2017)

de la Bédoyère, G., 'The Emperors' Fatal Servants', *History Today*, March 2017 Issue, pp.58–62.

Bentley, P., 'A Recently Identified Valley in the City', *London Archaeologist*, Vol. 5, Number 1, pp.13–16, 1984.

Bidwell, P., *Roman Forts in Britain* (Stroud: Tempus, 2007)

Bidwell, P., 'The Roman Fort at Bainbridge, Wensleydale: Excavations by B.R. Hartley on the *principia* and a summary account of other excavations and surveys', *Britannia*, Vol. 43, pp.45–113, 2012.

Birley, A.R., *The* Fasti *of Roman Britain* (Oxford: Clarendon Press, 1981)

Birley, A.R., *Septimius Severus: The African Emperor* (London: Routledge, 1999)

Birley, A.R., *The Roman Government of Britain* (Oxford: Oxford University Press, 2005)

Birley, A.R., 'The Frontier Zone in Britain: Hadrian to Caracalla', in: de Blois, L. and Lo Cascio, E. (eds.), *The Impact of the Roman Army (200 BC–AD 476)*, pp.355–370 (Leiden: Brill, 2007)

Bishop, M.C., *The Secret History of the Roman Roads of Britain* (Barnsley: Pen & Sword, 2014)

Bishop, M.C., *The Gladius: The Roman Short Sword* (Oxford: Osprey Publishing Ltd, 2016)

Blagg, T., 'The Sculptured Stones', in: Dyson, T. (ed.), *The Roman Riverside Wall and Monumental Arch in London - Special Paper No. 3.*, pp.125–193 (London: London and Middlesex Archaeological Society, 1980)

Breeze, D.J., *Roman Scotland* (London: Batsford Ltd/Historic Scotland, 2000)

Breeze, D.J., and Dobson, B., *Hadrian's Wall* (London: Penguin Books, 2000)

Breeze, D.J., and Hodgson, 'Plague on Hadrian's Wall?', *Current Archaeology*, Issue 365, Vol. 30, pp.28–35, 2020.

Brodribb, G., 'A Survey of Tile at the Roman Bath House at Beauport Park, Battle, East Sussex', *Britannia*, Vol. 10, pp.139–156, 1979.

Burgess, R.W., 'Principes cum Tyrannis: Two Studies on the *Kaisergeschichte* and Its Tradition' in *The Classical Quarterly*, Vol. 43, pp.491–500, 1993.

Campbell, D.B., *Mons Graupius AD 83* (Oxford: Osprey Publishing Ltd, 2010)

Campbell, D.B., 'The Fate of the Ninth', *Ancient Warfare*, Vol. 4, No. 5, pp.48–53, 2011.

Campbell, D.B., *The Fate of the Ninth: The Curious Disappearance of One of Rome's Legions* (Glasgow: Bocca della Verita Publishing, 2018)

Connolly, P., *Greece and Rome at War* (London: Macdonald & Co (Publishers) Ltd, 1988)

Cornell, T.J., 'The End of Roman Imperial Expansion', in: Rich, J., and Shipley, G. (eds.), *War and Society in the Roman World*, pp.139–170 (London: Routledge, 1993)

Cornell, T.J., and Matthews, J., *Atlas of the Roman World* (Oxford: Phaidon Press Ltd, 2006)

Cotton, J., 'A miniature chalk head from the Thames at Battersea and the "Cult of the Head" in Roman London', in Bird, J., Hassall, M., and Sheldon, H. (eds), *Interpreting Roman London: Papers in Memory of Hugh Chapman*, pp.85–96, 1996.

Cowan, R., *Roman Legionary, 58 BC–AD 69* (Oxford: Osprey Publishing, 2003)

Cowan, R., *Imperial Roman Legionary, AD 161–284* (Oxford: Osprey Publishing, 2003)

Cowan, R., *Roman Battle Tactics 109 BC–AD 313* (Oxford: Osprey Publishing, 2007)

Cunliffe, B., *Greeks, Romans and Barbarians: Spheres of Interaction* (London: Batsford Ltd, 1988)

Cunliffe, B., *Europe between the Oceans* (New Haven: Yale University Press, 2008)

Cunliffe, B., *Britain Begins* (Oxford: Oxford University Press, 2013)

D'Amato, R., and Sumner, G., *Arms and Armour of the Imperial Roman Soldier* (Barnsley: Frontline Books, 2009)

D'Amato, R., *Imperial Roman Naval Forces 31 BC–AD 500* (Oxford: Osprey Publishing, 2009)

D'Amato, R., *Roman Army Units in the Western Provinces (1)* (Oxford: Osprey Publishing, 2016)

D'Amato, R., *Roman Heavy Cavalry (1)* (Oxford: Osprey Publishing, 2018)

D'Amato, R., *Roman Army Units in the Western Provinces (2)* (Oxford: Osprey Publishing, 2019)

Davies, M., 'The Evidence of Settlement at Plaxtol in the Late Iron Age and Romano-British Periods', *Archaeologia Cantiana*, Vol. 129, pp.257–278, 2009.

Dougherty, M.J., 'Jerusalem AD 70', in: Jestice, P.G. (ed.) *Battles of the Bible*, pp.194–215 (London: Amber Books, 2008)

Elliott, P., *Legions in Crisis* (Stroud: Fonthill Media Ltd, 2014)

Elliott, S., *Sea Eagles of Empire: The Classis Britannica and the Battles for Britain* (Stroud: The History Press, 2016)

Elliott, S., *Empire State: How the Roman Military Built an Empire* (Oxford: Oxbow Books, 2017)

Elliott, S., *Septimius Severus in Scotland: The Northern Campaigns of the First Hammer of the Scots* (Barnsley: Greenhill Books, 2018)

Elliott, S., *Roman Legionaries* (Oxford: Casemate Publishers, 2018)

Elliott, S., *Julius Caesar: Rome's Greatest Warlord* (Oxford: Casemate Publishers, 2019)

Elliott, S., 'Clash of the Titans: The Battle of Lugdunum, AD 197', in *Ancient Warfare* magazine, Vol. 13, Issue 3, pp.27–35, 2020.

Elliott, S., *Romans at War* (Oxford: Casemate Publishers, 2020)

Elliott, S., *Pertinax: The Son of a Slave Who Became Roman Emperor* (Barnsley: Greenhill Books, 2020)

Elliott, S., *Roman Britain's Missing Legion* (Barnsley: Pen & Sword, 2021)

Elliott, S., *Roman Conquests: Britain* (Barnsley: Pen & Sword, 2021)

Erdkamp, P. (ed.), *The Cambridge Companion to Ancient Rome* (Cambridge. Cambridge University Press, 2013)

Fields, N., 'Headhunters of the Roman Army', *Minerva* magazine, November/December, pp.9–12, 2006.

Fields, N., *Carrhae 53 BC: Rome's Disaster in the Desert* (Oxford: Osprey Publishing, 2022)

Frere, S., *Britannia: A History of Roman Britain* (3rd edn) (London: Routledge, 1974)

Frere, S., 'M. Maenius Agrippa, the Expeditio Britannica and Maryport', *Britannia* magazine, Vol. 31, pp.23–28, 2000.

Gaffney, V., Fitch, S., and Smith, D., *Europe's Lost World: The Rediscovery of Doggerland* (York: Council for British Archaeology, 2009)

Garrison, E.G., *History of Engineering and Technology: Artful Methods* (Boca Raton, Florida: CRC Press, 1998)

Geoffrey of Monmouth, *The History of the Kings of Britain: An Edition and Translation of De gestis Britonum (Historia regum Britanniae)*, trans. N. Wright, (Woodbridge, 2007)

Gill, D., 'A Natural Spur at Masada', in *Nature* journal, Vol. 364, pp.569–570, 1993.

Goldsworthy, A., *Roman Warfare* (London: Cassell, 2000)

Goldsworthy, A., *The Complete Roman Army* (London: Thames & Hudson, 2003)

Goldsworthy, A., *Caesar* (London: Weidenfeld & Nicolson, 2006)

Goldsworthy, A., *Augustus* (London: Weidenfeld & Nicolson, 2014)

Graafstaal, E., 'What Happened in the Summer of AD 122: Hadrian on the British Frontier – Archaeology, Epigraphy and Historical Agency', *Britannia* magazine, Vol. 48, pp.76–111, 2018.

Grainge, G., *The Roman Invasions of Britain* (Stroud: Tempus, 2005)

Green, P., *Alexander to Actium* (London: Thames & Hudson, 1990)

Haywood, J., *The Historical Atlas of the Celtic World* (London: Thames & Hudson, 2009)

Head, D., *Armies of the Macedonian and Punic Wars* (London: Wargames Research Group, 2016)

Heather, P., *The Restoration of Rome* (London: Macmillan, 2013)

Hingley, R., 'Roman Britain: The structure of Roman imperialism and the consequences of imperialism on the development of a peripheral province', in: Miles, D. (ed.), *The Romano-British Countryside: Studies in Rural Settlement and Economy*, pp.17–52 (Oxford: BAR/ Archaeological and Historical Associates Ltd, 1982)

Hingley, R., *Globalizing Roman Culture – Unity, Diversity and Empire* (London: Routledge, 2005)

Hingley, R., *Londinium: A Biography* (London: Bloomsbury Academic, 2018)

Hodgson, N., 'The British Expeditions of Septimius Severus', in *Britannia* magazine, Vol. 45, pp.31–51, 2014.

Holder, P., 'Auxiliary Deployment in the Reign of Hadrian', in: J.J. Wilkes (ed.): *Documenting the Roman Army: Essays in honour of Margaret Roxan*, Bulletin of the Institute of Classical studies Supplements, London, pp.101–146, 2003.

Holland, T., *Dynasty* (London: Little, Brown, 2015)

Holland, T., *Dominion* (London: Little, Brown, 2019)

Hornblower, S., and Spawforth, A., *The Oxford Classical Dictionary* (Oxford: Oxford University Press, 1996)

James, S., *Rome and the Sword* (London: Thames & Hudson, 2011)

Jestice, P.G., 'Introduction', in: Jestice, P.G. (ed.) *Battles of the Bible*, pp.6–18 (London: Amber Books, 2008)

Jones, B., and Mattingly, D., *An Atlas of Roman Britain* (Oxford: Oxbow Books, 1990)

Kaye, S., 'The Roman Invasion of Britain, AD 43: Riverine, Wading and Tidal Studies Place Limits on the Location of the Two-Day River Battle and Beachhead', *Archaeologia Cantiana*, Vol.136, pp.227–240, 2015.

Kamm, A., *The Last Frontier: The Roman Invasions of Scotland* (Glasgow: Tempus, 2011)

Kean, R.M., and Frey, O., *The Complete Chronicle of the Emperors of Rome* (Ludlow: Thalamus Publishing, 2005)

Keppie, L., *The Making of the Roman Army, from Republic to Empire* (London: Batsford, 1984)

Keppie, L., 'The Fate of the Ninth Legion: A Problem for the Eastern Provinces?' in: Keppie, L. (ed.) *Legions and Veterans: Roman Army Papers 1971–2000*, p.247 (Stuttgart: Franz Steiner Verlag Wiesbaden GmbH, 2000)

Keppie, L., *The Legacy of Rome: Scotland's Roman Remains* (Edinburgh: Birlim, 2015)

Kiley, K.F., *The Uniforms of the Roman World* (Wigston: Lorenz Books, 2012)

Knusel, C.J., and Carr, G.C., 'On the Significance of the Crania from the River Thames and its Tributaries', *Antiquity* magazine, Vol. 69, pp.162–9, 1995.

Kolb, A., 'The Cursus Publicus', in: Adams, C., and Laurence, R. (eds) *Travel and Geography in the Roman Empire*, pp.95–106 (London: Routledge, 2001)

Kulikowski, M., *Imperial Triumph: The Roman World from Hadrian to Constantine* (London: Profile Books, 2016)

Lambert, M., *Christians and Pagans* (New Haven: Yale University Press, 2010)

Le Bohec, Y., *The Imperial Roman Army* (London: Routledge, 2000)

Levick, B., *Julia Domna: Syrian Empress* (London: Routledge, 2007)

Luttwak, E., *The Grand Strategy of the Roman Empire: From the First Century AD to the Third* (Baltimore: John Hopkins University Press, 1976)

McWhirr, A., and Viner, D., 'The Production and Distribution of Tiles in Roman Britain with Particular Reference to the Cirencester Region', *Britannia* magazine, Vol. 9, pp.359–377, 1978.

Marsh, G., and West, B., 'Skullduggery in Roman London', *Transactions of the London and Middlesex Archaeological Society*, Vol. 32, pp.86–102, 1981.

Mason, D.J.P., *Roman Britain and the Roman Navy* (Stroud: The History Press, 2003)

Mattingly, D., *An Imperial Possession: Britain in the Roman Empire* (London: Penguin Books, 2006)

Mattingly, D., *Imperialism, Power and Identity: Experiencing the Roman Empire* (Princeton: Princeton University Press, 2011)

Matyszak, P., *Roman Conquests: Macedonia and Greece* (Barnsley: Pen & Sword, 2009)

Merrifield, R., *The Roman City of London* (London: Ernest Benn, 1965)

Millett, M., *The Romanization of Britain* (Cambridge: Cambridge University Press, 1990)

Millett, M., *Roman Britain* (London: Batsford, 1995)

Milne, G., and Richardson, B., 'Ships and Barges', in: Milne, G. (ed.) *The Port of Roman London*, pp.96–102 (London: B T Batsford, 1985)

Moody, G., *The Isle of Thanet: From Prehistory to the Norman Conquest* (Stroud: Tempus, 2008)

Moffat, B., 'A Marvellous Plant: The Place of the Heath Pea in Scottish Botanical Tradition', *Folio* magazine, Issue 1, pp.13–15, 2000.

Moorhead, S., and Stuttard, D., *The Romans Who Shaped Britain* (London: Thames & Hudson, 2012)

Myers, S.D., 'The River Walbrook and Roman London' PhD thesis, (Unpublished: University of Reading, 2016)

Noble, G., Golderg, M., and Hamilton, D., 'Pictish Symbols: Inscribing Identity beyond the Fringe of Empire', *British Archaeology*, July/August, p.45, 2019.

Oleson, J.P., *The Oxford Handbook of Engineering and Technology in the Classical World* (Oxford: Oxford University Press, 2009)

Oman, C., *England before the Norman Conquest* (London: Methuen, 1938)

Ottaway, P., *Roman Yorkshire* (Pickering: Blackthorn Press, 2013)

Oosthuizen, S., *The Emergence of the English* (Leeds: ARC Humanities Press, 2019)

Parfitt, K., 'Folkestone During the Roman Period', in: Coulson, I. (ed.) *Folkestone to 1500: A Town Unearthed* pp.31–54 (Canterbury: Canterbury Archaeological Trust, 2013)

Parker, A., *The Archaeology of Roman York* (Stroud: Amberley Books, 2019)

Parker, P., *The Empire Stops Here* (London: Jonathan Cape, 2009)

Pausche, D., 'Unreliable Narration in the *Historia Augusta*', *Ancient Narrative* journal, Vol. 8, pp.115–135, 2009.

Perring, D., 'London's Hadrianic War', *Britannia* magazine, Vol. 41, pp.127–147, 2017.

Pitassi, M., *The Roman Navy* (Barnsley: Seaforth, 2012)

Pollard, N., and Berry, J., *The Complete Roman Legions* (London: Thames & Hudson, 2012)

Potter, D., *Rome in the Ancient World: From Romulus to Justinian* (London: Thames & Hudson, 2009)

Potter, T.W., and Jackson, R.P.J., 'The Roman Site of Stonea, Cambridgeshire', *Antiquity*, Vol. 56, Issue 217, pp.110–120, 1982.

Rankov, B., 'A Secret of Empire (imperii Arcanum): an unacknowledged factor in Roman imperial expansion', in: Hanson, W.S. (ed.) *The Army and Frontiers of Rome: Papers offered to David J. Breeze on the occasion of his sixty-fifth birthday and his retirement from Historic Scotland*, pp.163–172 (Portsmouth, Rhode Island: Journal of Roman Archaeology Supplementary Series, no. 74, pp.163–172, 2009)

Redfern, R., and Bonney, H., 'Headhunting and amphitheatre combat in Roman London, England: new evidence from the Walbrook valley', *Journal of Archaeological Science*, No 43, pp.214–26, 2014.

Reid, R., 'Bullets, Ballistas and Burnswark: A Roman Assault on a Hillfort in Scotland', *Current Archaeology*, Vol. 27, Issue 316, pp.20–26, 2016.

Robertson, A.S., 'The Bridges on the Severan Coins of AD 208 and 209', in: Hanson, W.S., and Keppie, L.J.F. (eds), *Roman Frontier Studies* (Oxford: BAR/Archaeological and Historical Associates, pp.131–140, 1980)

Rodgers, N., and Dodge, H., *The History and Conquests of Ancient Rome* (London: Hermes House, 2009)

Ross, S., and Ross, C.,' Recent Roman Discoveries During the A1 Upgrade in North Yorkshire', *Current Archaeology*, Vol. 30, Issue 359, pp.18–22, 2020.

Rowsome, P., 'Mapping Roman London: Identifying its Urban Patterns and Interpreting Their Meaning', in: Clark, J., Cotton, J., Hall, J., Sherris, R., Swain, H., (eds) *Londinium and Beyond. Essays on Roman London and its Hinterland for Harvey Sheldon*, Council for British Archaeology Research Report, Vol. 156, pp.25–32 (York, 2008)

Russell, M., 'What Happened to Britain's Lost Roman Legion?' *BBC History Magazine*, May issue, pp.40–45, 2011.

Salway, P., *Roman Britain* (Oxford: Oxford University Press, 1981)

Scarre, C., *The Penguin Historical Atlas of Ancient Rome* (London: Penguin, 1995)

Scarre, C., *Chronicle of the Roman Emperors* (London: Thames & Hudson, 1995)

Sheldon, H., 'Enclosing Londinium', *London and Middlesex Archaeological Society Transactions*, Vol. 61, pp.227–235, 2010.

Sheppard, S., *Roman Soldier versus Parthian Warrior* (Oxford: Osprey Publishing, 2020)

Sidebottom, H., *The Mad Emperor: Heliogabulus and the Decadence of Rome* (London: Oneworld Publications, 2022)

Southern, P., *Roman Britain* (Stroud: Amberley Publishing, 2013)

Southern, P., *Hadrian's Wall: Everyday Life on a Roman Frontier* (Stroud: Amberley Publishing, 2016)

Starr, C.G., *The Roman Imperial Navy 31 BC–AD 324* (New York: Cornell University Press, 1941)

Stathakopoulos, D.C., *Famine and Pestilence in the Late Roman and Early Byzantine Empire* (London: Routledge, 2004)

Strong, D.E., 'The Monument', in: Cunliffe, B. (ed.) *5th Report on the Excavations on the Roman Fort at Richborough, Kent* pp.40–73 (Oxford: Oxford University Press, 1968)

Tibbs, A., *Beyond the Empire: A Guide to the Roman Remains in Scotland* (Marlborough: Robert Hale, 2019)

Todd, M., *Roman Britain 55 BC–AD 400: The Province Beyond Ocean* (Glasgow: Fontana Press, 1981)

Tomlin, R.S.O., *Roman London's First Voices* (London: Museum of London Archaeology, 2016)

Wallace-Hadrill, A., (ed.), *Patronage in Ancient Society* (Routledge: London, 1989)

Watson, G.R., *The Roman Soldier: Aspects of Greek and Roman Life* (Ithaca, New York: Cornell University Press, 1969)

Weber, W., *Untersuchungen zur Geschichte des Kaisers Hadrianus* (Leipzig: B.G. Teubner, 1907)

Wheeler, R.E.M., *London: Volume 3, Roman London* (Royal Commission on Historical Monuments of England, London, 1928)

Whitby, M., *Rome at War AD 293–696* (Oxford: Osprey Publishing, 2002)

Wilkes, J.J., 'Provinces and Frontiers', in: Bowman. A.K., Garnsey, P., and Cameron, A. (eds), *The Cambridge Ancient History Vol. XII, The Crisis of Empire, AD 193–33*, pp.212–268 (Cambridge: Cambridge University Press, 2005)

Windrow, M., and McBride, A., *Imperial Rome at War* (Hong Kong: Concord Publications, 1996)

Wolff, C., 'Units: Principate', in: le Bohec, Y. (ed.) *The Encyclopedia of the Roman Army Vol. 3.*, pp.1037–1049 (Hoboken, New Jersey: Wiley-Blackwell, 2015)

Index